KT-366-073

Model Building in Sociology

BASIC IDEAS IN THE HUMAN SCIENCES
Editors: Alasdair MacIntyre and Patrick Doreian

MODEL BUILDING
IN SOCIOLOGY

Peter Abell
Senior Lecturer, Department of Sociology
University of Essex

WEIDENFELD AND NICOLSON
5 Winsley Street London W1

© Peter Abell 1971

All rights reserved. No part of this publication
may be reproduced, stored in a retrieval system,
or transmitted, in any form or by any means,
electronic, mechanical, photocopying, recording
or otherwise, without the prior permission of the
copyright owner.

ISBN 0 297 00397 6

Printed in Great Britain by
Cox and Wyman Ltd,
London, Fakenham and Reading

Preface

There are two well-established traditions in the teaching of sociology – at least in Britain. These are, first, an emphasis on the philosophy of physical science with a view to establishing whether or not sociology can be scientific in the sense of this discipline, and second, an emphasis on statistical technique. Unfortunately, the two traditions seem rarely to meet; so in this book I have made an attempt to bring them together. As the reader will no doubt soon realise, I am neither a philosopher nor a statistician, and consequently run the risk of incurring the wrath of professionals in both fields. But I hope they will at least bear with the endeavour. I could easily be convinced of the wrongheadedness or even downright falsity of much of the detail of my book; but I doubt if I could be persuaded of the illegitimacy of the enterprise. I remain convinced that what is required in sociology, at the moment, is an infusion of philosophically sophisticated technique. I would not like to claim this book provides it, but I do at least hope that it may stimulate others in this direction.

Although I do not ascribe to the view that sociology can be a science in the sense of physics or chemistry, largely because I believe it is a conceptual absurdity to think of laws applicable in all places at all times, I do believe that much can be learned from the physical sciences. Broadly speaking, my belief is that sociology should be concerned to fabricate a 'rational' social existence – societies in which people understand the influences under which they labour and the consequences of what they do in complex situations. Admittedly this state of affairs remains at the moment, little more than a pipe-dream, but a detailed

Preface

analysis of causal sequences (as developed in the text) appears to me to be the best way of proceeding in that direction. Thus, for me, there is no separation between sociological analysis and the fashioning of a better social existence.

The structure of the book is straightforward. Chapter 1 introduces what I term the hierarchy of scientific sophistication. (I must apologise for the expression, but I failed to find an alternative, less pretentious one that conveyed my meaning.) Subsequent chapters explore the levels in this hierarchy: Chapter 2 outlines a framework for units of analysis; Chapter 3 is concerned with concepts; Chapter 4 moves on to consider the problem of measuring concepts, i.e. converting them into variables. Chapter 5 provides an analysis of theoretical concepts in sociology, and Chapter 6 then considers propositions which relate two concepts. In Chapter 7, I have discussed the problems of relating propositions. Chapter 8 considers, in outline, the salient features of sociological covariation. Finally, Chapter 9 deals with causal modelling.

I should like to emphasise that this is not a book on statistics. Although the later chapters involve a knowledge of modern econometric technique, they are written in a manner accessible to readers with a more elementary statistical knowledge.

I would like to express my gratitude to Alasdair MacIntyre, Pat Doreian and Michael Lane for their painstaking scrutiny of early drafts of the manuscript. I must especially thank Alasdair MacIntyre for the feeling of intellectual excitement that he brought to my University in his all too short a stay here. I must, of course, make the usual restrictions – I am solely responsible for any mistakes, inconsistencies in reasoning and lapses of judgement in the text. Finally, my sincerest thanks to Marion Haberhauer whose ability to translate my written language into typed English must remain a monument to secretarial perseverance.

Peter Abell 1971

Contents

Contents

1. The Model Building Perspective

1.1 Introduction

It is a truism, perhaps barely worth stating, that in our everyday life we attempt to describe and explain the world around us in terms of *concepts*; this is true both of the physical and social worlds. Science also uses concepts – sometimes those we are all familiar with, sometimes not – but science is also characterised by a systematic endeavour to relate these concepts into sets of interrelated propositions; an endeavour which, for the want of a better expression, I will term model building.[1] Not necessarily theoretical model building, for we may very well wish to erect models that contain only observational[2] concepts, i.e. no theoretical concepts at all.

In this essay, I want to outline some of the logical features of a model building perspective in sociology. I purposely call it a perspective for it is only one among many other markedly different perspectives in the discipline. This particular perspective is, of course, much under-developed in contemporary sociology but the advances we all look for, particularly in theoretical sociology, can surely only come when we recognise that it is not sufficient merely to spin more and more precisely articulated theoretical concepts; rather we must embed our concepts in models which show how they are related, and how the models represent or generate that complicated entity which we all know as social reality.

As the title of the book suggests, we are limiting the scope of our inquiry to situations where we only have cross-sectional data; i.e. we exclude consideration of models based on over-time or longitudinal data. This restriction is unfortunately necessary to keep the length of the text within reasonable bounds, but in later chapters we will briefly consider causal models involving data collected at more than one point in time in order to show, by contrast, the full logic of cross-sectional models.

Having data at only one point in time does, of course, impose severe limitations on the model builder, but it is still the general practice in sociology to collect only such data. The problems of collecting significant data over time are well known and it seems that even though we may, in the future, expect less reliance to be placed on cross-sectional and more on over-time data, the former will often be all that is available to the model builder.

It is nevertheless important to recognise a basic assumption behind the collection and manipulation of cross-sectional data – an assumption that is not often made explicit. It can perhaps be best highlighted by comparing and contrasting the typical way in which models are expressed in sociology and the physical sciences.

Let us assume that two variables X and Y are related in some way. Now the physical scientist will characteristically express the relationship between them in terms of differential equations. Perhaps the most general model he could adopt would be

$$\frac{dX}{dt} = kY \qquad (1.1)$$

$$\frac{dY}{dt} = k'X, \text{ where } k \text{ and } k' \text{ are constants.} \qquad (1.2)$$

That is, he expresses rates of change of one variable as a function of the other. Thus in the actual elaboration of the model he recognises the time dependency of the relationship between X and Y.

The sociologist, on the other hand, is far more likely to express the relation between the variables in terms of a simple equation, like

$$X = bY \qquad (1.3)$$

where b is a constant (errors being ignored).

Thus, on the face of it, he discounts any time dependency of the relationship.

But the implicit assumption behind expressing models in this form is that the variables X *and* Y *are in aggregate equilibrium.* So when we put pairs of values of X and Y into an equation like (1.3), in order to evaluate the parameter b, we assume that they are in equilibrium. It is not often recognised that when, for example, a correlation coefficient between two variables is determined, the value of this coefficient will be time dependent unless the variables are observed in an equilibrium relationship. If the relationship between X and Y can be represented by the above two differential equations then, *at equilibrium,*

$$\frac{dX}{dt} = \frac{dY}{dt} = O,$$

so $$kY = k'X \qquad (1.4)$$

thus, $$X = \frac{k}{k'}Y. \qquad (1.5)$$

So comparing the equilibrium equation (1.3) with this expression we see that $b = k/k'$. Thus in determining the value of b from *equilibrium* values of X and Y we in effect determine the ratio of the two *rate constants* k and k'.

The problem of aggregate equilibrium between variables will be taken up later on, but for the moment it is imperative to recognise that the computed value of a parameter like b (or an equivalent correlation coefficient) can only be regarded as a *structural parameter* of a model if we have evidence that the variables are in aggregate equilibrium. If variables accommodate instantaneously or almost instantaneously to one another there is no problem; the appropriate equilibrium values will always be observed. If, on the other hand, the accommodation consumes time, then this is not so and we must search for independent evidence for equilibrium.

There seems to be very little recognition of this problem in sociology. The ease with which correlations between variables are taken as significant parameters without any reason to suppose the variables have reached a joint equilibrium distribution is disturbing. This is particularly the case where attitudes are related to some variable characterising a social-structural environment. Our common knowledge tells us that a stable attitude will only result as a consequence of an experiential process – the attitude will become established over time. For example, the relationship between 'status crystallisation' and 'political liberality' (Lenski, 1954) will, in all probability, exhibit this characteristic. One does not expect a person to become 'politically liberal' as soon as he finds himself in a state of low crystallisation. Rather, he becomes 'liberal' as a consequence of a cumulative social experience of the strain inherent in such a position. The fact that variables take time to come to their equilibrium distributions often implies that there exists a complex set of intervening variables.

1.2 The Hierarchy of Scientific Sophistication

We may start our inquiries with what I term the *hierarchy of scientific sophistication* (Figure 1.1) which gives us some idea of the complexity of the processes we have to go through in erecting sociological models.

The most fundamental decision that has to be faced at the outset of any sociological investigation is the specification of the *units of analysis* – for example people, social groups, organisations, roles, etc. Perhaps our analysis may involve more than one type of unit; for instance, both organisations and roles or people in the organisations may be involved, in which case our analysis is correspondingly more complex. It is fairly evident that a great deal of sociology is concerned with situations where, as it were, we have to consider differing types of units of analysis. A most common enterprise is to explain a person or role incumbent's behaviour in terms of his social structural environment, which is perhaps a complex institutional or organisational setting. So we must expect when building models of human behaviour to jump back and forth between different units of analysis.

It should be noted, moreover, that the units of analysis

adopted in a sociological investigation may themselves be defined in terms of rather complex theoretical ideas. When we take 'social groups' as our basic units we then, in effect, adopt a fairly extensive theoretical definition; the problems of selecting units of analysis cannot be clearly separated from the problems of conceptual elaboration. Indeed, we are all familiar with the long-standing debate in sociology as to what constitute *the units* of social systems or structures.

These problems will be considered later but for the time being let us assume that we can clearly demarcate a population of units to which our concepts are supposed to be appropriate and move on to consider these.

The basic exploratory device of the sociologist is the *concept*; for example, group cohesion, group conflict, rates of suicide, alienation, and so on. Concepts apply to (are predicates of) units of analysis – in the broadest sense they are properties of, or relations between, units of analysis. They are thus the basic descriptive categories we employ in our explorations of the social world. The problems of where they come from and how to use them in sociological inquiry must, of course, occupy our attention in subsequent chapters.

Figure 1.1 The Hierarchy of Scientific Sophistication

	Example
⎰ Units of Analysis	'Social' groups
⎱ Concepts	Group cohesion; inter-group conflict; intra-group conflict
|	
(measurement)	
|	
Variables	'Degree' of group cohesion, inter-group conflict and intra-group conflict
(relating variables)	
|	
Propositions	*Increases* in inter-group conflict *lead to increases* in group cohesion
(relating propositions)	
|	
Interrelated Propositions	*Increases* in inter-group conflict *lead to increases* in group cohesion and *increases* in group cohesion *lead to* decreases in intra-group conflict
|	
(axiomatisation)	
|	
Axiomatised Propositions	(See text, Chapter 7)

The next stage in sophistication is to obtain *measures* of concepts by converting them into *variables*. This is done by assigning a range of *values* to the concepts and a little further on we shall see how complex a problem this can be, particularly in sociology. In Figure 1.1 then, we can speak of 'degrees' of inter-group conflict, etc. The process whereby values are assigned to concepts is known as measurement and in the social sciences it is often referred to as the *problem* of measurement, because with many concepts one encounters rather acute difficulties in obtaining measures (i.e. variables). Sociological concepts do not very readily lend themselves to measurement, but we may note here that when speaking of measurement in sociology we do not confine ourselves to commonsense ideas about measurement; using real numbers and their properties is only part of the story.

Once our concepts have been measured the next step is to relate them, as variables, in *propositions*. For example, in Figure 1.1, the proposition is that group cohesion and inter-group conflict are related. The proposition states that increases in one variable *lead to* increases in another, which seems to imply some notion of causality; that is, a causal connection between the variables. Clearly any proposition must contain some sort of connective relating its constituent variables and we shall subsequently have to pay a great deal of attention to their nature and form. But for the moment it may be noted that a proposition contains two concepts or variables and some sort of connective.

The next stage in the hierarchy is to try to obtain *interrelated propositions* and, as our example (Figure 1.1) indicates, one of the most obvious ways of accomplishing this is to consider two propositions with one common variable – 'group cohesion' in this case. This, however, is only one way and very much the simplest. It is really at this point that the idea of a *model* enters. For models of sociological phenomena are nothing more and nothing less than a complex set of interrelated propositions. Many people speak of multivariate propositions, but I prefer to limit the word 'proposition' to the case where only two variables are related and speak of models when more than two variables are involved.

The final stage in the hierarchy of scientific sophistication is axiomatised propositions. It is often both elegant and intellectually efficient to obtain axiomatised systems of propositions where a set of axioms entail[3] a further set of propositions. Such systems are, however, relatively rare in sociology, though Zetterberg (1965) has popularised a very limited conception of axiomatic theory whereby two propositions containing a common variable, of the form 'if A leads to B, and if B leads to C', are taken as 'axioms' entailing the proposition 'A leads to C'. We shall, however, have to give these ideas some very close scrutiny as this sort of entailment depends on the interpretation put on the expression 'leads to'.

It is true to say that, though much contemporary sociological activity is concerned with coining concepts and also converting them into variables with a view to testing isolated propositions, very little indeed goes beyond this. Theories comprising sets of interrelated propositions are at the moment relatively rare in sociology, but in terms of the more demanding criterion of scientific activity, it is only when we arrive at this level of analysis that we can really start saying we have anything approaching a theory. Of course, much of what goes for sociological theory is, in reality, a quest for fruitful theoretical and observational concepts and must be seen as such. But the answer to the question as to their fruitfulness can ultimately only be settled in terms of their utility in constructing models of social reality. We want to know how social reality works – its mechanisms – and it is only by adopting a model building perspective that this quest can be carried through. We must remember, though, that the ultimate value of our endeavours will depend upon the intelligence with which we originally select our problem area, the units of analysis and the concepts we regard as appropriate to the problem.

In the next few chapters we will consider in more detail some of the problems associated with moving up the hierarchy of scientific sophistication.

2. Units of Analysis

2.1 Introduction

Any piece of sociological research must commence with some decision about the basic units of analysis involved; these are the entities to which our concepts or variables pertain. As was mentioned earlier, units may be of differing 'complexity' and invariably contain, in the way they are abstracted from the totality of reality, embedded theoretical notions such as in the use of the unit 'social group'. For a very long time now, theoreticians have tried to insist that the most basic units in a sociological analysis are not individual persons but rather something like positions, statuses, roles, collectivities, norms, values and so on. And there is surely some element of truth in the statement that empirical sociology has traditionally been extremely limited in its selection of basic units of analysis. The vast majority of empirical studies start with individual people though, to be fair, these are often supposed to represent more abstract entities – such as when somebody is interviewed to determine the 'nature of his role'. We are not, however, directly concerned with this debate here. What is required is a general logical framework into which differing substantive conceptions of units may be fitted. Furthermore, this framework must enable us to move back and forth between different levels of analysis so we can accommodate situations like those outlined in Chapter 1, where it was suggested that an individual person's behaviour may be explained in terms of his organisational setting. It is not altogether clear how this involves different units of analysis, except that, on the face of it, both organisations and persons are involved. The question is, how are they related? In part, all this clearly has something to do with the way basic units are aggregated into more complex ones.

But before going on to consider such a framework, it must be emphasised how important it is to specify, as far as possible, the boundaries of the set of units of analysis towards which the particular research (the model building) is directed. That is to say the population at risk must be specified. A great deal of sociological research (especially attempts at replication) goes awry because of an initial failure to specify the precise nature of the population. In effect, this is a plea for clear and precise definitions of population though this is admittedly often difficult to accomplish. For example, Lenski (1954) has demonstrated a connection between 'status disequilibrium'[1] and 'political liberality' in a sample population drawn in Detroit. Status disequilibrium is the variation in rank on a *set* of status dimensions – the higher the variation across the set then the less equilibriated a person is, and vice versa. The basic idea is that persons who are highly disequilibriated suffer punitive social experiences as a consequence of differential treatment on each dimension and become politically liberal with a view to changing the social structure. But does Lenski intend his findings to be generalisable to other urban populations or not? If not, what are the peculiar features of Detroit that make it a unique population in this respect? Clearly, Lenski did intend his findings to be generalisable, perhaps to *all* those populations that exhibit a multiplicity of status rankings, but if such a population were encountered with a significant level of disequilibrium and little or no political liberality (apart from problems of definition and aggregate equilibrium between the variables) what would our reaction be? In practice, we would try to explain the apparent anomaly, and one way of doing this would be to point out that some feature of the original Detroit population, necessary for the presence of a relationship between disequilibrium and political liberality, did not hold. But perhaps if we had originally been more careful in specifying the 'nature' of the Detroit population, we might not have had occasion to study the particular example we did. All this may seem very obvious to the reader, but a casual perusal of the sociological literature seems to warrant this emphasis. Often authors do not justify or define – even in a minimal sense – the nature of the populations to which they believe their findings are applicable.

Another way of putting all this is in terms of the classical hypothetico-deductive model of scientific explanation. Readers will, no doubt, recognise the above stipulations as one aspect whereby the *set of initial conditions* are specified (see Chapter 6) under which a hypothesis or law is supposed to hold. These are normally regarded as a set of necessary and sufficient conditions for the applicability of the law. We will, however, have occasion later on to consider the rather subtle nature of this necessity and sufficiency in sociological explanations.

Populations of units of analysis may be specified in two ways:

(i) *Intensionally:* When the population is defined in terms of an explicit set of criteria or properties – for example, the set of all persons living in urban areas (urban areas being defined in terms of a set of characteristics); and

(ii) *Extensionally:* When all the units in the population are explicitly listed – for example, a list of the words on this page.

Needless to say, the two modes of specification are often closely connected, for we may define the list of words on this page as 'the set of all words on this page'. But the importance of general intensional definitions is that they are empirically open, and naturally facilitate extrapolation of research findings through space and time. One should, therefore, as far as is possible, endeavour to base sociological research on general intensional definitions of populations. But of course there is always a danger in this; for if all the necessary conditions for the presence of the relationship we are looking for are not caught in the definition of a population, then all the problems alluded to above will emerge.[2] For instance, if the population 'all persons living in urban areas' is adopted when the concern is to establish a relationship between status disequilibrium and political liberality, then it might well be under-specified. We might have been too permissive in our attempts to permit generalisability of the relationship.

Of course, we are often not in a position to specify, in full detail, the universe to which we think our particular findings are applicable. In these conditions all that can be asked for is prudence and caution and perhaps an explicit statement about the problem. Reasons why the findings might or might not be generalisable to certain other, apparently 'similar', populations should be given. In this way a pivot is provided not only for replication but for the extension and elaboration of the findings (in our case the model).

Even if a population can be clearly defined and its boundaries located, in practice we can rarely (as is well known) subject the whole of it to analysis; our endeavours are most often directed to a *sample*. And normally speaking, of course, the sample should be representative of the population. A detailed analysis of what constitutes this representativeness would take us into considerations of sampling theory and I will assume the reader is familiar with the basic ideas of sampling theory and the logic of testing for significance.[3] One point that may be brought out here, though, is that when the nature of a population is fully specified then the more knowledge we have about it and the more sophisticated our sampling procedures can be. We can use our knowledge of the population at risk to provide us with a stratified sample, thus facilitating more significant analysis.

To summarise:

(1) As far as possible, the precise nature of the population of units, to which the concepts/variables and ultimately propositions apply, should be made explicit.

(2) If the study is not carried out on the full population of units then a 'representative' sample should be utilised, taking into consideration our knowledge of the nature of the population.

2.2 A Logical Framework for Primary Units of Analysis

We now return to the problem of providing a logical framework for selecting and aggregating units of analysis. It was previously remarked that the major conceptual problem is that we often want, in some way, to aggregate our primary units of analysis into collectivities of one sort or another so that, for instance, both the individual (primary unit) and the structure that 'surrounds' him can be conceptualised. Formal methods provide the most efficacious means of devising such a framework. In this way the logical features of aggregation can be abstracted, which should then be applicable to any set of primary units we care to use.

We start then with:

1. A set $X = \{x_i\}$ of *primary units*.

$i = 1, 2, \ldots, n$, for example, the population of a given city. There are then two ways in which the units in set X can be characterised:

(a) in terms of their *properties*[4]

(b) in terms of the *relationship(s)* between them.

2. *A primary aggregate* of units is defined as a subset of X (or X itself) possessing a certain common property or properties: for example, persons living in a certain precinct of the city.

3. *A primary structure* (structure for short) of units is defined in terms of:

(a) the set X or a subset of X;

(b) *at least one* binary relation R on the set or subset of X creating a set of associated pairs[5] of the form x_iRx_j: for example, the set of persons in a city who *interact* (the binary relation) in face to face situations.

The distinction between structures and aggregates is important. Though the term *collectivity* is often used to cover both in sociology, we should be very clear concerning the logical distinction between them. When encountering the word 'collectivity', one should ask whether a structure or an aggregate is implied. Sometimes the two ideas are utilised together when, for instance, a social group is defined as a set of individual persons (primary units) with both a structure (the interaction relationship) and a common property (all members having a common 'interest'). When a collectivity is defined in this manner, we will refer to it as a *primary empirical collectivity*. It often becomes an empirical problem in itself to study the co-ordination of such collectivities – how, for instance, the interaction structure in the group is related to the distribution of intensity of interests. Much of the complexity of sociology revolves around this sort of analysis, whereby structures are related to attributes or properties of the units in the structure. In subsequent chapters we will try to provide techniques for sorting out the complexities of this sort of analysis.

One of the most convenient ways of depicting primary units, aggregates and structures is in terms of ideas of elementary *graph-theory*.[6]

The primary units in set X may be depicted as points in a plane (Figure 2.1(i)). The position of the points in the plane has no significance, but it is often analytically useful to group them in certain ways. Aggregates may then be depicted as in Figure 2.1(ii) where two are defined, A and B. Finally, Figure 2.1(iii) depicts a structure where the points are connected by lines (*arcs*) representing the binary relation; this is called a graph-theoretic structure.

We may wish to describe more than one type of relationship holding between the units and so generate more than one structure. When this is the case the constituent structures may be referred to as *structures over the particular relationship R_i* (where R_i is named). For instance, an 'interaction' and a 'friendship' relation can be defined over the same set of people.

We are in a position to give a more formal definition of a graph (structure).

A graph consists of:

(1) a set of points in a plane (usually finite), and

(2) a set of lines (arcs) joining some or all of the pairs of points.

If the points are distinguished one from another by naming them, the graph is said to be *labelled*. The properties of primary units may be regarded as providing a *vector labelling* of the points. So a *vector labelled* graph is one comprising a set of points, a vector of properties associated with each point and a set of arcs joining some or all of the points.

Figure 2.1 Primary Units, Aggregates and Structures

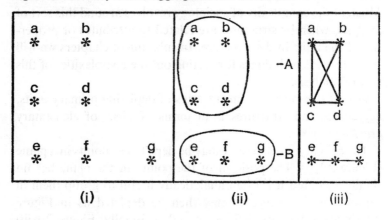

(i)	(ii)	(iii)

Figure 2.2 Some Di-graphs

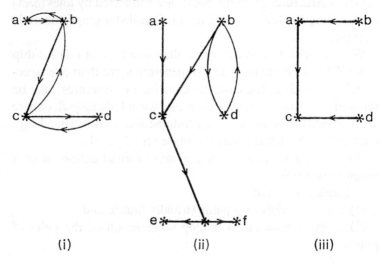

(i)	(ii)	(iii)

Our example in Figure 2.1 contains what are termed *symmetric arcs*, i.e. if a particular unit *a* is related to *b* then *b* is also related to *a* (for formal definitions of symmetry properties of relations see Chapter 4, p. 42). The relationship of 'social interaction' seems by definition to be symmetric. But we might want to consider structures where the relationship is not necessarily symmetric (for example, relationships of subordination and superordination) and consequently introduce 'direction' onto the arcs of the structure. If we do this, we define a *di-graph*. Figure 2.2 depicts some labelled di-graphs. It should be noted that if there is an arc running both ways between a pair of points we can introduce a type of symmetry with a di-graph. Figure 2.2 may be taken to represent a 'Friendship choice structure' where an arc is *incident out of* point *a* and *incident in to* point *b* if *a* chooses *b* as a friend, and if *b* reciprocates this choice there will also be an arc incident out of *b* and incident into *a*.

A di-graph may thus be defined in terms of:

(i) a set of points in a plane, and

(ii) a set of *directed* lines (arcs) connecting some or all the pairs of points.

Graphs and di-graphs provide a very powerful way of depicting a structure on a set of primary units.

There is, however, an alternative way of picturing structures. Whenever one can draw an *n*-point graph, it can equally well be represented as an $n \times n$ matrix A, where the elements $a_{ij} = a_{ji} = 1$ if point *i* is related to point *j* (i.e. there is an arc between them), and $a_{ij} = a_{ji} = 0$ if point *i* is not related to point *j*. Clearly the matrix will be symmetric about the main diagonal. Analogously an *n*-point di-graph can be depicted as a matrix, but in this case, a_{ij} is not necessarily equal to a_{ji} since there can be an arc incident out of point *i* and incident into point *j*, but not the reverse. The matrix is thus not, in general, symmetric.

The matrices for the graph in Figure 2.1(iii) and Figure 2.2(i) are depicted in Figure 2.3.

It should be noted that the entries down the main diagonal take the value 0. If we allow *reflexive* relations (arcs) then these

Figure 2.3 Some Matrices Representing Structures

	a	b	c	d	e	f	g
a	0	1	1	1	0	0	0
b	1	0	1	1	0	0	0
c	1	1	0	1	0	0	0
d	1	1	1	0	0	0	0
e	0	0	0	0	0	1	0
f	0	0	0	0	1	0	1
g	0	0	0	0	0	1	0

The matrix corresponding to the graph in Fig. (2.1 (iii))

	a	b	c	d
a	0	1	0	0
b	1	0	1	0
c	0	1	0	1
d	0	0	1	0

The matrix corresponding to the di-graph in Fig. (2.2 (i))

entries may take on a value of unity. A reflexive relation is one where something is related to itself (see Chapter 4, p. 43).

It is a matter of convenience whether a structure is depicted as a graph or a matrix. For fairly small structures ($n < 10$) a graph or a di-graph is often most helpful, but above this size the network of relations often becomes so complex that a graph loses any analytical utility and the matrix representation is more useful.

Starting with a set of primary units, we may, therefore, define either a set of graphs or matrices, one for each definable relation holding between the units. So far, then, our framework formally consists in:

   (i) a set of primary units,

  (ii) a set of properties of the primary units,

 (iii) a set of relations holding between the primary units.

From these we can construct:

  (iv) a set of primary aggregates,

   (v) a set of primary structures,

  (vi) a set of primary empirical collectivities.

The way in which these aggregates and structures are in fact constructed depends, of course, on the empirical problem in hand. But it should be emphasised once again that concepts like 'social group' often imply a complex interrelationship between the properties of the units and various relationships holding between them. Thus, for example, a social group may be demarcated in terms of *connected* (see next section) interaction, cognitive and affective structures and the possession of similar attitudes of one sort or another. The concept thus cuts across a series of primary structures and aggregates.

2.3 Some Properties of Structures

It is convenient next to consider some important concepts concerning structures.

  (i) *Connectivity:* If we consider graphs first of all, a graph (symmetric structure) is said to be connected if there is a *path* (i.e. a continuous sequence of arcs) connecting *all* pairs of points in the graph. The graph in Figure 2.1(iii) is *not* connected. But, in fact, there are, in the total graph, two connected sub-graphs consisting of 4 and 3 points. A connected sub-graph of a graph (sub-structure of a structure) is called a *component*. Thus, the graph in Figure 2.1(iii) contains two components, the sets {a, b, c, d} and {e, f, g}.

Turning now to di-graphs, the situation is clearly a little more complex, for meaning can be attached to the *direction* of paths in the structure.

A di-graph is said to be *strongly connected*[7] if there exists a *directed path* (i.e. a continuous sequence of arcs all directed in the same direction) running both ways between all pairs of points in the di-graph. The di-graph depicted in Figure 2.2(i) is strongly connected.

A di-graph is said to be *connected* if there exists a directed path running one way *or* the other between all pairs of points in the graph. The di-graph depicted in Figure 2.2(iii) is connected.

A di-graph is *weakly connected* if there exists a *semi-path* (i.e. a continuous sequence of arcs, irrespective of the direction of the arc) between all pairs of points in the path. The di-graph in Figure 2.2(iii) is weakly connected.

The degree of connectivity can be defined for all the different types of connectivity by taking the ratio of pairs of points actually connected to the total number possible. The degree of connectivity is an important summary parameter of structures since social groups normally have a fairly high degree of connectivity, at least in some of their constituent relations.

(ii) *Completion:* A graph or di-graph is said to be *complete* if all the pairs of points are connected by an arc. Thus in a graph of *n*-points there will be $n(n-1)/2$ arcs and in a di-graph there will be $n(n-1)$ arcs.

So a complete structure is always connected. Harary (1959) has suggested that social groups tend to completion and the ways in which different types of relationships in structures influence the connectivity and completion patterns is an important area of sociological investigation in its own right (Abell, 1969a).

2.4 Extension of the Framework to Higher Order Structures
The basic distinction between primary units, aggregates, structures and empirical collectivities has now been established. Much of the complexity of social structures, however, results

from the fact that one can speak of properties of and relationships between these structures, aggregates and empirical collectivities themselves.[8] For example it is quite natural to use the idea of social groups or organisations having 'collective' properties and relationships with each other.

In general, we may start with a set of primary units, define a set of structures or aggregates (in terms of one or more binary relations or properties) and then *secondary structures* by invoking the idea of a binary relationship between the primary structures. Similarly, secondary aggregates can be defined by considering aggregates of primary aggregates with common properties, and secondary empirical collectivities in terms of both relationships between and properties of primary structures of aggregates. Figure 2.5 gives an example of this. Clearly there is no reason why one should not go on to define structures or empirical collectivities or aggregates of even 'higher order', by considering relationships between secondary structures, and so on. The diagrammatic form of Figure 2.4 is convenient for depicting secondary structures where the bold line represents the relationship between two structures circumscribed by the broken line.

Figure 2.4 A Secondary Structure

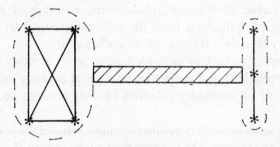

There is, however, a further rather crucial distinction to be made between *relationships that hold between structures as structures* (as above) and relationships that hold between the primary units of different structures. The best way to make this distinction clear is by an example. Suppose we define two social groups in terms of an interaction relationship where there is a connected interaction structure internal to each group and no interaction between the groups. Figure 2.1(iii) could be an example of this state of affairs, i.e. each component is a social group. We might now ask who 'recognises' who in the total structure, and thus obtain a further structure, the 'cognitive structure', which may well have links between the two components. Clearly, whenever we consider more than one type of relationship in a structure, situations like this might arise. The cognitive links hold between the primary units of the different social groups. But this sort of cross group or cross structural linking is to be distinguished from the linkages in secondary structures where the relationship holds between the structures as total entities. Even here, of course, it may be that the linkage between the structures 'implies' certain patterns or types of linkages between individual units in the structures. For instance, if we say one group dominates another, it may imply that all members of the first group dominate all members of the second, or it may not. When we say one group 'dominates' another, we often do not mean this at all. Rather we mean the first group as a *total entity* dominates the second as a *total entity* in some functional setting, and it would not be correct to imply that appropriately directed domination relationships would hold between each pair of individuals from the different groups.[9] By way of summary then, our framework now allows for:

(i) a set of secondary units (defined in terms of either or both primary relations and properties on a set of primary units);

(ii) a set of secondary relations holding between secondary units;

(iii) a set of secondary properties characterising the secondary units – for example, the properties of social groups. Lazarsfeld and Menzel (1961) refer to these as global properties.

Secondary properties can be of two types:

(a) Those properties that are derived from properties of or relationships between the primary units. For example, when social groups are characterised by the mean value of a property of their constituent primary units or their connectivity.

(b) Emergent properties *not* derivable from properties of or relationships between units. Although the idea, for example, of social groups having emergent properties has played a fairly prominent role in social theory, there has been little attempt to operationalise it. But we should distinguish between emergent properties that are *in principle* not derivable from distributions of primary properties or relations and those that *in practice* are not. Many philosophers, of course, disavow the former altogether and despite repeated pleas for their 'existence' in sociology no research, as far as I am aware, has ever led to a satisfactory formulation. A so-called emergent property usually invites an attempt to reduce it to properties of individual units. The history of physical science is replete with such attempts.

So, secondary structures and aggregates and empirical collectivities can be defined in terms of (i), (ii) and (iii) above.

Furthermore, the process can logically be extended to third order structures, fourth order structures and so on.

This, then, completes the logical framework within which we can select units of analysis. It allows us, for example, starting with a set of individual persons possessing certain properties, to define social groups (structures) on this set in terms of certain binary relations and to define the higher order groupings by specifying relationships between the groups.

The richness of sociological analysis often springs from considering different types of structures and aggregates starting with a simple set of primary units like persons. We can, of course, start with primary units that possess some structure and construct more complex structures out of these – indeed, in one sense an individual person is a complex psychological structure.

The table in Figure 2.5 gives an outline summary of the framework alongside an elementary example.

2.5 Types of Analysis

It is important to recognise the types of sociological analysis

Figure 2.5 Framework for Units of Analysis

FRAMEWORK	EXAMPLE
1. A set of primary units	A set of persons
2. A set of properties of the primary units	A set of 'relevant' characteristics of the individuals (i.e. a set of concepts characterising persons), e.g. sex, age, attitudes, etc.
3. A set of primary relations between the primary units	A set of relations between the persons, e.g. interaction, friendship, superordination, subordination, etc.
4. A set of aggregates of the primary units defined in terms of one or more of their common properties	Aggregates in terms of one property, e.g. all persons of the same sex, or same age: aggregates in terms of more than one attribute, e.g. all persons of the same sex *and* age, etc.
5. A set of structures of primary units (primary structures)	The structures developed on the set of persons by the interaction, friendship, superordination-subordination relations. (There will be as many structures as definable relations)
6. A set of primary empirical collectivities	'Social groups' defined in terms of say interaction *and* friendship structures *and* similar attitudes
7. A set of secondary relations holding between either primary aggregates, structures or empirical collectivities	Superordination/subordination between social groups
8. A set of secondary structures	The structures developed on the set of primary structures, aggregates and empirical collectivities by the secondary relations, e.g. relationships between social groups, etc.
9. Higher order units and relations	Structures or aggregates of social groups (e.g. organisations or societies)
10. Higher order structures and aggregates	Structures or aggregates of organisations or societies

invited by the previously outlined framework. We will deal with most of them in subsequent chapters but a summary at this point will give some idea of its analytical richness. There are five types of analysis possible:

(i) *Classical Analysis of Distributions of Properties:* All the properties of the units will have a particular distribution across the full set of units. So one can speak of appropriate summary parameters characterising these distributions, e.g. means and variances. These parameters will, in general, be a function of the *level of measurement* (Chapter 4, p. 49) of the properties. The summary parameters may be taken as properties of aggregates or empirical collectivities as when, for instance, the mean value of 'level of commitment' is used to measure 'group cohesion'. It is perhaps worth pointing out here that many distributions in sociological contexts are not particularly regular, which often makes the use of summary parameters difficult. As is well known, a normal distribution is perfectly defined in terms of its mean and variance and so a collectivity with an individual property distributed in this manner can, 'without loss of information' be characterised by the mean and variance of the distribution. For more irregular distributions higher-order moments of the distribution must be defined. Sociologists have, however, failed to elaborate theoretical ideas at the collectivity level which can take account of such moments. Despite pioneering efforts by Coleman (1964), one of the major deficiencies of contemporary sociological theory is the lack of any general theory of aggregation of 'micro level' distributions into 'macro level' parameters.

(ii) *Analysis of Distributions of Structural Properties:* The two important concepts here are *indegree* and *outdegree*. The indegree of a unit in a structure (point in a graph) is the number of relations (arcs) of a particular type incident into the unit. The outdegree of a unit is the number of relations of a particular type incident out of the unit. Clearly, where there is more than one type of relationship we may speak of indegree and outdegree for each relationships. The outdegree will be given by the row sum of the appropriate matrix and the indegree by the column sum. Thus the outdegrees in Figure 2.1 (iii) are: $a = 3$, $b = 3$, $c = 3$, etc. The indegrees are $a = 3$, $b = 3$, $c = 3$, etc. The total indegree in a structure must obviously be numerically equal to the total outdegree.

B

The distributions of indegree and outdegree over different types of relationships can be described in given structures. The importance of this type of analysis can easily be appreciated when one recognises that the relations may well be 'social relations' between people. So the analysis describes the distribution of the types of structural environment people find themselves in. Connectivity and completion conceptions are also important in this context.

(iii) *Classical Analysis of Covariation of Properties of Units:* The covariation of the properties of units of analysis can be analysed in the standard fashion using appropriate statistical techniques.

(iv) *Contingently Relating Structures:* Much social theory is couched in terms of one structure exerting an influence over another; for instance, economic relations determining cultural relations. We will see (Chapter 6) that our framework enables us to analyse correlations and ultimately causal relations between structures.

(v) *Contingently Relating Structures and Properties of Units:* A typical problem in social theory is to try to relate the attitudes, beliefs, values, etc., a person or collectivity possesses in virtue of its relationships with other units. Our framework also enables us to analyse situations like this (Chapter 6).

2.6 Changing Units of Analysis
There is one further issue worthy of brief comment; this is the problem of so-called *ecological correlation* (Robinson, 1950). A full treatment will not be given here as it has been dealt with very fully elsewhere.[10]

The problem of ecological correlation arises whenever we take aggregates as our units of analysis and try to infer from an established relationship between two variables at this level to the same relationship holding at the level of the constituent units of the aggregates. To use the earlier example, it is not, in general, possible to infer from an established relationship between the proportion of people in status disequilibrium and the proportion who are politically liberal, where our units of analysis are social groups, to a relationship positing a connection between disequilibrium and political liberality for individuals.

Assume, for the sake of simplicity, that status disequilibrium and political liberality are dichotomous variables[11] and we have the hypothetical data in Figure 2.6 for four groups.

Figure 2.6 Data Using Groups as Units of Analysis

	Groups			
	1	2	3	4
Proportion of persons politically liberal	0.1	0.2	0.3	0.6
Proportion of persons in status disequilibrium	0.1	0.2	0.3	0.6

The data clearly suggest a perfect positive linear relationship between the two variables. And on the basis of this we might be tempted to postulate a relationship between status disequilibrium and political liberality *for individual persons in the groups.*

But now assume that the data depicted in Figure 2.7, giving the joint distributions for the two variables *within* each group, can be obtained.

We note that the marginal distributions are perfectly compatible with the proportions expressed in Figure 2.6. But the internal joint distributions by no means suggest a uniform positive relationship between $\bar{E}$ and L. Group 1 shows a positive correlation between disequilibrium and liberality; group 2 a negative correlation; group 3 a positive correlation and group 4 a perfect negative correlation.

It would thus be invalid to infer a within-group correlation between these two variables on the basis of data taking the groups themselves as units of analysis. However, it is the inference that is invalid, not the correlation at the group level.

Figure 2.7 Data Using Individuals as Units of Analysis

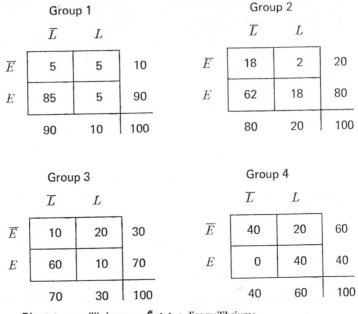

E is status equilibrium; $\bar{E}$ status disequilibrium;
L is political liberality; $\bar{L}$ is political illiberality.

We might well be interested in the relationship at the group level for its own sake.

But it is imperative in sociological research to be aware of this problem: it is very easy casually to make inferences between different levels of analysis. This is not always illegitimate and the reader is referred to Goodman (1959) for further details.

3. Concepts

3.1 Introduction

There is an extensive literature on the problems of concept formation, both within the boundaries of sociology itself, and in the philosophy of science,[1] and the reader must be referred to these sources for a detailed consideration of the various problems.

We will make the elementary distinction, however, between:
 (i) theoretical concepts (T-concepts) and
 (ii) observational concepts (O-concepts),
where O-concepts are 'given' in immediate sense experience, but T-concepts are not. This is, of course, altogether too simple a statement, as we know it is by no means an easy matter to decide on a set of observational concepts in sociology; there is much disagreement within the discipline as to the precise nature of the observational domain. Furthermore, so-called O-concepts often contain embedded theoretical ideas, and even the most rudimentary observational procedures often rest upon a series of theoretical assumptions. The whole debate about the nature of social reality and the way social actors constitute this reality[2] is germane to this problem. But just as, in the last chapter, we bypassed the problem concerning the most fruitful sociological units, we do so here, for we are much more concerned with a logical framework within which the debate can be set. We will therefore, assume that a set of O-concepts appropriate to the problem in hand[3] can be clearly distinguished.

If they are to have any value in an empirical science, T-concepts must be 'ultimately expressible' in terms of O-concepts. The phrase 'ultimately expressible' is, of course, vague and needs much elaboration. The standard practice in sociology is to *operationalise* T-concepts in terms of O-concepts. The word 'operationalise' however covers a wide variety of procedures and it is the conception itself that really needs elaboration. This terminology is used rather than the more obvious phrase 'defined in terms of' since, in the practice of sociology, the relationship between T-concepts and O-concepts is often so loosely codified that the notion of definition is altogether too strong. Furthermore, in a subsequent chapter it will be argued that it is often desirable in model building not to adopt explicit definitions of T-concepts.

T-concepts need not necessarily be immediately expressible in terms of O-concepts, since we may distinguish between those that are 'immediately expressed' in terms of *other* T-concepts and those that are expressed in terms of O-concepts. Of course, the former sort must *ultimately* be expressible in terms of T-concepts that are themselves operationalised in terms of O-concepts. For example, Blauner (1964) has suggested that the T-concept 'alienation' is expressible in terms of (implies?) other T-concepts like 'powerlessness', 'meaninglessness', 'normlessness', and 'isolation'; and that these concepts in turn can be operationalised in terms of sets of O-concepts. This gives the hierarchy depicted in Figure 3.1.

The major question is: what is the nature of the *lines* in the above diagram – that is, the *inferences* between the concepts in

Figure 3.1 A Theoretical Hierarchy

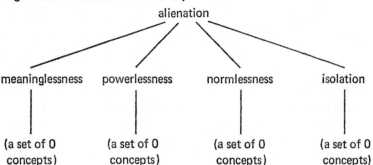

the hierarchy? Northrop (1947) calls the inference between T-concepts and O-concepts *epistemic correlation* but his analysis tells us little of the precise nature of the inferences. It is, however, easier to consider these problems in terms of variables rather than concepts and so we may, with advantage, postpone our deliberations until the next chapter. There is, however, a notable feature of the above hierarchy which is fairly characteristic of any attempt to set out the structure of social theory. Technically the structure is a *tree* which implies, among other things, that there are no horizontal links between the points (concepts). This is not surprising for the lack of horizontal links corresponds to a lack of theoretical propositions (except for the ones relating 'alienation' to 'meaninglessness', etc.); a horizontal link between say 'powerlessness' and 'normlessness' would imply a proposition relating these two T-concepts. But as we remarked earlier, social theory exhibits a marked paucity of propositions. The modal activity of social theorists has been devising interesting T-concepts, not working out relationships between them. In one sense, the aim of a model building perspective is to establish horizontal links in structures like the one above. As long as 'social theories' look like trees, we have few theoretical propositions, and, in the strict sense, little social theory!

Of course, theoretical concepts like meaninglessness, powerlessness, etc., are often regarded as *dimensions* of the concept alienation and if this is so, then they are not necessarily meant to enter propositions but 'elucidate' the deeper lying concept. Theoretical propositions would enter the picture when the concept alienation itself was related to other concepts which in turn may be 'multi-dimensional'. Unfortunately, however, the idea of dimensions of T-concepts is not always used in a very precise manner; sometimes it implies an analytic and sometimes a synthetic relationship between the T-concept and its dimensions (see Chapter 5). In the former case the lines in Figure 3.1 between 'alienation' and 'meaninglessness' etc. stand for logical implication, in the latter for a contingent connective. But the problem naturally arises as to when it is correct to treat concepts as dimensions of deeper lying theoretical concepts and when to treat them as concepts in their own right, in the sense that they can be related to other concepts. It has been argued elsewhere (Abell, 1969b) that sociologists have traditionally been too eager to use the dimensional approach, but unfortunately one often encounters severe technical difficulties in taking the other approach. We will return to this problem later.

3.2 Types of Concepts
A further major distinction may be drawn between:
  (i) explained concepts, and
  (ii) explanatory concepts.
Explained concepts are those concepts which denote the phenomena (the presence of, absence of, or variation of) that we wish to explain in terms of *explanatory concepts*. Thus explained concepts and explanatory concepts normally appear (as variables) in sociological propositions. The same distinction is sometimes made in terms of dependent and independent variables, the former being explained and the latter being explanatory. However, this terminology is often misleading, since so-called independent variables are, in fact, not always statistically independent. So we will adopt the above terminology. *Sociological models will normally relate an explained concept or set of explained concepts to a set of explanatory concepts.*
  The distinction may also be drawn between:
  (i) internal concepts, and (ii) external concepts.
  By *internal concepts* I mean those concepts that actors themselves employ to describe and explain their behaviour, action and social environment;[4] by *external concepts* I mean concepts, other than internal concepts, deployed by, say, the sociologist, to describe and explain behaviour and social phenomena. The most obvious examples of the former are reasons, intentions, purposes, etc., whilst an example of the latter might, perhaps, be demographic pressure.
  The boundary between internal and external concepts is not often very clear; this is particularly true when the sociologist

himself is in some sort of commune with his subject matter. For then he can play a pedagogic role and constantly enrich the conceptual repertoire of the actors – so that concepts that are initially the sole proclivity of the sociologist become 'everyday' concepts of the actors. Perhaps the Freudian concept of the unconscious is a good example of this.

External concepts may be further subdivided as follows:

(a) External concepts which are *logically related* to an internal or set of internal concepts. That is, they are 'logical constructs' of internal concepts; the relationship between the internal and external concept is *analytical*. I will call the use of such concepts *constructivism;* and

(b) External concepts which are *not logically related* to any internal concepts.

When Winch (1958) refers to 'technical concepts' that 'imply a prior understanding of those concepts which belong to the activities under investigation' and Schutz (1967) refers to 'secondary concepts', they seem to be referring to external concepts of type (a).

The distinction between type (a) and (b) is not, however, easy to sustain. For there is the problem revolving around the interpretation of the phrase 'logically related to'. Winch's synonym for this seems to be 'prior understanding' and Schutz's, 'logical construct', but these expressions do not seem to take us very far. Technically, however, this often turns out to be the problem of variable formation in sociology, so we will consider it in that context in Chapter 5.

3.3 Types of Sociological Explanation

If the explained/explanatory and internal/external dimensions of concepts are cross-classified it leads to the four-fold classification depicted in Figure 3.2.

There are thus, on the basis of this classification, three (one is impossible)[5] types of approach to sociological model building. It is well worthwhile taking a brief look at these for each carries with it characteristic implications for the practice of sociology.

Figure 3.2 Types of Sociological Explanations

EXPLANATORY CONCEPT

		internal	external
EXPLAINED CONCEPT	internal	radical internalism I	II
	external	(impossible)	radical externalism III

Type 1 (*Radical Internalism*): If this approach were adopted to the exclusion of all others, then both the explanatory and explained concepts would be part of the 'actor's view of things'. In other words, the sociologist would be limited to describing and explaining the social domain in terms of the concepts used by the actors themselves. Thus his explanatory schemes could in no way transcend those of the actor. The sociologist would not be at liberty to recognise and describe or explain phenomena that were not part of the 'cognitive map' of the actors. Perhaps this perspective would allow him to bring some phenomena under a different explanation or description from those of the actors; for instance, he might suggest the 'real reasons' why somebody was behaving in a certain way, using reasons that differ from those given by the actor. But such reasons would have to be comprehensible to the actor and part of his stock of concepts 'appropriate' to the behaviour in question and furthermore, explanations of this appropriateness could also only be in terms of internal concepts. Needless to say, the radical internalist perspective would drastically circumscribe the theoretical activities of the sociologist.

Although it is, of course, often important to take into consideration the actor's descriptions and explanations, the sociologist would regard this as only a starting point of his activities and feel at liberty to go beyond these (MacIntyre, 1967). In particular, he might note some feature of a social situation that the participant actors do not, or even the lack of some feature shown to him by a comparative perspective not possible for the untutored actor. Clearly the sociologist can either ignore these or adopt an externalist standpoint; it would surely be incumbent upon the radical internalist to give reasons for ignoring them.[6]

All this aside, a key question is: can the sociologist legitimately provide an *alternative* to the actor's explanation of some phenomenon? Logically this would usually involve a type II situation,[7] where the explained concept (denoting the phenomenon) is internal and the sociologist's explanatory concept(s) external. So we may now turn to this type.

Type II (External Explanations): If the sociologist were limited to this perspective then he would necessarily be constrained to explain only those phenomena that the actors themselves conceptualise but remain free in his selection of explanatory concepts. Thus, if an actor has an explanation of the phenomenon in question, it becomes possible for the sociologist and the actor to have differing explanations. We can distinguish two situations; first, where the external concepts are in some way 'constructed' out of the internal concepts and second, where the external concepts are logically independent of any internal explanatory concepts at all. In the former case, we would be dealing with Winch's technical concepts or Schutz's secondary concepts. We will study in subsequent chapters the limitations that might be imposed on this sort of constructivism, but it should be noted that such constructions are normally made to provide concepts of *greater generality* than the actors themselves employ.

The second case, where the explanatory concepts are logically distinct from those of the actor, is a common form of explanation, particularly in anthropology; for instance, when the anthropologist provides an external explanation of rain dances.

Much social functional 'explanation' also has this structure; as for instance when attempts are made to explain the presence of some social institution involving the so-called functional requisites of a system not recognised by the participant actors.

There is an important logical problem associated with non-constructivist external explanations for, when such an explanation is provided by the sociologist as an alternative to an internal explanation, we are naturally tempted to ask which is the 'correct' one. Consider, for instance, the anthropologist who explains the incidence of lighting of fires in a primitive culture in terms of temperature drop; he establishes a perfect correlation between a specified drop in temperature and the lighting of fires and stands content with this as an explanation. However, suppose a rather more discerning anthropologist learns the people's language and actually asks them why they light fires, to which they reply that they do so to keep the 'bad spirits' at bay. Now which explanation is correct? There seem to be various ways out of this problem. Firstly, one can adopt the internalist stance and ignore completely the correlation between the behaviour pattern and drop in temperature. Secondly, one could search for criteria for accepting one rather than the other and thirdly, one could attempt some sort of reconciliation of the two forms of explanation.

Let us return to our example. Suppose the first anthropologist points out to the second one that *according to our present understanding of human biology* the peoples in question would actually perish if they did not light fires to protect themselves from the cold, and therefore 'really' they must light the fires for this reason; the implicit claim being that if anybody were to reject this explanation then he would be inconsistent if he did not also reject a great deal of our 'knowledge' of human biology. In general, the logical force of such an appeal is to the effect that one should accept those explanatory concepts (in this case, drop in temperature) which also play a role in a more extensive theoretical framework (the theory of human biology in this case). So the first anthropologist might argue: my explanation in terms of temperature drop is clearly more powerful than the one in terms of 'spirits'. But, of course, it is also true that the concept of 'spirit' might well play a very extensive role in the belief system of the primitive peoples and we might then, if we pursued this line of argument find ourselves in a comparative analysis of 'our' and 'their' belief systems. It may therefore be difficult, on this sort of criterion, to establish a clear-cut case for the greater analytical power of 'our' framework. A deep understanding of the role of the concept of spirits in the people's scheme of things might still stand as a highly 'rational' (i.e. rational in their terms) intellectual edifice. One way out of all this is perhaps to try to establish rules of correspondence between the internal concept like 'spirit' and external one like 'drop in temperature'. But, presumably, for such a strategy to have any intellectual appeal it would require the establishment of correspondences over a wide set of concepts in both belief systems. Such a strategem would, of course, be one mode of what I have called constructivism.

An alternative way would be to try to involve both internal and external concepts in the same model. In the present example we might adopt something along the following lines: a drop in temperature leads to perception of the threat of spirits which in turn leads to lighting of fires. If we interpret 'leads to' as some sort of causal connection then we have a three variable causal chain with 'perception of spirits' as an intervening variable between 'drop in temperature' and 'lighting of fires'. So the claim of the first anthropologist to have established a link between the two extreme variables in this sequence is quite compatible (under certain restrictive circumstances to be studied later) with the internal explanation. I am not of the view that reconciliations between external and internal explanations can always be carried through but often they can and we should, as model builders, be constantly on the look-out for opportunities of doing this.

An externalist might still react to this endeavour by saying – well, it seems to me that 'drop in temperature' is good prediction of 'lighting fires' and I have, therefore, no need of the variable 'perception of spirits'. There are two points to be made about this. Firstly, a technical point: if the relationships between the three variables are not deterministic but only probabilistic, then 'drop in temperature' will *not*, in general, be as good a predictor as 'perception of spirits' of 'lighting of fires' (see Chapter 8). Secondly, consider the case where the perception of spirits is a function of a complex belief system and suppose some exogenous factor changes or destroys this system (shall we say industrialisation) so that the people no longer believe in the spirits and thus as a consequence, they *cease to light fires even though the temperature drops.* Now the externalist would not be able to explain this cessation; for him there was a 'law-like' connection between 'temperature drop' and 'lighting of fires', so he would ascribe to the subjunctive conditional 'if there were a drop in temperature there would be lighting of fires'. The internalist, on the other hand, would seem to be in a far more powerful position for he could predict that loss of faith in the spirits would lead to cessation of fire-lighting. But it is not as simple as that, for we may recall our earlier supposition that these people would perish in the cold if they did not light fires. So perhaps they would rapidly learn this and still come to light fires, then it would appear that there was some force in the externalist's standpoint. Of course, they might not light fires, but find some alternative way of keeping out the cold, thus still rendering the externalist major proposition incorrect. So where do we stand? *The important point is that it is only by comprehending the significance of the internalist concepts that we can begin to understand why the people changed their way of keeping out the cold but, at the same time, the external concepts are needed for understanding why the alternative strategies in the changed behaviour pattern are necessary.*

We will adopt the view in this essay that where possible both internal and external concepts should be used in sociological model building.

Type III (Radical Externalism): In this case, both the explained and explanatory concepts are external. The sociologist will necessarily use this sort of explanation when he tries to account for some feature of a social system that is not recognised by the actors. For example the distinction between 'strategic' and 'cataclysmic' approaches has become popular in conflict theory, the latter being, in essence, an externalist approach. An intelligent use of both approaches to model building is perhaps desirable, but always keeping open the possibility of bringing the two together by the use of a constructivist stratagem.

4. Variables

4.1 Introduction

So far we have considered the diversity of units of analysis which are available to the sociologist and have taken a brief look at the types of concepts which he can use to characterise these units.

The next stage in the hierarchy of sophistication is to convert concepts into variables, for it is as variables that our concepts will eventually appear in propositions and models.

Concepts are 'turned into' variables by *mapping* them into a set of *values*. The notion of mapping is a very general one which describes the process whereby one can move from one set of entities to another. For example, naming objects is a mapping of a set of objects into a set of names. Since the idea of mapping is a very useful one, it is perhaps worth while taking a brief look at it.

A mapping of one set into another, say A into B, is a rule which associates each element of A with an element of B. If the rule ascribes only one element in B (an *image*) for each element in A, the mapping is *single valued*. Pictorially we can represent the mapping as in Figure 4.1.

Figure 4.1 A Single-Valued Mapping

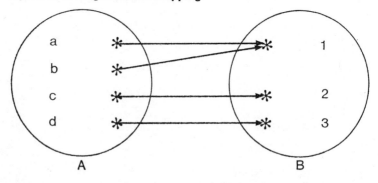

This mapping is single-valued whereas the one in Figure 4.2 is not, for *a* and *b* each have two images.

Figure 4.2 A Many-Valued Mapping

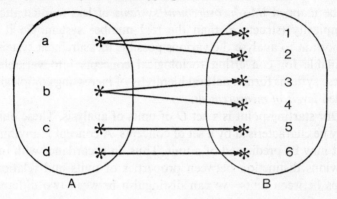

When a mapping between a set *A* and a set *B* is such that the set of images (the *range*) in *B* is the entire set then the mapping is said to be of *A onto B*. Note, however, that when we speak of a mapping of *A into B* we do not necessarily imply that the mapping is not *onto* – 'onto mappings' are a special case of mappings of one set into another.

A single-valued mapping of sets *A onto B* is 1 to 1 if no image in *B* is an image of more than one element of *A*. The mapping that characterises the process whereby concepts are 'converted' into variables is normally a single valued one; it takes a set of clearly defined states of the concept into a formal set of symbols (values). And this set of symbols or values has some sort of *mathematical structure*[1] defined upon it.

This is the process normally known as *measurement*, though it must be emphasised that the idea of measurement is used in a very broad sense in sociology. Most of us, when we say things are measurable, mean we can assign numbers to them; we believe we can map a set of objects (units of analysis) according to some property (concept) they possess into the set of *real numbers*. So the values we assign are the ones we associate with the real number system. For example, we may measure the length (concept) of a number of rods (units). Unfortunately, however, many sociological concepts do not lend themselves to measurement in terms of the real numbers and they have, consequently, to be mapped into *measurement systems* of less mathematical complexity (structure) than the real number system. So it is important to analyse the various possible measurement systems available for converting sociological concepts into variables. These systems form a natural hierarchy of increasing complexity called *levels of measurement*.

Our starting-point is a set O of units of analysis. These units may be characterised by a set of concepts. A concept is anything that may be predicated of a unit. Thus, in accordance with our previous distinction between properties of units and relationships between units, we can distinguish between two different types of measurement.

(a) *Pure Measurement*: defined as a mapping of set O, according to some common property(ies) of the elements of O, into a measurement system.

For instance, if we were measuring the length of a number of rods (set O) the property/concept 'length' of each rod would be mapped into a segment of the real number system giving us what is termed a ratio measure (see below). In accordance with the framework we developed in Chapter 2, set O may comprise:

either (1) primary units, e.g. people,

or (2) secondary or higher order units (i.e. structures, aggregates or empirical collectivities), e.g. interaction structures, or social groups.

The properties of secondary or higher order units may be either:

(i) summary parameters of the properties of the sub-units, e.g. the mean and variance in attitude on some topic of group members;

(ii) summary parameters of the structure of the sub-units, e.g. the degree of connectivity or completion of a social structure;

(iii) emergent properties (see Chapter 2, p. 21).

(b) *Structural Measurement*: defined as a mapping of set O according to some relationship holding between some (or all) of the elements of set O into a measurement system.

For example, structural measurement would be involved when measuring the 'degree of interaction' between members of a social group. So with structural measurement one is concerned with the relationships holding between units of analysis. Clearly the relationships may hold between primary units or higher-order units. (See Chapter 2, p. 18.)

It is thus imperative to distinguish between, on the one hand, properties that units of analysis have *relative* to one another (e.g. height, weight) leading to pure measurement systems; and on the other hand, *relationships* holding between units (e.g. interaction with, communication with) which lead to structural systems. However, we may use some structural parameter (e.g. degree of completion or connectivity) to characterise a set of structures leading to a pure measurement system over the set.

Although 'properties of' and 'relationships between' units can normally be distinguished one from the other, properties can nevertheless often be construed as relationships and vice versa. For instance, the property of a person – the capital he holds – may be used to indicate the extent to which he dominates (a relationship) some other person. Also, conversely, the fact that A communicates with B may be utilised to describe A as having the property of 'communicating'.

Before we go on to consider the nature of various measurement systems available to the sociologist, it is helpful to make a rather long digression into the formal properties of binary relations. This will not only facilitate our understanding of measurement systems, but also help us in the general discussion in subsequent chapters.

4.2 Some Elementary Properties of Binary Relations

A *binary relation R* on a set $M = \{m_i\}$, $i = 1, 2, \ldots, n$ defines two mutually exclusive and exhaustive sets of associated pairs of elements from M of the form

$$m_i \, R \, m_j \quad \text{(read: } m_i \text{ is related to } m_j)$$
$$m_i \, \bar{R} \, m_j \quad \text{(read: } m_i \text{ is not related to } m_j)$$

If the relation R is *complete* over M then the set of pairs of the form $m_i \, \bar{R} \, m_j$ is empty. We have already seen that a convenient way of depicting a binary relation on a set is in terms of a graph or di-graph. (See Chapter 2, p. 13).

Three important properties of binary relations can be defined:
  (i) symmetry,
  (ii) antisymmetry,
  (iii) asymmetry.

(i) A binary relation R on a set M is said to be *symmetric* if, for any pair of elements that are related,

$$(m_i \, R \, m_j) \Rightarrow (m_j \, R \, m_i)$$

(for '$\ldots \Rightarrow \ldots$' read, 'if ... then ...').

That is, if m_i is related to m_j then m_j is related to m_i. Symmetric relations are of quite common occurrence in sociology, e.g. 'lives with', 'is sibling of', 'is married to', 'interacts with'.

We should note, of course, that

$$(m_i \, \bar{R} \, m_j) \Rightarrow (m_j \, \bar{R} \, m_i).$$

(ii) A binary relation R on a set M is said to be antisymmetric if, for any pair of elements that are related,

$$[(m_i \, R \, m_j) \cdot (m_j \, R \, m_i)] \Rightarrow [m_i = m_j].$$

(for '$\ldots \cdot \ldots$', read, '... and ...').

That is, if m_i is related to m_j and m_j is related to m_i then m_i is *equivalent* to m_j. (The properties of the equivalence relation will be defined below.)

The prototypical case of an antisymmetric relation is the relationship '$\geqslant$' (greater than or equal to) on numbers.

Examples of sociological interest are relations that contain the term, 'at least as', e.g. 'at least as highly valued as', or 'at least as powerful as'.

(iii) A binary relation R on a set M is said to be *asymmetric* if, for any pair of elements that are related,

$$(m_i \, R \, m_j) \Rightarrow (m_j \, \bar{R} \, m_i).$$

That is, if m_i is related to m_j then m_j is *not* related to m_i.

The most common sociological example is 'preference'; if m_i is preferred to m_j then m_j is not necessarily preferred to m_i.

There are two further important properties of binary relations: reflexivity and transitivity.

(iv) A binary relation R on a set M is said to be *reflexive* if, for any element,

$$m_i \, R \, m_i.$$

That is, m_i is related to itself.

(v) A binary relation R on a set M is said to be *transitive* if, for any three elements,

$$[(m_i \, R \, m_j) \cdot (m_j \, R \, m_k)] \Rightarrow [m_i \, R \, m_k].$$

That is, if m_i is related to m_j and m_j is related to m_k, then m_i is related to m_k.

We normally expect preference (asymmetric) relations to be transitive, for if m_i is preferred to m_j and m_j to m_k then we 'expect' m_i to be preferred to m_k. Indeed, some authors have felt so sure of this that they have tried to define rationality and irrationality in these terms. According to them, a rational ordering of preferences must be transitive. However, there is a fair body of evidence to suggest that people do not always observe transitivity in their preferences (Luce, 1959).

A clear distinction should be made between relations that analytically (i.e. by their very meaning) have certain properties and relations that contingently happen to have these properties. 'Interaction' is analytically symmetric but 'choice of friend' is not; nevertheless it may turn out, in a given empirical context, that friendship choices are symmetric. The search for symmetry properties of this sort is, of course, an important empirical endeavour in its own right.

The Equivalence Relation One of the most fundamental relations in any scientific practice is equivalence; objects that fall under the same concept are regarded as equivalent. Thus classification is based upon the idea of equivalence – those things that we classify in the same category are regarded as, in some sense (i.e. according to some property), equivalent.

An equivalent relation is

    (i) symmetric,

    (ii) reflexive, and

    (iii) transitive.

Consider equality in numbers, for instance: if $a = b$, $b = a$ (symmetry), $a = a$ and $b = b$ (reflexivity), and if $a = b$ and $b = c$ then $a = c$ (transitivity).

One of the most intriguing features concerning classification in sociology is how actors themselves create classifications of their social environment. What are the properties of social objects that actors concentrate upon in setting up equivalences entailed by their classifications? This problem is, of course, one aspect of the internalist approach to sociology. We may thus re-cast this issue by posing the question – what are the social determinants and consequences of the way actors create equivalence classes? These are two major questions in ethnomethodology (Garfinkel, 1967). Elsewhere I have suggested in outline a formal theory concerning these problems, where only in very special circumstances are the full properties of equivalence constituted by actors. Usually their 'classifications' are 'fuzzy at the edges' (Abell, 1969a).

Ranking and Binary Relations The properties of binary relations enable us to define three types[2] of ordering which play a central role in measurement theory. They are

    (i) the linear order

    (ii) the weak order, and

    (iii) the partial order.

(i) *A linear order* is defined as a complete, transitive, asymmetric relation on a set. Complete (cf. Chapter 2, p. 18) means that all pairs of elements in the set are in relation (i.e. *compar-*

able). For example, if we rank official positions in a hierarchy according to their social status, we might expect to obtain a linear order. Consider the five positions:

{Director (*A*), General Manager (*B*), Sales Manager (*C*), Research Department Director (*D*), and Salesman (*E*)}.

Then a possible status ranking would be

$A > B > C > D > E$ (where $>$ = 'is of greater status than').

Note, however, that this ranked sequence only contains an implicit recognition of transitivity – it implies that any member of the sequence to the left of another is of greater status, so $(A > C)$ and $(C > E)$, etc. A more laborious but perhaps more informative way of depicting the same linear order is in terms of the matrix in Figure 4.3.

Figure 4.3 A Matrix Corresponding to a Linear Order

	A	*B*	*C*	*D*	*E*
A	–	1	1	1	1
B	−1	–	1	1	1
C	−1	−1	–	1	1
D	−1	−1	−1	–	1
E	−1	−1	−1	−1	–

If we designate the entry of the *i*th row and *j*th column of this matrix r_{ij}, then $r_{ij} = 1$ if $i > j$; $r_{ij} = -1$ if $j > i$ and r_{ij} is left blank if $i = j$ (the relation is not reflexive for we cannot regard somebody as having greater status than themselves). Only the entries r_{ij} or r_{ji} need be known since by the definition of asymmetry one determines the other. The reason why all the +1 entries appear above the main diagonal and the −1 entries below, is because the ordering of the rows and columns of the matrix corresponds exactly to the ranking of the linear order. If it did not, this symmetry would be lost. If a ranking is a linear order then we can always find an ordering of the rows and columns of its associated matrix portraying this sort of symmetry.

(ii) *A Weak Order* is defined as a complete, reflexive, transitive, antisymmetric relation in a set.

The difference between a weak order and a linear order is that the former allows for equivalence within the ranking whereas the latter does not. Thinking in terms of our example of a status ranking once again, it is conceivable that some of the official positions could have an equivalent status. For example, suppose the General Manager (B) and the Sales Manager (C) have an equivalent status, then one possible ranking is

$A \geqslant (B = C) \geqslant D \geqslant E$ (where $\geqslant$ = 'is of greater or equal status') i.e., $B \geqslant C$ and $C \geqslant B$.

The matrix representation is depicted in Figure 4.4.

Figure 4.4 A Matrix Corresponding to a Weak Order

	A	B	$\dot{C}$	D	E
A	1	1	1	1	1
B	−1	1	1	1	1
C	−1	1	1	1	1
D	−1	−1	−1	−1	1
E	−1	−1	−1	−1	1

The entry of the ith row and jth column $r_{ij} = 1$ if $i \geqslant j$ and $r_{ij} = -1$ if $j \geqslant i$. Thus, if $r_{ij} = r_{ji} = 1$, i and j are in an equivalence relation. Note that in this case entries have been put down the main diagonal as we need to define reflexivity in the ranking to give us equivalence classes. Further, it should be noted that equivalence within a weak order is also transitive so, if $A = B$ and $B = C$, then $A = C$.

In practice, a weak order can be described as a linear order of equivalence classes where some of the equivalence classes may contain only one element.

(iii) *A partial order* is defined as an incomplete, reflexive, transitive, antisymmetric relation on a set. The important difference between a weak order and a partial order is that the latter is incomplete, i.e. at least one pair of elements is *not comparable*. Thinking in terms of our status ranking once again, we might find that the status of the General Manager (B) and the Sales Manager (C) are not comparable in the same way that all the other positions are comparable with one another. One possible ranking would be

$$A \geqslant (B \, I \, C) \geqslant D \geqslant E$$

where $B \, I \, C$ means that B and C are incomparable. A convenient way of depicting a partial order is as a special type of graph, where points in a plane represent the elements, and lines the anti-symmetric relation; and where it is understood that any point lower down the page is connected by the antisymmetric relation to any point above it.

So the above partial order may be depicted as in Figure 4.5.

Figure 4.5 A Partial Order

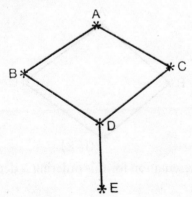

The matrix representation of this partial order is in Figure 4.6; where I represents the non-comparability relation and the $+1$

Figure 4.6 A Matrix Corresponding to a Partial Order

	A	B	C	D	E
A	1	1	1	1	1
B	-1	1	I	1	1
C	-1	I	1	1	1
D	-1	-1	-1	1	1
E	-1	-1	-1	-1	1

and -1 entries have the same meaning as before. The reader should satisfy himself that I is an equivalence relation.

It is possible, of course, to obtain a mixed partial and weak order. For example, if B and C were of incomparable status and D and E of equivalent status we may write

$$A \geqslant (B I C) \geqslant (D = E)$$

which is expressed graphically in Figure 4.7.

Figure 4.7 A Mixed Partial and Weak Order

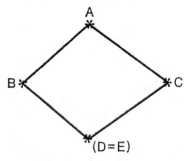

The matrix representation for this ordering is depicted in Figure 4.8;

Figure 4.8 A Matrix Corresponding to a Mixed Partial and Weak Order

	A	B	C	D	E
A	1	1	1	1	−1
B	−1	1	*I*	1	1
C	−1	*I*	1	1	1
D	−1	−1	−1	1	1
E	−1	−1	−1	1	1

where the notation is as before.

Needless to say, it is imperative to distinguish between the noncomparability and the equivalence relations.

This concludes the section on binary relations so we may now return to the central problem of this chapter.

4.3 Measurement Systems

Measurement has already been defined as the process whereby concepts are mapped into a set of values; these values, along with some associated structure, comprise a measurement system. A measurement system is normally selected so that the structure associated with it has empirical meaning in the sense that it reflects (bears a one to one relationship to) the structure in the phenomena being measured. In addition, the distinction between pure measurement (i.e. mappings of properties of objects) and structural measurement (i.e. mappings of relationships between objects) has been established. For the moment we will concentrate upon pure measurement; our aim is to erect a hierarchy of measurement levels, running from the least structured at the bottom to the most structured at the top.

Now since our ordinary everyday understanding of measurement involves the use of real numbers let us start, without being too technical, by noting five of their important properties.

1. *Zero* Numbers have a unique origin in zero.

2. *Order* The real numbers have the property of a linear order running positively and negatively from zero.

3. *Infinity* The linear orders are of unlimited extent in both directions from zero.

4. *Distance* Distances (i.e. differences) between numbers are ordered; they are, in fact, characterised by an antisymmetric relation whereby the distance between any pair of numbers is greater than, less than, or equal to ($\geqslant$) the distance between any other pair of numbers.

5. *Density* The real numbers are dense in the sense that, for any two numbers one cares to name, one can always find one in between. There are no 'gaps' in the real number system.

It is upon these five properties that the structure of the real numbers is based. The full panoply of arithmetical operations – addition, subtraction, multiplication, division, etc., is, as we shall see, closely related to them.

Thus in a strict sense, if we were to limit ourselves, in measurement, to the structure of the real numbers we should have to be able to give empirical meaning to all these properties.

In sociology, however, a far less restrictive approach is usually adopted towards measurement, whereby the 'full' use of the above properties is not always regarded as essential. It is only at one pole of the hierarchy of measurement levels that the full structure of the real number system is appropriate. The hierarchy is depicted in the Figure 4.9, and we will now go on to consider the properties of the various levels.

4.31 THE SIMPLE NOMINAL LEVEL

Traditionally the nominal level has been regarded as the 'lowest' level of measurement. For the sake of complete rigour, however, the simple nominal level may first be defined.

The Simple Nominal Level is a one to one mapping of set O onto a set of symbols (values), e.g. names.

Thus each object in set *O* is given a unique value or name. This level of measurement merely names objects in the real world, no

Figure 4.9 Simple Measurement Systems

Name	Description	Structure	Use of Numbers	Invariant Transformation	Arithmetical Operations	Examples
Simple Nominal	Naming objects uniquely	None	As 'names' for objects only	None	None	John, Jack, Mary, etc.
Nominal	Classification of objects	Equivalence relation internal to the 'classes'	As 'names' for classes only	Permutation transform	None	Sex, religious denomination
Ordinal	Ranking of objects	Linear order, may have zero	Any monotonically increasing/decreasing sequence	Monotonic transform	None	Friendship, power, etc.
Interval	Metric scale with distance	Order and distance	Order and distance properties of numbers. Scale invariant to ratio of distances between numbers	Linear transform of the form $y = a + bx$	Addition Subtraction	
Ratio	Metric scale with distance and zero	Zero, order and distance	Order, distance and zero properties of numbers. Scale invariant to ratios of points on the scale	Linear transform of the form $y = bx$	Addition Subtraction Multiplication Division	Height, weight, population, etc.

attempt being made to classify them. In effect, everything in the real world is regarded as unique. Perhaps those sociologists who regard sociology as a descriptive enterprise where 'all social phenomena are unique' are in some sense utilising this level.

If one were tempted to use the real numbers as values at the simple nominal level, then they could only be used as 'names'; the properties of order, distance, density, infinity and zero have no meaning.[3] Thus any collection of numbers in any order with or without zero would be equally effective; to name *n* objects, *any permutation of any* n *numbers* would suffice.

Despite its lowly nature, however, the simple nominal level is of importance as it lies at the foundation of the structural levels of measurement which are concerned with the relationship between a set of named objects (see Chapter 2, p. 14 – labelled graphs).

4.32 THE NOMINAL LEVEL

The nominal level of measurement is defined as a single-valued mapping that takes set O *into a set of values* (*according to some property of the elements of* O) *but where more than one object may be assigned the same value.*

When two objects are mapped into the same value, it implies that they are, in some way (i.e. according to some property) equal, identical or equivalent. That is, the equivalence relation holds between objects mapped into the same *class* (assigned the same value). But since it is also stipulated that each object may be assigned to one class only (the mapping is single valued) then the mapping will separate the elements of set *O* into mutually exclusive and exhaustive classes.

Thus, whenever an attempt is made to classify objects in sociology the structure of equivalence is forced upon subsets of them. For example, if an attempt were made to classify a set of people according to religion (concept) then a possible nominal 'variable' would be Catholic, Anglican and Non-Conformist. And people classified under any one of these headings would be regarded, at least in respect to their religion, as equivalent. Of course, different nominal variables of religion could be elaborated – ones using different classes altogether or ones using more *discrimination*, i.e. more classes. There is one important point to note however, nominal variables must always be exhaustive – there must be a class into which each object can be mapped. Clearly, in the above example we might encounter people who are neither Catholics, Anglican nor Non-Conformists. Then it is necessary to elaborate at least one further class. It may, in this case, be a residual class of 'others'. But in general in sociological analysis, one should try to avoid such a class – especially if empirically it contains a relatively high proportion of the population (set *O*). Such a variable would be regarded as lacking sufficient discrimination. Often, of course, one has eventually to use a residual category to make a classification exhaustive but, in general, the smaller the proportion of 'others' the better.

It is also imperative to make sure that a nominal variable corresponds to a clearly defined concept. A necessary condition for this is that the mapping should be unequivocally single valued. That is, there should be no possibility of putting the same object into more than one class.

Thus if somehow we came up with a nominal variable 'urban', 'Catholic', and 'Protestant', then this would be unacceptable as the categories are not mutually exclusive. Indeed, we could treat the variable – 'urban', 'not urban' as a *different variable* (i.e. a different concept) from religion and perhaps look for relationships between the two.

Classifications are often based upon a rather complex set of properties of the objects and we have, in effect, to make a decision about which objects are most similar and which most different. This, needless to say, is a complex business, but the nominal variable is then being treated as a theoretical one. Of course the nominal variable, religion, may be construed in this way. Rather than merely taking people's declared allegiance a whole range of their religious attributes (behaviour) may be studied in an attempt to erect a *summary* classification. But we would be much more likely to do this if we were looking for the variable of 'religiosity' and again we might want to relate religion (i.e. declared allegiance) to religiosity!

If numbers are used to denote the classes of a nominal variable then, as with the simple nominal level, the properties of order, distance, density, infinity and zero have no meaning. Any collection of numbers could be used to denote the classes. In fact, it would perhaps be best to speak of using numerals rather than numbers. And, of course, any permutation of a set of numerals would be adequate for naming the classes; so we speak of a nominal scale as being invariant to permutation transform of numbers.

4.33 THE ORDINAL LEVEL

The ordinal level of measurement may be defined as a single-valued mapping of set O, according to some property of the elements of O, into a linear order of values.[4]

Ordinal variables allow us to say that there is more or less of something, but not how much more or less; they are very common in sociology. Thinking in terms of numbers, the ordering property holds, but nothing is known about the distance between the values. This means that an ordinal variable can be represented by any increasing/decreasing sequence of numbers. Technically, they are invariant to monotonic transform of numbers. As long as the sequence of numbers used increases or decreases in the right direction with the variable in question, it is a suitable representation of the variable.

We may, however, distinguish ordinal variables with a zero point and those without one. In the former case any increasing series of numbers starting with zero will be suitable, and in the latter any increasing sequence starting with any number whatsoever.

All this is rather abstract so now let us see how ordinal variables can appear in sociology. Consider the concept of friendship and ask the question, 'How can one obtain measures of friendship?' (i.e. convert the concept into a variable). Well, our common sense tells us that friendship is something more than a 'nominal variable' since we are normally prepared to speak of different levels of intensity of friendship – perhaps running from indifference to extreme friendship (or even love). We would be prepared to say that we are *more* or *less* friendly with *A* than *B* but would be rather loath to say by how much. This would suggest that we naturally operate with an ordinal variable of friendship. In fact, much the same argument applies to many of our everyday concepts. Most social relationships and evaluations are of an ordinal variety and some of the major sociological concepts appear to be 'naturally' of the ordinal species. Think of 'power', 'influence', 'satisfaction', 'authority', and so on.

It is thus reasonable to anticipate that ordinality will play a strategic role in sociology.

The possibility of constructing higher order variables (i.e. interval or ratio) out of what at a common-sense level naturally seems to be ordinal, should not necessarily be precluded. In fact, the conversion of what are naturally (i.e. for the actors themselves) ordinal variables into interval and ratio variables can be seen as part of the internalist versus externalist debate we encountered earlier. A radical internalist standpoint towards sociology dictates that the structural limits of the actors' ordinality should be the sociologist's also. But on the other hand, from a constructivist standpoint, the process of converting an actor's ordinal variable into an interval or ratio variable would be an example of the *constructivist* stratagem.

Returning to our example of friendship – how could it be converted into an ordinal variable? Let us concentrate upon the simplest technique, for we are here only concerned with the logic of measurement systems, not with the details of scale construction (for this see, for example, Torgerson, 1965). Let us assume we ask a person to indicate his feelings of friendship towards specific persons and we offer him the following response categories: extremely; very much; fairly; not very much; indifferent. Then we may suppose the response categories form a *linear order* of intensity of friendship. (Note: the variable scale is

c

a *linear order* of values though if we think of mapping persons, i.e. the friends, into the scale then they would, in general, form a weak order, since, in general, some persons would be mapped into the same category in the linear order.) We may thus alternatively view an ordinal scale as:

(i) a weak order in terms of mapped objects; or

(ii) a linear order of variable scale categories.

If we are tempted to use numbers to indicate the categories of the above ordinal scale, then they may be scored in integers from 0 (indifference) to 4 (extremely). That is,

$$4 > 3 > 2 > 1 > 0.$$

But note, only the ordering properties of the numbers are relevant.

In fact, as we have noted, any decreasing sequence of numbers would suffice.

For this reason, care should be exercised in using numbers to represent an ordinal variable. The distance between the numbers has no meaning. Thus we have no right to suppose that on the original scoring the category scored 2 represents a state of friendliness one half of that represented by the category scored 4. Since the distance between the numbers has no meaning we cannot speak of units of friendship and none of the arithmetical operations, addition, subtraction, multiplication and division, are applicable.

Furthermore, there are no natural aggregation operations which are appropriate to ordinal variables. So summary measures must be confined to rather unsatisfactory statistics like the median or mode. The lack of such an operation is indeed the chief analytical limitation of ordinal variables and it is for this reason that sociologists are frequently persuaded to 'assume' an interval or ratio variable when it is actually only ordinal. Most of classical statistics is only strictly applicable when measurement techniques move beyond the ordinal level so there is clearly a high premium on obtaining higher level variables.

It is very important to recognise these limitations: if the

sociologist is limited to ordinality then he cannot legitimately adopt any theoretical concepts that depend on the normal arithmetic manipulations, and statements of the form, '*A* is twice as friendly towards *B* as he is towards *C*', are strictly meaningless.

If the ranking has an infinity of classes, the property of infinity can, of course, have meaning for an ordinal variable. In practice, however, this is rarely the case. It is worth noting how the absence of the concept of infinity is related to the lack of any natural aggregation operation at the ordinal level. The infinity property of real numbers (as a measurement scale) permits an indefinitely large series of aggregation operations (additions) on the scale, always leading to a resultant scale point – we can never run out of measurement values. Arithmetical addition requires the notion of infinity so the operation can always be defined. But since there is no natural aggregation operation associated with an ordinal scale, the infinity property is not necessitated in the same way. In fact, it is perhaps the case that many sociological variables have an upper bound. Considering 'power' for instance, perhaps we could 'aggregate' the power of a group by 'adding' more people to it, each bringing an additional increment of power; but there is an upper limit to this process beyond which the power of the group does not increase (see below).

There seems to be no *logical* reason why an ordinal variable should not exhibit a sort of density. For we could always insert another ranked class between any two classes in a given scale. But empirically this is often impossible – the discriminations of the scale are the limit of our observational techniques.

There is, however, a rather important way in which the simple idea of an ordinal variable as a weak or linear order can be extended.

If it is possible to rank not only units of analysis but the 'distances' between the ranked categories, then clearly we have a 'stronger' variable than the straightforward ordinal one. For example, if we once again asked somebody to rank the formal

positions A, B, C, D and E in an organisation and he gave the rankings
$$A > B > C > D > E$$
then we could go on to ask the ranker to rank the 'distances between the positions. The appropriate type of question would be, for example, 'Does the status of A exceed the status of B by a greater or lesser amount than the status of C exceeds the status of D?' In this manner, we could obtain a linear or weak order of the so-called *first differences*. If we designate them

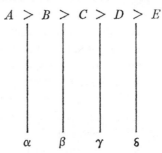

then one possible ranking of the first difference (assuming transitivity) is
$$\alpha > \beta > \gamma > \delta.$$

This is, of course, a special case where the distances between the categories increase in value as the value of the categories increase. Variables where one has both the ranking of the categories and the first differences are sometimes known as *ordered metric* scales (Coombs, 1964). Clearly there is no *logical* reason why the differences between the first differences should not be ranked also. So if we designate these:

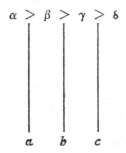

one possible ranking might be

$$a > b > c.$$

The process may then be extended so that the resultant two differences may also be ranked. However, the likelihood of empirically obtaining rankings beyond the first difference is rather remote. If we ask people to rank second differences for example, they are likely to lose track.

The ordered metric scale gives us more information than the straightforward ordinal scale. The characteristic statement for an ordinal scale is '*A* is greater than *B*' but, for an ordered metric, '*A* is greater than *B* by a greater amount than *B* is greater than *C*'. Ordered metric variables enable us to obtain a 'feel' for the distance qualities of the variable. A special case would, of course, be where all the first differences are equal and we may treat at least these parts of the variable as an interval one.

4.34 INTERVAL AND RATIO LEVELS

The interval and ratio levels may be conveniently considered together as the distinction between them is rather academic. If an interval measured variable can be obtained then it is almost invariably possible to obtain a ratio level variable as it is merely an interval scale with a defined zero point. Sometimes both types are referred to as *Cardinal*.

With an interval scale, in addition to ordering, the distance property of numbers also has meaning.

Interval measurement is a single-valued mapping of the set O, *according to some property or properties of the objects of the set, into a set of numbers such that the order and distance properties of numbers have meaning.*

This implies that any increasing/decreasing sequence of numbers which preserves the *ratio of the distances* between the corresponding numbers will provide an adequate representation of an interval scale.

For example, the sequences (2, 3 and 4) and (4, 6 and 8) would be equally suitable for measuring a particular property. The ratio of the distance between consecutive numbers in both sequences is identical, i.e. unity. Clearly, starting with any sequence of numbers we can multiply them by a further constant number and the ratios of the corresponding distances will be identical. So an interval scale is invariant to multiplication by a constant. Furthermore, the ratio of distances criteria will be preserved when adding a constant number to each member of a particular sequence. For example, on adding 3 to the original sequence we obtain 5, 6 and 7.

An interval scale is thus invariant to:

(i) multiplication by a fixed number, and

(ii) addition of a fixed number.

This means that, in general, one interval scale can be converted into another by a linear transform $y = a + bx$ where a and b are constants and x and y are corresponding points on two interval scales.

We noted earlier that the major limitation of ordinal variables is their lack of any aggregating operation, which effectively precludes much of the analytical power of summary measures. The arithmetical operations of addition and subtraction are, however, fully operable at the interval level. So we can add or subtract on a given scale and it will give the corresponding point on any linear transform of the form $y = bx$ of that scale. For instance, if we add 2 and 2 giving 4, in the scale (2, 3, 4), then the corresponding addition on the scale (4, 6, 8) is to add 4 and 4 giving 8, i.e. the linear transform ($y = 2x$) of 4 on the original scale. A similar argument does *not* apply to the transform $y = a + bx$ though; for example $y = 2x + 3$ gives a corresponding addition of 7 and 7 giving 14 not 11.

We cannot, however, speak of ratios with an interval scale. This is made clear by comparing the two equivalent interval scales (2, 3, 4) and (5, 6, 7); the ratios of the last to the first term in the two scales is not identical (i.e. $4/2 \neq 7/5$). This means that we cannot meaningfully multiply and divide. *It is the ratios of distances that are invariant on interval scales, not ratios of points on the scale.*

Since arithmetical addition is the natural aggregation operation at the interval level of measurement, the infinity property of numbers becomes logically important. It renders all possible additions logically possible. The density property also means that there is no limit imposed by the nature of the scale on the degree of discrimination of any measuring technique.

The *ratio level* of measurement has the properties of order, distance and zero of the real numbers.

Ratio measurement is a single-valued mapping of the set O, *according to some property or properties of the elements of* O *into a set of numbers such that the order distance and zero property of numbers have meaning.*

The ratio level is invariant to a linear transformation of the form $y = ax$ where a is a positive constant and y and x are corresponding points on two scales. As well as addition and subtraction we can utilise multiplication and division with a ratio scale since, as the zero is fixed, the ratios of corresponding points on two scales will be identical. Consider, for instance, the scale $y = (0, 1, 2, 3, 4)$ and $x = (0, 2, 4, 6, 8)$ then $y = (\frac{1}{2})x$ and the ratio $4/1$ on y is equal to $8/2$ on x, etc.

Consequently, an important feature of a ratio scale is that it permits us to make statements about proportions of the form '*X* is twice as much as *Y*'.

This, then, concludes our analysis of the classical measurement hierarchy.

4.4 Some Extensions of Classical Measurement

The ideas surrounding classical measurement theory are those of congruence, or otherwise, with the real number system. The key properties of this system are order, distance and zero and, to a lesser extent, density and infinity; so the full operations of arithmetic only emerge when all these properties are appropriate.

Perhaps the most dramatic point of change in the classical hierarchy is between the ordinal level and the interval level, for it is at the latter level that the compounding operations of addition emerge; there is no analogous operation at the ordinal level.

Arithmetical addition is, of course, only one possible type of compounding operation. It has a great deal of mathematical structure associated with it, and perhaps we can gain some insight into problems of measurement by considering the general properties of operations rather than just this one. We may be able to detect compounding operations with less associated structure than numerical addition and consequently more appropriate to sociological problems.

But let us first note the empirical significance of operations in the context of measurement. Consider a concept like mass; it is not difficult to see the reason why a measurement system incorporating the operation of addition is so appropriate for measuring it; *we can locate operations in the real world that correspond (bear a one to one relationship) to the operation of addition in arithmetic.* We can take pieces of matter and place them together on, say, a balance, and compare them with other pieces of matter. There are thus two major components of this real world operation (usually called weighing):[4]

(i) compounding or aggregating masses,

(ii) comparing different masses and aggregated masses.[5]

In the simplest interpretation these bear a one to one relationship to *adding* and *finding equality* on real numbers. A little later we will make a more rigorous and formal analysis of the concept of an operation. Meanwhile note that the major problem in sociology is that very few concepts/variables permit operations in the real world comparable to weighing. There are often no natural 'compounding' and 'comparing' experiments whereby, for instance, we can take two people of a certain 'power' and say that together they have an amount of power equivalent to a third person.

Our inability to locate operations in the social world is partly attributable to the old problem – the difficulty of performing experiments in the social domain; but, in addition, the indicators of sociological concepts we normally consider, like 'power', do not exhibit the *consistency* characteristics implied by a general compounding operation.

For instance, we might perform an experiment whereby

individuals and combinations of individuals are repeatedly put in a conflict situation and in each case the winner determined; if it is found, on the basis of a series of such experiments, that A always beats B, B always beats C and C always beats D and, furthermore, the *full* transitivity of such a series is also established, then we have a perfect linear order:

$$A > B > C > D.$$

Now let us score these, $D = 1$, $C = 2$, $B = 3$ and $A = 4$.

If we wish only to regard this as an ordinal scale then any monotonic transform of this sequence of numbers would, of course, suffice. If, however, we attempt to interpret these numbers as an interval scale we should be able to define arithmetical addition. So we would expect, if we matched C and D together against B, to find that they 'draw', i.e. they are of equal power. Also B and D together should 'draw' with A, and B and C together should beat A – perhaps in the ratio 5/4?

So if these types of experiments could be meaningfully carried out and we could obtain *consistent* results in the sense that, having erected the initial scale of power, the predictions for all the logically possible combinations of individuals gave results in accordance with the original scale, then we could treat the scale as an interval one. It is possible, of course, that the results of the experiments would be consistent with a different scoring of the original scale. The intellectual exercise then becomes one of finding the scoring consistent with the results of a given set of experiments.

We might be able to devise a gaming experiment along these lines and *just* might obtain consistency. But the chances of carrying out experiments of this sort *in situ* are, of course, remote. Suppose A, B, C and D are nation-states, and we want to obtain a measure of their relative *average* power over a period for which they were repeatedly in conflict, individually and in alliance, and for which we have the appropriate data. I think most of us would be extremely surprised if we could erect a simple numerical scale demonstrating consistency over all the alliances. Perhaps we could obtain a simple linear order scale, moving from the most powerful to the least powerful, but nations are powerful for different reasons – some have good armies, some effective air forces, some both. Now in dyadic conflict of one against one, it might be that effective air power is the key factor, so the simple linear order based upon this sort of conflict really corresponds to effective use of air power. But in alliance, it may be that certain concomitant combinations of ground power and air power provides the key factor and we would then not obtain simple consistency. The moral of this would seem to be to consider different aspects of power: in the technical language, different dimensions. Thus the concept of power becomes multi-dimensional. So we could ask ourselves the question as to the nature of the measurement structure on each of these dimensions. But it is most likely that the data will not give us any information appropriate to a compounding on these dimensions taken separately – e.g. nations do not form alliances and fight using either their armies or air forces only. The problems then are immense, but it appears that it may be helpful to consider less structured operations than addition which would have less demanding consistency criteria. We may search for formal operations that have a meaningful counterpart in the social world and which permit some sort of compounding or aggregation, giving us a scale that is, as it were, between the ordinal and interval levels.

To summarise the argument so far:

(i) The major analytical advance of an interval scale over an ordinal scale is the compounding operation of addition.

(ii) For compounding operations to be meaningful on a scale there must normally be empirical counterparts of the operation in the real world which exhibit the required consistency patterns.

It is worth noting the significance of studying measurement from this standpoint. In effect, it views a measurement system as an *axiomatic structure* (see Chapter 7). The axioms of the structure are the statements that assign numbers to the scale values; the 'theorems' are the combinational statements that exhibit a consistency (are derivable from the scale values). Two points follow from this. Firstly measurement is in fact a *theoretical structure* and should be viewed as such. The truth or falsity of the theorems provides a test of the measurement theory. If a consistent pattern is not found (i.e. a theorem is untrue) then this refutes at least one axiom of the measurement theory. Secondly, since measurement is a 'theoretical idea' it should not be seen as an issue apart from theoretical elaboration in sociology.

4.41 OPERATIONS

Now let us turn to the general conception of a *binary operation on a set*. Attention will be confined to binary operators as it is logically probable that higher order operations can be reduced to binary ones.

We have already encountered the idea of an ordered pair on a set. With a set A of n elements there is a potential set of n^2 ordered pairs designated $A \times A$ (sometimes called the Cartesian product).

Let B *be the set or a subset of* A $\times$ A. *Then any single-valued mapping of* B *into* A *is called an operation on* A. The range of the operation is the set of image elements of the mapping.

An operation is thus merely a mapping of pairs of elements of a set into the set itself. For example, if the set consists of integers then addition is a binary operation whereby any two integers can be added to give a third integer (except if one of the original integers is 0 when the operation gives the other summed integer). All this might seem rather pedantic but, by viewing arithmetical operations as only one member of a class of operations, we can study the various amounts of structure built into different operations. And, according to our above stipulations, this structure must usually have some empirical counterpart to render the operation meaningful in a measurement system.

So now let us start with the general idea of an operation and step by step build in a structure motivating the exercise in terms of the concept power.

In general we may write an operation $\oplus$ on a set A

$$a \oplus b = c$$

for all a, b and c in set A.

Closure If there is a mapping for all pairs in $A \times A$ into A then the operation is said to be closed. For instance, addition on the infinite set of integers is closed since the sum of any pair of integers is an integer.

Even this most elementary restriction on an operation is problematic when we come to sociological examples. Assume for instance that four states of powerfulness, A, B, C and D can be detected (perhaps these are internal concepts). *Now if we want a compounding operation on this set of states to be closed then the result of the compounding process must be either* A, B, C *or* D *and must be defined for all the pairs of states.* This is clearly counter-intuitive for if we assume a ranking of the states of the form $A > B > C > D$ then we would expect $A \oplus D$ to be greater than A. So our mapping would not be closed to the initial *empirical* set of states of powerfulness. If we scored the states according to the integers or real numbers then the problem would be solved, for these are infinite sets. But we should note that an operation on such sets will create 'states' of aggregate powerfulness that have no individual empirical reference. If we allow an operation on a set of internally defined states of a concept to produce non-internal aggregate states then this is one aspect of taking an externalist standpoint in sociology. It is in fact a form of constructivism; the external states are logical constructs (i.e. constructs according to the rules of the operation) of internal states. We must, in using an operation of this sort, be satisfied as to the sociological meaningfulness of obtaining the non-internal states.

It was mentioned above that sociological variables may often have upper bounds. This would mean that any compounding operation definable on the states of the variable would have an upper bound rendering the operation closed over a finite set of states. This is the common-sense situation where the 'addition' of 'some more' of something does not always make a difference. Certain measures of the concept power might well exhibit this property.

One model that satisfies conditions like these is the operation of the general form

$$a_i \oplus a_j = a_i \text{ if } a_i > a_j,$$
$$a_i \oplus a_j = a_j \text{ if } a_j > a_i.$$

So the operation on an ordered set $(A > B > C > D)$ would be given by the Table depicted in Figure 4.10.

Figure 4.10 An Operation on a Set

$\oplus$	A	B	C	D
A	A	A	A	A
B	A	B	B	B
C	A	B	C	C
D	A	B	C	D

This may be termed a domination model, since the 'largest' always dominates the smaller in the operation. There is a certain amount of evidence that affective variables behave in this manner (Abell, 1969a).

Of course there are many other possible operations – one for each logically possible type of Table of the above form: the restriction is, in all cases, that the compounding operation cannot produce states outside the initial empirically defined set of states.

One of the ways in which social theory and measurement can be brought closer together is by *empirical study* of compounding operations of this sort. Perhaps operations are not generally closed but there are severe limits on the number of states beyond the initial empirical set that can be meaningfully defined. The infinite sets of integers and real numbers thus permit far too much licence.

If we think in terms of power again, then *a priori* one might feel this variable has fairly straightforward metric properties at low levels; but the scale might, as it were, converge for high values in the sense that a point exists above which an additional increment of power to a collectivity will have very little overall effect. In fact this would be detected if power were related to another variable in non-linear manner (see Chapter 8).

What seems fairly clear is that sociologists are going to have to become far more ingenious in studying the properties of compounding properties of measurement scales.

Commutativity A binary operation $\oplus$ on a set A is said to commute if

$$a \oplus b = b \oplus a$$

for all a, b in A.

For example, addition on real numbers or integers is commutative. Essentially, a relation is commutative if it does not matter in which order one considers the pairing of elements. Contrast subtraction on numbers $(2 - 3 \neq 3 - 2)$.

Now to think in terms of compounding operations on a variable like power; if an operation is commutative then it does not matter in 'which order we compound states of powerfulness'. So in an alliance between two nations A and B there is no difference between A forming an alliance with B or B with A. If ever we suggest the legitimacy of interval or ratio scales for measuring a variable like power then we necessarily imply commutativity of the empirical compounding operation, namely addition in the arithmetic.

Associativity A binary relation $\oplus$ on a set is said to be associative if it satisfies the associative law

$$(a \oplus b) \oplus c = a \oplus (b \oplus c)$$

for all a, b, c in A.

For example, addition on integers or real numbers is associative. The essence of the associative law lies in the implication that it does not matter in which order an operation is carried out over a set of entities. Thus we get the same result if we add 2 and 3 getting 5 and then add 3 giving 8, as when we add 3 and 3 getting 6 and then add 2 to obtain 8.

To appreciate the significance of associativity of compounding relations we might consider our conflict experiment for the measurement of power, where the compounding operation is supposed to reflect the consequences of alliance formation. In this context, associativity implies something like the following: in specified conflict situations an alliance formed first of all between a and b and then between this alliance and c should have the same power (conflict-winning efficacy) as an alliance initially formed between b and c with the later incorporation of a. Now it does not take much imagination to realise that these two social processes of alliance will not necessarily have properties of equivalence, so if we tried to reflect the objective structure by a measurement system incorporating associativity we might well be committing the sin of imposing too much structure. But, as we emphasised before, this is an empirical question and the applicability or otherwise of measurement systems involving associativity must be seen as such.

Units and Zero An element e of a set A which satisfies

$$e \oplus x = x \oplus e = x$$

for all x in A is called a *unit element* for the operation $\oplus$.

If a set does contain a unit element with respect to a given operation $\oplus$ then it is necessarily unique. For if there were two unit elements e and e', $e' = e$ since if we put $e = e'$ in the above definition $e \oplus e' = e$. But $e' \oplus x = x \oplus e' = x$ for all x in A so putting $x = e$ we obtain $e \oplus e' = e$, thus $e = e \oplus e' = e'$. So any unit element is unique.

An element n of a set A which satisfies

$$n \oplus x = x \oplus n = n$$

for all x in A is called a *zero element* for the operation $\oplus$.

Zero elements are also unique. For if n and n' are both zero elements for $\oplus$ then $n = n'$, since if we put $x = n'$ in the above definition we obtain $n \oplus n' = n$. But n' satisfies $n \oplus x = n = x \oplus n' = n'$ for all x in A, so if we put $x = n$ we obtain $n \oplus n' = n$. Thus $n = n \oplus n' = n$.

We have already seen the importance of zero elements in the ratio level of measurement. Only if a measurement system contains a zero is the binary operation of multiplication applicable.

4.5 *Algebraic Structures*

If different combinations of the properties closure, commutativity, associativity, zeros and units are applied on a set over one or more operations, then we can define various algebraic structures. The real numbers appropriate to the interval and ratio scales are just one of these structures. So we can now see the real number systems as one pole in a series of measurement systems, running in increasing order of structure but all lying in some sense above the ordinal level. We will now take a brief look at some of these and indicate the uses to which they have and could be put in sociology.

(i) *A gruppoid:* Is defined as an operation on a set (written $(G, \oplus)$ where G is a non-empty set and $\oplus$ a binary operation). A gruppoid thus has very little structure associated with it and would correspond to a compounding operation with no underlying regularity like associativity, etc. One might obtain such low-structure mappings in sociological contexts. Our power model might turn out empirically (especially a complex *in situ* situation) only to have the structure of a gruppoid.

(ii) *A semi-group:* A semi-group is a gruppoid $(G, \oplus)$ where the operation is *associative*. If the ordering of a compounding operation has no significance then we might expect to obtain the structure of a semi-group. Semi-groups are a characteristic structure in modern theories of linguistics and if, as is often suggested, there is some isomorphism between linguistics and certain structural problems in sociology, we might expect semi-groups increasingly to become of some significance in sociology. They have also proved suggestive in the topological analysis of complex social structures (Abell, 1969b).

(iii) *A group:* A group is a semi-group $(G, \oplus)$ which satisfies the following conditions:

(a) the operation is associative;

(b) it has a unit element, e;

(c) every element of G has an *inverse*, i.e. for each x in G there exists an element $\bar{x}$ in G called an inverse of x, such that

$$x \oplus \bar{x} = \bar{x} \oplus x = e.$$

(d) If in addition $\oplus$ commutes, then we speak of commutative groups.

Groups have already found a certain amount of use in sociology. The work of Harrison White (1963) on kinship-systems uses the idea of a permutation group and the Boolean addition[6] over sets of (1, 0) matrices (i.e. structures) forms a group where the matrix with all zero entries is the unit element.

(iv) *Other structures:* There are many other algebraic structures involving one or more operations building up to the real number system. It would, however, be out of place to examine these here. But we might expect that in the most general sense measurement in sociology will, in the future, involve algebraic structures of varying complexity. But this is a very specialised area of current research and we must refer the reader to the excellent mathematical literature on abstract algebra.

4.6 Measurement of Structural Variables

In the opening paragraphs of this chapter the distinction was drawn between pure and structural measurement but so far only pure measurement has been considered. We may now, therefore, extend our findings to structural measurement by considering the measurement properties of relations between the objects in set O.

It has already been noted that one of the most convenient ways of depicting a structure is in terms of a graph or di-graph, where points in a plane represent units of analysis and lines (arcs) joining the points represent the relations.

Thus a type of structure (or graph) can be defined for each level of measurement leading to the classification in Figure 4.11.

Simple binary structures we have already met – if the nominal variable comprises more than two categories then we can define a structure for each category type. For instance, with a classification of exchange types, economic, political and kin (i.e. exchange

Figure 4.11 Structural Levels of Measurement

Level of measurement	Structure (graph)
Nominal	Simple binary structure graphs and di-graphs
Ordinal	Ordinal structures – a linear order or weak order of valuations on the relation
Ordered metric, etc.	Ordered metric structure – an ordered metric associated with the relations in the structure
Interval and Ratio	Cardinal structures – ratio or interval level measures on the relation

of women) we would define three simple binary structures (graphs) – one for each type of exchange.

Ordinal structures (Abell, 1968) are a little more complex, they comprise

    (i) a set of units O,

    (ii) a relation mapping O into itself, and

    (iii) a weak order or linear order of valuations,

$$\phi_1 > \phi_2 > \phi_3 \ldots .$$

A value from (iii) is then attached to each relationship in the structure, arc in the graph, or entry in the associated matrix. Figure 4.12 shows an ordinal graph and associated matrix.

Ordinal structures reflect all those situations where a set of units are linked by relationships of varying intensity, but where cardinal measures (i.e. interval or ratio measures) cannot be

Figure 4.12 Some Structures

Name	Graph	Matrix
Simple binary (Nominal)		
Ordinal		
Interval and Ratio (Cardinal)		

Simple binary (Nominal) matrix:

	a	b	c	d	e
a	–	1	0	0	0
b	–	–	1	0	1
c	–	–	–	1	0
d	–	–	–	–	1
e	–	–	–	–	–

Ordinal:

linear order of values

$\phi_1 > \phi_2 > \phi_3 > \phi_4$

	a	b	c	d	e
a	–	ϕ_1	0	0	0
b	–	–	ϕ_3	0	ϕ_2
c	–	–	–	ϕ_4	0
d	–	–	–	–	ϕ_1
e	–	–	–	–	–

Interval and Ratio (Cardinal):

	a	b	c	d	e
a	–	1	0	0	0
b	–	–	2	0	5
c	–	–	–	3	0
d	–	–	–	–	4
e	–	–	–	–	–

Note: Although the above examples are all symmetric structures (graphs) the same measurement techniques can be extended to non-symmetric structures (di-graphs) obtained. For example, an interaction structure may well have this property, as perhaps may many hierarchical structures where we can obtain a ranking of the degree of authority that individuals or roles have over each other. It has recently been suggested (Abell, 1969b) that social role structures are of an ordinal variety.

A special type of ordinal graph is one where there are two linear orders of valuations, one positive and one negative. We may call such a graph an *algebraic ordinal graph*. These graphs are suitable for depicting situations where relationships between units are either positively or negatively evaluated. For example, the 'friendship' relationship where it is normally the case that friendship and hostility can be defined.

Little more needs to be said about ordered metric structures. The additional factor here is that the ranking on the relations is an ordered metric one, not merely a linear or weak order.

If either interval or ratio measures can be obtained for the relations in the structure, then we may speak of cardinal structures; these may be depicted either as graphs with the appropriate measures on the arcs or as valued associated matrices (Figure 4.12).

5. The Treatment of Theoretical Variables

5.1 Introduction

The treatment of theoretical variables calls for some special comment; T-concepts are, by definition, not directly observable and we have therefore to ask how they can be converted into T-variables in terms of O-concepts and variables.

Three approaches to this problem may be distinguished:

(i) The definitional approach whereby T-variables are explicitly defined in terms of O-variables.

(ii) The 'operationalist' approach whereby T-variables are 'operationalised' in terms of a set of O-variables.

(iii) The latent causal approach whereby T-variables are treated as latent causal agents inducing changes and covariations among O-variables.

Although these three approaches are not mutually exclusive (in particular (ii) lies rather uneasily between (i) and (iii)), it is useful to consider them separately while, in so doing, drawing parallels and connections.

5.2 The Definitional Approach to T-variables

The most obvious way of using T-concepts or variables is to explicitly define them in terms of O-concepts or variables; that is to establish an *analytical* link between the T- and O-concepts (variables).

Let us assume that a given T-concept can in some way, be defined, in terms of a set $O = \{O_i\}, i = 1, 2, \ldots, n$ of O-concepts. Furthermore, assume an appropriate logical structure on set O permitting us to make statements involving the elements of set O. In the simplest case we might take $\{O_i\}$ as simple dichotomous variables and consider statements merely conjoining the elements in the set as the structure. In general, we write $S\{O_i\}$ to indicate some specified structure on O. For example, population pressure of a nation (a T-variable) might be defined as the ratio of total population to total land area of the nation (O-variables) thus implying *ratio measures* of the O-variables and the operation of division. Formally, then, $S\{O_i\}$ becomes the *definiens* in a definition of a T-concept. It is, of course, imperative to consider the type of structure defined on set O and, to emphasise a point made earlier, that the nature of T-concepts or variables depends upon the level of measurement of the O-concepts in their *definiens*. If, for instance, ratio level measures cannot be defined on set O, then T-concepts implying this level of measurement are not strictly legitimate although it may be worth while to make an assumption of such measures.

There are three ways of attempting to define T-variables:

(i) Where $S\{O_i\}$ gives the *necessary* and *sufficient* conditions for T (i.e. $T \Leftrightarrow S\{O_i\}$).

(ii) Where $S\{O_i\}$ gives only the *necessary* conditions for T (i.e. $T \Rightarrow S\{O_i\}$).

(iii) Where $S\{O_i\}$ gives only the *sufficient* conditions for T (i.e. $T \Leftarrow S\{O_i\}$).

Although, in the strict sense of the word, only form (i) is a definition it is useful to use the word 'definition' in a broader sense to include the less restrictive forms (ii) and (iii).

One is naturally tempted to define T-concepts in the following manner (dropping the subscript for convenience):

$$Tx \Leftrightarrow [Cx \Rightarrow (S\{O\})\,x]. \tag{5.1}$$

That is: x can be predicted of T if and only if, when x is in conditions C, x will exhibit some specified structure on set O, where C and O are observational concepts. Thus the appearance of $S\{O\}$ in conditions C would be a necessary and sufficient condition for T.

Carnap (1937) has however demonstrated a difficulty with this type of formulation. It implies that for any entity not under conditions C (i.e. Cx has truth value false) the expression in the square brackets (the *definiens*) must be true. For by the rules of extensional logic if the antecedent of a conditional statement is false then the statement itself must be true. So under these conditions the object would be predicated of T. To avoid this clearly unsatisfactory state of affairs, Carnap suggested the form

$$Cx \Rightarrow [Tx \Leftrightarrow (S\{O\})x] \qquad (5.2)$$

which reads: if x is under conditions C then x is a T if and only if x exhibits a specified structure on set O. Statements of this form are sometimes called *reduction-sentences*. This formalisation avoids the above difficulty. Furthermore the treatment has the advantage that it gives only a partial definition of T, as it only explicitly defines T for those xs that happen to fall under conditions C, leaving it open that T might be predicated of xs under other conditions; the conditions C only provide a sufficiency for the statement in the square brackets. So we may envisage the definition of a given T-concept in terms of an *open* series of this sort of expression:

$$C_1\, x \Rightarrow [Tx \Leftrightarrow (S\{O_1\})x]$$
$$C_2\, x \Rightarrow [Tx \Leftrightarrow (S\{O_2\})x] \qquad (5.3)$$

$$\cdot$$
$$\cdot$$
$$\cdot$$

$$C_n\, x \Rightarrow [Tx \Leftrightarrow (S\{O_n\})x].$$

This formalisation seems fairly close to actual practice in sociology. Consider, for instance, a series of questions C_1, $C_2, \ldots, C_n$ with appropriate answers O_i for demonstrating the presence of T; the above series of statements would represent the logic of this situation very well indeed. For example, if a person (x) were asked a question in suitable conditions (together comprising C_i) then that person may be predicated of T if he gave a response O_i etc. And since the series of partial definitions of this form is logically open this corresponds well with our experience that we can, when trying to define a T-concept, normally ask many more or different questions. Alternatively each sentence may be regarded as a definition of a 'value' of the variable T on a given scale.

This sort of formalisation also has the advantage that it permits us to take a cross-cultural or comparative perspective on T-concepts. For when we speak of the problem of using the 'same' T-concept in different cultural settings surely we mean nothing less and nothing more than that the presence of T must be demonstrated in different conditions. So a series of reduction sentences may be appropriate for defining a T-concept in one cultural setting and at the same time be perfectly compatible with a different set of reduction sentences in another cultural setting. Our formalisation thus accommodates the classical problem of cross-cultural definition in sociology.

Even though the present formalisation only partly defines any given T-concept it is still a very demanding criterion and is perhaps rarely obtained in sociology. Some of the simpler T-concepts can often be defined in this manner, but it is unlikely that the richer sociological concepts like alienation, anomie, etc., can.

The demanding nature of this definitional form springs from the use of logical equivalence (i.e. necessity and sufficiency). For, if we think in terms of questions and answers once again, it stipulates that, given the appropriate question and conditions, the appropriate answer is a necessary and sufficient condition for the T-concept. So if the conditions were fulfilled and the question fixed and then an inappropriate answer resulted, the presence of the T-concept would be immediately invalidated. Our practical experience in using questionnaires as a research tool tells us that this is often far too demanding a property to set upon our data. We prefer to think, at least implicitly, in terms of a probabilistic relationship between T-concepts and replies to questions or indeed any other type of appropriate behaviour. We may, however, try to relax the definitional approach by dropping criteria of necessity *and* sufficiency and replacing it by one or the other.

So if $S\{O\}$ gives only the sufficient conditions for T we may formalise the 'definition' as follows:

$$Cx \Rightarrow [(S\{O\})\,x \Rightarrow Tx] \qquad (5.4)$$

which reads: if x is under conditions C then if x exhibits $S\{O\}$, then x is a T. This formalisation has the effect of leaving the definition even more open than the previous one for in conditions C, $S\{O\}$ is only a sufficient condition for T so there could even in these conditions be other structures on O, say $(S'\{O\})$ indicating the presence of T. Thus, if we are permitted to use the word 'definition' in this context, it means there can be alternative definitions of a T-concept in the same conditions. Such definitions may be described as *contextually sufficient definitions*.

If $S\{O\}$ gives only the necessary and not the sufficient conditions for the presence of T then we may formalise the 'definition' as

$$Cx \Rightarrow [Tx \Rightarrow (S\{O\})\,x] \qquad (5.5)$$

which reads: if x is under conditions C then if x is a T it will exhibit the structure $S\{O\}$. This form of definition in effect postulates $S\{O\}$ as 'only part' of T, for it is necessary but not sufficient – there will be some other component of T but $S\{O\}$ must also be present. We may say that $S\{O\}$ provides a *contextually necessary definition*, the context being C.

Strict definitions of the three sorts under consideration have not proved particularly useful in sociology. It is the practice to think in terms of a rather looser relationship than that of necessity and sufficiency between a T-variable and observational variables.

It is important finally to emphasise the analytic (i.e. as opposed to synthetic) nature of the link between T- and O-concepts (variables) implied by the present approach. Thinking, once again, in terms of the theoretical structure in Figure 3.1 the 'lines' represent analytical links. So it would be a *conceptual* absurdity, if either $T \Leftrightarrow S\{O_i\}$ or $T \Rightarrow S\{O_i\}$ holds, to assert T and deny $S\{O_i\}$; and, if $T \Leftarrow S\{O_i\}$ or $T \Leftrightarrow S\{O_i\}$ holds, an absurdity to assert $S\{O_i\}$ and deny T.

Population pressure, for example, *means* (at least in part) the ratio of total population to land area. It would be nonsense to 'search for' population pressure independently of population and land area. The analytic approach to theoretical terms has important implications for theoretical structures (see Section 5.5).

5.3 The Operationalist Approach to T-variables

Although this approach is not always logically distinct from the definitional one, it has sufficient unique features to warrant independent consideration. It should be noted, however, that the word 'operationalism' is used in a restricted sense; it is sometimes called measurement by *fiat*.

The logical feature of the operationalist approach to T-concepts or variables is normally somewhat as follows:

1. Consider a T-concept, e.g. social class.

2. Assume that concept T can be 'operationalised' by a set $I = \{i_i\}, i = 1, 2, \ldots, m$ of *indicators* selected from a set of *items*, e.g. social class can be operationised in terms of income, occupation, education, etc. Decide on *measures* of the elements of set I, e.g. decide on measures of income, occupation, education, etc.

3. Adopt a technique of mapping all logically possible combinations of indicator values into an *index* measure. That is, adopt a technique of *index* construction – map points in the n-dimensional *indicator space* into the *index space*. This mapping is normally many to one, i.e. it is an information condensing technique.

A full consideration of the details of operationalisation would involve us in the theory of scaling but this would be out of place here as we are really only concerned with the overall logical features of the process. Readers interested in the actual techniques of scaling are referred, for example, to Torgerson (1958).

The operationalist approach is not always explicit about the logical stature of the link between the T-concepts and O-concepts. On the one hand, the relationship between social class and income, occupation, education, etc. appears to be construed as *analytic*; part of what we mean by social class is certain profiles of these latter variables. The technique is then close to that presented in the previous section; the difference being that the link between social class and given properties is likely only to be probabilistic. The picture is thus somewhat as follows: under conditions C if a person is of a particular social class T then there is a 'high probability' that he will have a specified educational, occupational, income profile. The *definiens* is linked to the subject of the definition by a 'given' probability. But the fact remains (if this interpretation of social class is correct) that nobody would think of 'searching' for social class independently of these or other similar variables. On the other hand, when the T-concept 'intelligence' is operationalised in terms of performances on IQ tests then the implication often seems to be that intelligence *causes* particular performances. So intelligence is synthetically related to performance. If this view is correct it would be sensible to 'search for' direct observation of intelligence independently of the performance on IQ tests. In this case operationalism is close to if not coincidental with the latent causal view of T-concepts. We will return to these problems in Section 5.5.

For the moment the process of operationalisation can be conceptualised as a series of inferences depicted in Figure 5.1. We will now consider each of these inferences in turn.

Figure 5.1 The Inferences Involved in Operationalisation

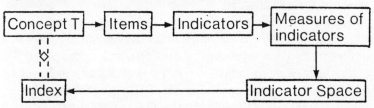

Concept to Items Here the problem is of selecting items that 'meaningfully' tap the ideas behind the concept, i.e. items that have high logical *validity*. This is, of course, where much of the creativity in the practice of sociology occurs. There are, however, standard texts[1] on the criteria whereby we select items in social research so the problem will not be considered further.

Items to Indicators Normally in social research we initially select more items for 'tapping' a concept than are ultimately used. That is, a subset of indicators is selected from the set of items. Items are selected in terms of one's *a priori* ideas about the T-concept in question. An item is said to have high validity if it serves well to represent the T-concept. But how can we decide when this is the case? An answer to this question cannot be given until the problem of creating indices has been considered; so we will return to it later (p. 91).

Indicators to Measures of Indicators This inference is in effect the problem of measurement in a special context. Indicators are concepts and must be converted into variables by mapping each into a measurement system. We may therefore, distinguish between the homogeneous case, when all the indicators are measurable at the same level, and the heterogeneous case, when they are not. Our above example of social class seems to be heterogeneous; income can naturally be measured at the ratio level and also perhaps education, if the number of years of formal education is taken as the measure. Occupation, on the other hand, can only be measured at the ordinal level (a status ranking of occupations). Our indicator space will, in such cases, be a rather complex entity. We often, of course, make assumptions about measurability to render an indicator space homogeneous. For instance, we might categorise income, occupation and education into ranked dimensions – High, Medium and Low. Indeed, in general, it is advisable in social research to render the indicator space homogeneous by making simple approximations of this sort, for the indicator space has eventually to be 'condensed' into the index space anyway. So, some of the condensation is carried out at the initial stage. One cannot draw any hard and fast rules about this as it is largely a matter of creativity in the research. But it is pointless to retain very fine distinctions on one indicator when the others are comparatively crude since, in the end, some aggregating operation will necessarily take place in the convergence to the index space; a chain is never stronger than its weakest link.

In the case of heterogeneous indicator spaces, the question naturally arises as to whether the indicators measured at a higher level of measurement should be simplified to a lower level or whether assumptions should be made to the effect that the lower level indicators are measured at a higher level. The answer to this question depends largely on the type of index we want. If an index at the low level will suffice then the first strategy should be utilised. If, on the other hand, a high-level index is required, attempts should be made in the second direction – but, of course, always with great caution. When in doubt, perhaps both strategies should be employed, different indices constructed and used comparatively in the model building.

Measures of Indicators to Indicator Space Once we have decided upon the measurement characteristics of our indicators then the nature and dimensions of the indicator space are set.

With *n* indicators having values $v_1, v_2 \ldots v_n$ respectively, our indicator space can be conceptualised as an *n*-dimensional space with

$$V = v_1 \cdot v_2 \cdot v_3 \ldots \cdot v_n$$

logically possible 'points'.

For example, if income, education and occupation are each measured as high, medium and low, then the logically possible number of 'points' in the indicator space (i.e. patterns of values in the indicators characterising units of analysis) is 27.

Indicator Space to Index The purpose of creating an index out of an indicator space is to condense the information in the former; i.e. to simplify it.[2] But we also want to preserve as much information in the index as possible. Thus, in constructing an index, we are faced with two inversely related factors – the attempt to simplify and the attempt, at the same time, to preserve information. The degree to which information is preserved in an index is the degree to which one can infer from an index score to an indicator pattern. The degree to which an index simplifies is the extent to which the diversity of patterns (points) in the indicator space is reduced by the index. To take a very simple example: if one had six points in an indicator space, *a, b, c, d, e* and *f* and these were converted into two index scores *A* and *B*, then a diversity of six has been reduced (simplified) to two, but we have lost information since by knowing something is an *A* we only know for example it is either an *a*, or *b* or a *c* – not which one. The essence then of constructing an index is to reduce an *n*-dimensional indicator space to one 'underlying' variable (the index).

Four types of index can be distinguished depending on their different measurement structure:

(i)   *Nominal indices:* The values are merely classifications.

(ii) *Ordinal indices:* The values have a linear ordering.

(iii) *Interval indices:* The values have the structure of the interval scale, i.e. distance and ordering.

(iv) *Ratio indices:* The values have the structure of the ratio scale, i.e. ordering, distance and zero.

Clearly, one would expect there to be a close relationship between the measurement structure on the indicator space and that on the index. So now let us look at some of the elementary logical features of index formation.

Perhaps the easiest way to accomplish this is by reverting once again to our example of social class. But in order to keep the argument as simple as possible, let us assume that we have only two indicators, say income and education, and each is measured on a scale – none, low, medium and high. There are thus sixteen 'points' in the indicator space.

Although in using the scale 'none' to 'high' only ordinality is implied, let us begin by assuming we have a homogeneous *ratio-measured indicator space*. (Only homogeneous indicator spaces will be considered as in the last section we recommended the homogenisation of heterogeneous spaces.)

If discrete cardinal measures of income and education are assumed as follows: none = 0, low = 1, medium = 2, and high = 3, then we would quite naturally construct the additive index depicted in Figure 5.2, thus obtaining a simple index running integrally from zero to six. Furthermore, we could

Figure 5.2 An Additive Index

		0	1	2	3
	3	3	4	5	6
Income	2	2	3	4	5
	1	1	2	3	4
	0	0	1	2	3

Education

clearly extend this very elementary technique to as many indicators as we please, so that the score for a particular unit of analysis is obtained from the sum of its scores on the component indicators. In general,

$$m. = \sum_{j=1}^{n} v_j \qquad (5.6)$$

and where $m.$ is the index score, v_j is the score on the jth indicator.

It is important, however, to realise the assumptions upon which such a simple procedure is based.

(a) The indicators are measurable at the ratio or interval level, and

(b) each indicator is comparable with all the others. That is, it is 'meaningful' to obtain additive scores across the set of indicators. For instance, the index scores 2 can be obtained in one of three ways – 2 on income and 0 on education; 1 on income and 1 on education; and 2 on education and 0 on income. *And for the purposes of the index there is no discrimination made between these three patterns.* It is in this sense that indices surrender information. If it is not *sociologically* meaningful to surrender information in this way then such an index should not be constructed. This, of course, raises once again the problem of concept formation in sociology: is it meaningful to lump together 2 on income and 0 on education with 2 on education and 0 on income? The construction of an index in this manner may be construed as an example of constructivism if the indicator dimensions are internal concepts. The index scores are external concepts which are logical constructs of internal concepts. The important point is that the information surrendered in the index mapping is *not* sociologically important. In our simple example, for instance, the distinction between 2 on education, 0 on income and 1 on income, 1 on education must not have any importance. By importance we, in practice, mean one of two things:

(a) If the index in question to be used is an *explanatory* variable then it should be a better predictor of (explanation of) variance in the explained variables than any of the indicators taken separately (see Chapter 8 for an elaboration of this point).

(b) If the variable is an *explained* one, then we should have good sociological reasons for not wanting to explain variance of the component indicators. This will usually happen when the variable plays a strategic role in a wider theory. Social class is perhaps a very good example of this.

In general, with two indicators, one of t categories and one of s categories, there will (assuming a simple cardinal scale) be $(s + t)$ index scores summarising the $(s \times t)$ indicator scores. And generalising to n indicators with S_i categories each, there will be $\sum_{i=1}^{n} S_i$ index scores summarising $\prod_{i=1}^{n} S_i$ indicator scores.

A ratio index should, of course, be invariant to linear transforms of the form $y = ax$ of all its component indicators.

For example, if the transform, $x' = 2x$ is applied to both the income and education indicators in the above example, instead of obtaining the additive index scores 0, 1, 2, 3, 4, 5 and 6 we obtain 0, 2, 4, 6, 8, 10 and 12. And note that the ratios of 'corresponding' points on these indices are equal (e.g. $6/1 = 12/2$). But the transform must be the same on both indicator scales. If, for example, we transformed only one of the indicators according to the transform $x' = 2x$ then the index scale would be 0, 1, 2, 3, 4, 5, 6, 7, 8 and 9.

Similarly an interval index will be invariant to linear transforms of the form $x' = ax + b$ (where a and b are constants), of *all* its indicators. For example, if the transform $x' = 2x + 1$ is applied to our original example, instead of an index with scores 0, 1, 2, 3, 4, 5 and 6 we obtain 1, 4, 6, 8, 10, 12 and 14. Now the ratios of distances are still equal (e.g. 6–4/8–6 = 1 = 2–1/3–2).

Of course, if discrete metric indicators can be obtained then normally a zero can be fixed and the distinction between interval and ratio indices becomes rather academic.

Ratio and interval level indicators are comparatively rare in sociology but, if they are obtained, it is a relatively simple matter to construct an additive index. It must be remembered, however, that the process of index construction is a many-to-one mapping and surrenders information.

Turning now to the case where the indicator space is ordinal, let us assume that income and education can only be measured ordinally as high, medium, low and none. The indicator space will now be depicted as in Figure 5.3.

Figure 5.3 An Ordinal Index Space

Income		none	low	medium	high
	high	HN	HL	HM	HH
	medium	MN	ML	MM	MH
	low	LN	LL	LM	LH
	none	NN	NL	NM	NH
		none	low	medium	high
				Education	

There are thus 16 'points' in the indicator space and the question arises, how can an index be obtained? Since the indicators are only ordered we must rule out any ideas of addition. It would therefore be unwise to begin by applying numbers

D

to the ranked categories since any increasing/decreasing sequence would do.

The problem is how to rank order the 16 points. If an asymmetric relation is imposed of the form: index point A is higher than point B if A is higher on at least one dimension and not lower on any other (Galtung, 1967), this relationship will be transitive giving the *partial order* depicted in Figure 5.4.

Figure 5.4 The Partial Order of an Ordinal Indicator Space

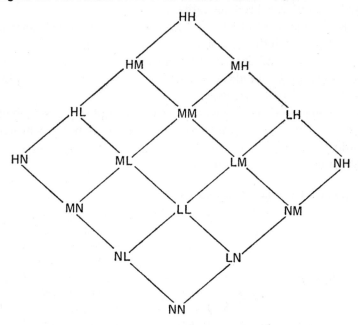

Mathematically this is a *lattice*[3] and is obtained by moving from the top right-hand corner of the original Table to its bottom left-hand corner.

The same type of structure can be generated however many ordinal categories there are on each indicator. And furthermore, a similar structure can easily be generated even when the number of indicators exceeds 2. The difficulty then in all cases is that only partial orders are obtained – not linear or weak orders – and so we have incomparable points in the indicator space. The problem remains how to impose equivalences in this underlying ordered structure for, as it stands, it provides no simplification.

If ranked equivalence classes (i.e. a weak order) are created across the points in the ordinal index space according to the rule (Galtung, 1967): class A > class B if and only if all points in $A \geqslant$ all points in B, then a *trichotomised* index would always result. The low value of the index corresponding to NN . . . and the high to HH . . . , and *all the intervening cases in the middle category*. This clearly provides only a very crude form of discrimination on the index. For, in general, with n ordinal indicators with r values each there are r^n points in the indicator space, therefore $(r^n - 2)$ points in the middle category of the index. Thus it appears that the above rule is rather over-demanding for practical purposes, especially as we might expect that in any empirical investigation the great majority of the cases will fall in the middle category.

So, for most practical purposes, the criterion that index class order implies element order under $\geqslant$ must be rejected.

If, therefore, we adopt the rule that A > B if and only if there are no points in B > A, then each 'level' in the lattice corresponds to a point in our index. So our original example of education and income gives a 7-point ordinal index running from NN at the bottom to HH at the top.

In general, with n indicators each with r categories there will be r^n points in the indicator space which will reduce to r levels in the partial order (lattice).

So far we have confined our attention to situations where all the indicators have an equivalent weighting. However, this is often an oversimplification. With interval and ratio indicators, weightings can, of course, be easily included in the index construction (e.g. a particular indicator may be given double weighting). In the ordinal case, things are not so straightforward. But a classical form of scale, the *Guttman* scale is, in essence, a technique of obtaining an ordinal scale when the indicators have a 'weighting'. Since, however, there are many standard texts available on this scale, we will not consider it here any further (see, for instance, Torgerson, 1958).

Turning now to consider a homogeneous nominal indicator space, we will concentrate solely upon dichotomous indicators since if there are more than two categories to an indicator then they are normally ranked.

An indicator space comprising n dichotomies will generally give 2^n points in the indicator space. The accepted practice for converting this space into an index is to score the nominal categories on each indicator as 0 and 1 (which often corresponds to non-endorsement and endorsement of a question on a questionnaire). We then simply continue as before and compute an *additive* index which will collapse the 2^n indicator points onto: $0, 1, 2 \ldots n$ index scores. Only the index scores 0 (indicator scores all 0) and n (indicator scores all 1) are in a one-to-one relationship with the indicator points. Consider, for example, four dichotomous indicators: the distribution of indicator space points on index values is as in Figure 5.5.

Figure 5.5 An Index Created out of Four Dichotomies

Index	Number of Indicator Points	Indicator Patterns
0	1	0000
1	4	1000, 0100, 0010, 0001
2	6	1100, 0011, 1001, 0110, 1010, 0101
3	4	1110, 0111, 1011, 1101
4	1	1111

One of the difficulties, therefore, with such an index is that the 'middle' range of index scores surrender more information than the extreme ones – and since one might expect in most empirical investigations to obtain most cases in these ranges the discriminating power of such an index is not good. It is for this reason that the Guttman technique is generally preferable. However, when we have no information as to the possible 'extent' to which a dichotomous indicator taps a concept this technique is often useful. It should be noted that a simple underlying metric is assumed in using the scores 0 and 1 in the indicator space. The sociological assumption here is that all endorsements are of equal value or intensity (i.e. 'yes' answers are equivalent in all questions).

This completes our brief introduction to the indicator space index inference. The reader should note, however, that there are many very sophisticated *scaling techniques* available to the sociologist and a very extensive technical literature on the subject. However, it is quite often perfectly adequate, given the nature of sociological data, to operate with the fairly simple models outlined here. It is pointless to utilise a very sophisticated scaling technique if the data do not warrant it, and if the end result of analysis is to be a largely qualitative appraisal. The decision as to how sophisticated to be is, of course, the responsibility of the researcher. But there are many examples in the sociological literature where very highly developed techniques have been adopted to 'scale' variables and then when the variables have been related, a simple high, low or negligible, correlation has been sought. In such cases, a simple but 'sociologically intelligent' (see next section) approach to the scaling would be just as adequate. A further advantage of simple scaling techniques is that we can easily understand the assumptions we have made and relatively quickly and inexpensively (in terms of time and money) make alterations to our scales.

Concept to Index We now have a set of index scores 'representing' our original T-concept. On the face of it, then, the concept has been 'operationalised' and the story is over. However, we may still wish to *evaluate* the index and its component indicators.

Evaluating an Index A very obvious question to ask is: How good is an index in operationalising its T-concept? Of course, since we have no knowledge of the T-concept apart from our knowledge of the index this question cannot be answered directly; so it is usual to go about answering it in an indirect manner. One way is to look at the correlation between the index and each indicator. But note that, since each indicator is a component of the index, there must necessarily be some residual correlation. (We could get around this by excluding each indicator from the index when studying these correlations but apart from the labour involved in this we would be in effect creating a new index each time.)

Normally indicators are accepted as 'good' if they show high correlations with the index. If an indicator is found that exhibits a correlation of unity with the index then it could be used equally as well as the index, which may be rejected because of its greater complexity. However, one may still wish to use the index if it has more discriminations on its scale than the indicator. For example, with dichotomous indicators, very high correlations are often obtained with an index, but the index is preferred because of its greater range of scores (discriminating power).

It is usual practice to reject those items that do not exhibit a high correlation with the index, thus reducing the initial set of items to a set of indicators. It should be noted, however, that in rejecting an item from an index (on the basis of its low correlation) the index is changed and we have therefore to recompute the correlations of the remaining indicators with the new index (i.e. the old index minus rejected items). This may in turn lead to unsatisfactory correlations between the remaining indicators and the new index – in that case the process has to be continued until a satisfactory set of indicators is located. If a particular item has a high logical validity (see below) for a given T-concept but exhibits a low correlation with the index then this is indicative of the multidimensionality of the T-concept. The T-concept has then to be treated as a multidimensional entity. For a technical discussion of these problems, the reader is referred to Torgerson (1958).

Looking for high correlations between indicators and an index in this manner is not the same thing as testing the *validity* of an index. In evaluating these correlations we are merely concerned to show that the index and component indicators order the units of analysis in the same manner. Validity means more than this. Broadly speaking, the term is used to describe how well *the index* represents the T-concept it is supposed to stand for. Unfortunately the term validity has been used in a variety of ways, but it is perhaps useful to distinguish between, on the one hand, *logical validity* and, on the other, *operational validity*. Logical validity is concerned with our *a priori* ideas of how an index and indicators express the meaning of a T-concept. Operational validity is normally tested by examining the correlation between the index and another variable (the criterion variable) to which T is supposedly related. Of two indices for a given T-variable, that which has the highest correlation with the criterion is normally taken to be operationally the most valid. However, this criterion seems to have gained support in situations where a given T-variable is related to only one further variable (criterion) in an isolated proposition. In model building it is often the case that the T-variable is related to many other variables and one index will not uniformly exhibit the highest correlation with all these other variables. Perhaps the index with the highest average correlation with all the other variables in the model could be regarded as the most valid but it is perhaps best in situations like this to adopt an explicit causal viewpoint about the relationship between T-variables and indices (see next section).

The other important property of an index is its *reliability*; by this is meant the extent to which a given index will *repeatedly* order the units of analysis in the same way. It refers to the stability of the index on different occasions and under different circumstances. Again the concept is dealt with in detail in the technical literature on scaling and the reader is referred to those sources for further details.

5.4 *The Latent Causal Approach to T-variables*

We now turn to the third way of treating T-variables, that is, to the explicit idea that T-variables act as latent causes of observational variables. The link between the Ts and Os is avowedly synthetic.

If it is explicitly assumed that the relationship between a T-concept and its indicators is one of causality, such that changes in T 'cause' changes in the indicators, then we may depict the situation as in Figure 5.6 – where we restrict our attention to two indicators O_1 and O_2 (Blalock, 1968):

Figure 5.6 A Theoretical Variable as a Latent Cause

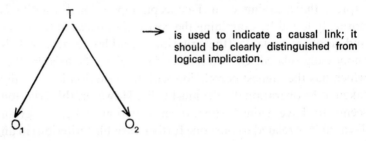

→ is used to indicate a causal link; it should be clearly distinguished from logical implication.

So the observed correlation between O_1 and O_2 is spurious. That is if some way of holding T constant could be found the correlation between O_1 and O_2 would disappear

i.e. Cor $(O_1 O_2 \cdot T) = O$ (ignoring sampling fluctuations).

Of course, to speak meaningfully of holding T constant there must be criteria for measuring T independent of O_1 and O_2. In other words, there must be some way of recognising the presence of T that does not involve the Os or anything logical implied by them, taken jointly or separately. But T is by definition a non-observable – so we appear to be in an impasse.

Blalock (1968) has argued, however, that it is often helpful to adopt the causal viewpoint even when there is no immediate possibility of measuring the T-variables directly. Complex theoretical models can be set out including non-measurable T-variables and measurable O-variables where correlations between the latter provide tests of the model. The advantage of this approach is that different indicators or indices are regarded as causal consequences of underlying T-variables and each is treated as important in its own right so the traditional problem of operational validity is circumscribed.

Let us take stock and highlight the difference between this approach to the status of theoretical entities and the one embedded in the two previously outlined approaches.[4] Here we are saying that a T-concept is, in fact, a contender for reality – admittedly a latent reality but it is definitely an existential entity (in some sense of the word). Moreover, it causes changes in Os which are not directly causally related and therefore we can only interpret their covariation in terms of T. But since T is not, at the moment, measurable we cannot 'test' this assumption. But a further advantage of the perspective is that it drives us towards finding independent techniques for measuring T.

The causal interpretation has a further advantage. We noted previously that 'indicators' do not normally perfectly intercorrelate; the causal model is perfectly compatible with this. For we can adopt the standard practice of introducing stochastic disturbances (μ_i) into our causal model as in Figure 5.7.

Figure 5.7 A Causal Model of a Theoretical Structure with Disturbance Terms

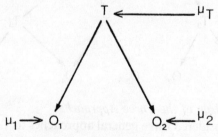

These, as we shall see later, can be conceptualised as either errors in observation (measurement) or further excluded causal variables acting randomly. These excluded variables may be either further T- or O-variables. In particular μ_T may comprise 'deeper' lying T-concepts/variables which are causally related to T. The perspective this opens up is the possibility of delving deeper and deeper into latent processes (cf. Durkheim), by the elaboration of these T-concepts. Our theoretical structures would have open ceilings.

A typical example may look something like the structure in Figure 5.8 where once again the arrows depict (synthetic) causal links between the variables. There is a point worth noting about O_4 – it is 'caused' by both T_4 and T_5 (i.e. it is theoretically *over-determined* (see Chapter 6)). Now if the operationalist approach were adopted, O_4 could stand as an indicator of *both* T_4 and T_5 but it is normally required that indicators operationalising distinct T-concepts be mutually exclusive. A methodological precept for the operationalist is that the same indicator should not be used to stand for different T-concepts for, if they did, he would 'build in' a connection between the T-concepts; it would not then be a completely contingent exercise to study their relationship. The latent causal approach, on the other hand, allows for theoretical over-determination.

Figure 5.8 A Complex Theoretical Structure

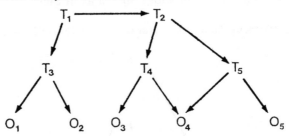

5.5 Comparison of the Three Approaches
We have considered three general approaches to T-variables and the question naturally arises in what circumstances each should be used. In many ways the latent causal approach is the most powerful but, unfortunately, the most difficult to deploy in the fullest sense of finding direct observations of the T-variables. I have argued elsewhere (Abell, 1969b) that such direct observation would be characteristically different in the social sciences from that in the physical sciences. In the latter, the observational

domain is characteristically reduced to micro-ontologies (atoms, molecules, etc.) so observations in the physical world can be construed as being caused by changes at the level of micro-ontology. In sociology, however, the characteristic latent ontology is a macro one – we try to construe people's behaviour in terms of their location in social collectivities. So for the latent causal approach to be effective we require ways of observing and characterising groups independently of the properties of their individual members. This is, of course, a restatement of the old problem of 'emergence' in sociology. Unfortunately at present there is no systematic meta-theory to help us in this direction. Properties of empirical collectivities, structures or aggregates are usually summary measures (means, variances, etc.) of the properties or relations between the component units. Another important class of latent variables contains psychological ones characterising the mental states (cognitive and emotional) of actors. I have suggested elsewhere (1969b) that recent developments in psycho-chemistry may in the future prove useful for 'directly' observing such states.

The force of the latent causal approach can, however, easily be appreciated by noting the *logical limitations* of the definitional approach.

If a given T-concept can be defined in the manner $T \equiv S\{o\}$ and T is related to another concept/variable X in a proposition of the form $(T \Rightarrow X)$ then we may write:

$$[(T \Leftrightarrow S\{o\}) \cdot (T \Rightarrow X)] \Rightarrow [S\{o\} \Rightarrow X] \qquad (5.7)$$

which is a tautology. *So T only plays a summary role*; it is, from a strictly logical standpoint, dispensable. Furthermore, if the variable X is defined in terms of a structure on a set a of observational concepts – $S\{a\}$ – then we may write:

$$[(T \Leftrightarrow S\{o\}) \cdot (T \Rightarrow X) \cdot (X \Leftrightarrow S\{a\})] \Rightarrow [S\{o\} \rightarrow S\{a\}] \quad (5.8)$$

which is also a tautology. This means, therefore, that both T and X are *logically* dispensable.

This logical dispensability is not quite so pronounced if the definitional form $T \Rightarrow S\{o\}$ is adopted. We may write

$$[(T \Rightarrow S\{o\}) \cdot (T \Rightarrow X)] \Rightarrow [S\{o\} \Rightarrow X] \qquad (5.9)$$

which is not a tautology. But, on the other hand,

$$[(T \Rightarrow S\{o\}) \cdot (X \Rightarrow T)] \Rightarrow [X \Rightarrow S\{o\}] \qquad (5.10)$$

is a tautology. So if a structure on a set of observational concepts is defined as a necessary condition for a T-concept then the T-concept is logically dispensable where it is the consequence, but not where it is the antecedent, in a proposition.

The third possible definitional form is $T \Leftarrow S\{o\}$, then we may write

$$[(T \Leftarrow S\{o\}) \cdot (T \Rightarrow X)] \Rightarrow [S\{o\} \Rightarrow X] \qquad (5.11)$$

which is a tautology, whereas

$$[(T \Leftarrow S\{o\}) \cdot (X \Rightarrow T)] \Rightarrow [S\{o\} \Rightarrow X] \qquad (5.12)$$

is not a tautology. So in this case the T-concept is logically dispensable if T is the antecedent but not when it is the consequence in a proposition.

All this means that the argument analogous to (5.8) for these two definitional forms is not tautologous. For example

$$[(T \Leftarrow S\{o\}) \cdot (T \Rightarrow X) \cdot (X \Leftarrow S\{a\})] \Rightarrow [S\{o\} \Rightarrow S\{a\}] \quad (5.13)$$

is not tautologous.

However, the definitional approach to T-concepts always, at least in part, renders them logically superfluous. With the latent causal approach the T-concepts are supposed to stand in a contingent relationship to the structure $S\{o\}$ and are thus not redundant. If one could devise techniques for observing T, the proposition relating T and $S\{o\}$ could be subjected to empirical test. Given the present state of social theory, however, it is (as Blalock, 1968, suggests) often a good idea to formulate complex theoretical structures as though one were adopting the latent causal approach even when it is clear that the T-variables cannot be measured directly. Then if a particular T-concept has many observational causal consequences and there is no hope of actually observing the T they can be combined into an index in the operationalist manner. But it is a good idea to keep clear in one's mind those T-concepts that are regarded as 'existential' (e.g. intelligence) and those that are merely summary concepts (e.g. population pressure).

5.6 Variables Characterising Collectivities

It was previously noted that a characteristic feature of socio-logical investigation is to attach concepts/variables to social collectivities. These are normally summary measures of some property of, or relationship between, the constituent units of the collectivity. So in the simplest interpretation such measures will be either measures of central tendency or dispersion of the property or relationship in question.

Measures of Central Tendency If the property of the constituent units is a cardinal measure then the *mean* is the most appropriate measure. The *median* is also a possibility. The mean is of course influenced by extreme values and, if data contain uncharacteristic extreme values, the median may be preferred to the mean.

However, the mean will be less susceptible to sampling fluctuations and if one is working with a sample then inferring to the population is not such an awkward business as with the median.

The median on the other hand has the distinct advantage that it is appropriate at the ordinal as well as the cardinal level.

No definitive rule can be given for the use of one of these parameters rather than the other. Each case must be approached with an open mind, and before making a decision the distributions should be examined to see which is the 'best' representation. Social theory rarely if ever, dictates the use of one rather than the other and in borderline cases both may be used and compared.

The *mode* is sometimes useful, especially when the variable concerned is a nominal one or with grouped data from cardinal or ordinal distributions. With multi-modal distributions the modes may be analytically more useful than a mean. Bi-modal distributions are relatively common in sociology where the variable in question runs from negative values through a 'zero point' to positive values. In such situations the proportion of cases in the modal categories may be the best parameters representing the distribution at the level of the collectivity. But in the face of very irregular distributions a central tendency measure is most probably of little analytical value.

The *harmonic* and *geometric* means are other possible measures at the cardinal level. Very little use has been made of these parameters in sociology.

Measures of Dispersion The *standard deviation* or *variance* measures are the obvious choice for cardinal variables. They gain their predominance amongst variance measures because of the role they play in the equation for the normal curve. But perhaps the *mean deviation* (i.e. the arithmetic mean of the absolute differences of each score from the mean) has a more obvious interpretation, and if no attempt is to be made to generalise from samples to populations this parameter may perhaps be used with advantage. There seems to be little justification for using simple measures like the *range* unless working with populations, for this parameter will be strongly influenced by sampling. In particular, the larger the sample the higher the probability of extreme cases and, consequently, the higher the range. The *quartile deviation* is not so susceptible to this problem, since it measures the range of the middle half of the units of analysis, it may be used when extreme cases are thought to be uncharacteristic or when there are other reasons for ignoring them.

If one is interested in the amount of dispersion relative to the mean then the *coefficient of variability* (i.e. the ratio of the standard deviation to the mean) may be a useful measure. There seems no reason why the relative variance (ratio of the variance to the mean) should not also be utilised.

The parameters mentioned so far, except for the range, are only strictly applicable with cardinal measures. For ordinal and nominal distributions the *information measure* is useful. It is defined as

$$I = \sum_i p_i \log_2 p_i$$

where p_i is the proportion of cases in category i and $\sum p_i = 1$.

Contextual Variables A recent analytical approach to situations where an individual's behaviour is a function of the behaviour of those in his social vicinity is the use of so-called variables. If a 'group' of individuals can be characterised by a variable X, then the contextual variable for any given individual i is defined as the mean of all the *other* individuals (i.e. excluding i) in the group.

Structural Properties We have already encountered, in Chapter 2, measures like degree of connectivity and completion which are structural summary parameters.

6. Propositions

6.1 Introduction

We are in a position to move one stage further up the hierarchy of scientific sophistication. We have considered concepts and how they may be converted into variables; now we turn to propositions.

Propositions normally contain
   (i) two concepts or variables, and
   (ii) a *connective* relating the concepts or variables.

From now on the term concept will be dropped in favour of the term variable for it is measured concepts (i.e. variables) that appear in propositions in the actual practice of sociology. Moreover, the *form* a proposition takes is a function of the level of measurement at which the variables can be measured. A proposition is called a T-proposition if it contains constituent T-variables and an O-proposition if it contains O-variables. The connective in a proposition may be either theoretical or observational. The most important T-connective is *'causes'* and we will have much to say about this later on. O-connectives are not observational in the sense that O-concepts are; they are always in some sense derived such as, for example, a *correlation measure*. Correlation coefficients are, of course, not observed in the strict sense but they are sufficiently different from, say, causal connectives for us to regard them as distinct. In fact the problems of inferring from *observed* correlation coefficients to *theoretical* causal links will become our central problem in subsequent chapters. Perhaps the most frequently occurring observational connective in sociology is the expression 'increases or decreases with', which is particularly appropriate when the variables in the proposition are measured at the ordinal level.

The Table in Figure 6.1 gives some examples of typical sociological propositions with their abstract form.

Figure 6.1 Some Sociological Propositions

Example	Abstract form	Status of connective
Intra-class consciousness is a function of inter-class conflict	A = intra-class consciousness B = inter-class conflict (A is a function of B) $A = f(B)$	'function of' observational
Intra-class consciousness increases with inter-class conflict	A increases with B (A correlates positively with B)	'increases with' observational
Intra-class consciousness decreases with inter-class conflict	C = intra-class conflict, (C decreases with B, C correlates negatively with B)	'decreases with' observational
Inter-class conflict causes class-consciousness	A causes B	'cause' theoretical
The kinship structure has the social function of social control	D = kinship structure E = social control (D has the social function of E) (N.B. difference between social function and function)	'social function' theoretical
All societies have an incest taboo	S = societies T = incest taboo all S are T $(x) [Sx \Rightarrow Tx]$	'if . . . then . . .' observational

Using these examples for the purposes of exposition we will now consider some general problems associated with the use of propositions in sociology.

6.2 Generality of Propositions and Sociological Explanation

In so far as sociology is a scientific enterprise, it is normally concerned to elaborate and test *general* propositions. Hence some preliminary introductory remarks about generality and sociological explanation are perhaps in place.

As is well known, philosophers of science distinguish between the following two sorts of scientific explanation:

(i) the *hypothetico-deductive* model whereby an event is explained as a specific instance of a 'general law', and

(ii) the *probabilistic* model whereby an event is said to have a high probability of occurring as an instance of a 'probabilistic law'.

In its simplest form, the hypothetico-deductive model enables us to deduce a statement describing an event of the form, if A then B, from the conjoin of a general proposition (law), of the form all As are Bs $((x)\,[Ax \Rightarrow Bx])$ and a set C of *initial conditions* under which the general statement or law is supposed to hold. The initial conditions usually comprise a set of instantial propositions. The key constituents of this form of explanation are thus:

(a) at least one general proposition (law) and

(b) a set of initial conditions C.

So we can say, in the context of the general proposition to the effect that all As are Bs under specified conditions C_1, that if something is an A then it will also be a B. It is therefore in this sense that general propositions are involved in the idea of 'explanation'.

There are, however, some points about this explanatory scheme well worth emphasising in the context of sociological inquiry and model building.

(1) It is usually specified that the general proposition in the scheme be a *Law*. But it is not altogether clear what comprises lawfulness in the physical sciences, let alone in the social sciences. All general propositions of the form 'all As are Bs' are not taken to be law-like. It is usual to make the distinction between

Problems of generalization.

'universal laws' and 'accidental generalisations'. Nagel (1961), amongst others, suggests that if a general proposition is a law it will normally justify the use of a *counterfactual conditional* of the form – 'If this were (had been) an *A* then it would (would have been) a *B*', whereas an accidental generalisation will not. Similarly, a law, in contrast to an accidental generalisation justifies the use of a subjective conditional of the form – 'If *A* should happen then so would *B*'. But these seem not to be not logical distinctions but ones rooted in our faith in the veracity of the general proposition. There are few cases in sociology where we would be willing to use the counterfactual and subjunctive conditionals in this manner. Even with a proposition like 'all societies have kinship structures' which, as far as I know, is universally true (given all *known* societies), we are rather reluctant to say 'if this were a society then it would have a kinship structure' in the face of the possible discovery of further societies. Perhaps some sociologists would be willing to make this statement and, if faced with something that looked like a society without a kinship structure, search for exceptions in terms of the *initial conditions* under which the 'law' holds (see below).

Again, it appears that our willingness to entertain a counterfactual (and thus a generalisation as a law) depends entirely on our attitude to the 'truth' of the generalisation. This is often a complex thing. But it is more often than not the case that, for a generalisation to be taken seriously as a law, it must be embedded in a theoretical structure whereby the generalisation is seen as derivable from deeper lying laws. It is a matter of theoretical support. Since there are few if any such structures at present in sociology, it is unlikely that we can distinguish between accidental and law-like generalisations along these lines. We are pleased to locate any sort of generalisation and the thrust of our endeavours at this stage in the development of the discipline must be towards specifying the initial conditions under which such generalisations hold. This brings us to the second point.

(2) Much sociological research is deficient in the sense that the researchers fail to specify the conditions under which their findings hold – which brings us to the heart of the problem of generality. Any general proposition is circumscribed, i.e. the situations in which it is applicable are reduced by a set of initial conditions. Given the theoretical development of sociology, the conditions under which 'general findings' are applicable is often very highly circumscribed indeed. The set of initial conditions is, in other words, very extensive. Now clearly the generality of a proposition and the 'extent' of the set of initial conditions are inversely related. The less restrictive the set C, the more general the proposition. But what do we mean by the 'extent' of the set of initial conditions? Well, we may, very roughly, know the number of instances of As that are ruled out by not conforming to the requirements of C, as being possible contenders for B-ship. There have been attempts to formalise these ideas but they do not really carry us very far in actual practice. But what we might note is that any sociological finding of the form '*some As are Bs*' can presumably be slotted into the hypothetico-deductive explanatory scheme by specifying enough initial conditions, thus rendering the original statement in the universal form 'all As are Bs'. Indeed, there is nothing to prevent us, on what has been said so far, from reducing the range of applicability of the finding to *one or even zero instances* by elaborating in sufficient detail the set of initial conditions.

Laws with no empirical instances whatsoever are not un-common in the physical sciences. They are accepted because of the role they play in a wider theoretical structure (cf. Newton's first law). The case of one instance (or very few) seems to arise in historical sociology where we might wish to explain a relatively unique historical occurrence. If explanations of such occurrences can be found involving general propositions they will normally be highly circumscribed by initial conditions but if the same conditions hold again (at some future or past time) then the general proposition would hold. From what has been said nothing follows concerning the practical likelihood of specifying these initial conditions. In one sense the *faith* of sociology is that at least the 'most important' variables can be specified.

We naturally tend to explain individual occurrences in terms of necessity and sufficiency. We say that a certain condition A was necessary for the appearance of B ($B \Rightarrow A$), or B was sufficient for A. Most logicians would accept, however, that a statement to the effect that a condition A is necessary for another B *entails* a universal statement of the form $(x)[Bx \Rightarrow Ax]$. So in using the language of necessity and sufficiency in such cases we imply generalisations. *The problem of explanations of unique or relatively unique occurrences is thus not one of the logic of the explanatory scheme but of finding the evidence to substantiate the scheme.*

6.3 Probabilistic Propositions and Sociological Explanation

In the actual practice of sociology we find very few examples of deterministic propositions of the form 'all As are Bs'. The much more characteristic form is a significant correlation between A and B (Cor (AB)) which, unless Cor $(AB) = 1$ or -1, suggests that sociological propositions and explanations are *probabilistic* rather than deterministic.

The general form of a probabilistic explanation is: the probability that an A is a B is 'high' (probabilistic law), or

$$\frac{\text{This is an } A}{\text{This } A \text{ is a } B},$$

where the horizontal line may be taken to mean 'makes it highly probable that'. Thus, on the face of it, the probabilistic explanatory scheme seems more applicable to sociological problems. For when we say that: $0 < \text{Cor}(AB) < 1$ there is a certain probability that an A is a B. However, such an assumption is rather over-simple.

Just as with the hypothetico-deductive model, where it is normally required that the generalisation be a law and not just an accidental generalisation, the probabilistic model requires that the major probabilistic statement be a law also. The precise nature of this lawfulness whereby any statistical relationship is distinguished from a probabilistic law is highly controversial. But a necessary, though perhaps not sufficient, condition for probabilistic lawfulness is that the probabilistic relationship between (in our example) A and B be relatively invariant over space and time. So the 'probabilistic process' described by the law can be characterised by some constant parameter (e.g. the half-life of radio-active decay). Now we know from the law of large numbers that the stability of such a parameter depends upon there being very many As and Bs but we also know that all sociological propositions by probabilistic standards refer to relatively small populations. So one can feel little confidence in finding probabilistic laws characterised by some temporally and spatially invariant parameters. Our common knowledge tells us that correlation coefficients do not exhibit any stability of this sort. This, of course, may also be due to lack of aggregate equilibrium between the variables but even with variables in equilibrium there is little likelihood of stability.

There is however a sense in which correlations or probabilistic relations between variables do exhibit the required stability. Although it is always unlikely that a numerical parameter (e.g. a probability number) can be invariantly attached to a relationship, nevertheless statistically significant relationships between the variables (at a specified probability level) often do exhibit a remarkable stability.

So we might remain content with such relationships. And, indeed, a great deal of sociology is conducted under this rubric where, for instance, we merely ask whether a correlation coefficient departs significantly from zero. But there is an alternative approach which is often more useful.

A conditional probabilistic relation $p(B/A)$ *may be regarded as an attempt to obtain a deterministic relation where all the appropriate initial conditions for the relationship have not been fully specified.* For instance, if we obtain a high positive correlation between 'status disequilibrium' and 'political liberality' then there are three distinct intellectual orientations we can take:[1]

(i) be satisfied and regard the relationship as inherently probabilistic and take the value of the correlation coefficient as a significant numerical parameter;

(ii) recognise that the value of the correlation coefficient is (even apart from sampling fluctuations) unlikely to show any numerical invariance over space and time, but note that the relationship between 'status disequilibrium' and 'political liberality' departs significantly from statistical independence;

(iii) seek to render the correlation coefficient nearer to unity by specifying additional initial conditions which must be present for the relationship between 'status disequilibrium' and 'political liberality' to hold. (We will see in subsequent chapters what this implies in terms of model building.)

The argument against adopting (i) as outlined above: we rarely expect actual correlation coefficients (or conditional probabilities) to be anything like stable over space and time and thus cannot expect them to enter propositions in the way that stable probabilities do in the physical sciences.

Strategy (ii) is more attractive. We might not be able to place much faith on the actual value of the correlation coefficient or associated probability number, but still feel that the departure from statistical independence of the relationship between 'status disequilibrium' and 'political liberality' is generalisable across space and time. But the difficulty here is that so many variables/concepts exhibit this property in most social systems that it becomes altogether too weak a criterion. So if we are to remain content with probabilistic propositions we still normally revert to a qualitative form of (i) where we say that correlations are high, medium or low. The demarcation between these categories is, of course, entirely arbitrary. But we may expect a correlation coefficient to show a relative invariance over space and time, within such bounds.

Strategy (iii) is often more useful in model building, for here we introduce additional constraints upon the generalisability of the relationship between the variables. We noted earlier that any probabilistic proposition can in principle be rendered deterministic by introducing enough constraints in the set of initial conditions. That is, by systematically finding reasons why some people who are status disequilibrated are not politically liberal. Technically this reduces to finding *interaction conditions or variables* and we will have much to say about this later on.

In most situations the sociologist has to remain content with correlational statements and in our subsequent deliberations we will start with this assumption. But it is often helpful to think in terms of an underlying deterministic proposition the correlational form being a consequence of underspecified initial conditions and additional 'causes' – see below.

6.4 The Form of Sociological Propositions

The most general way of stating the relationship between two variables is to say that one is a function of the other, e.g. $A = f(B)$. Of course, we can equally well write, $B = f(A)$, but in model building it is usual to distinguish between the *explained variable*, the variable whose variation we are trying to explain, and the *explanatory variable*, the variable we invoke to explain this variation. By convention the dependent variable is written on the left-hand side of a functional relationship and the independent variable on the right-hand side. So in the expression $A = f(B)$, A is the explained variable and B the explanatory one. Of course, propositions of this form tell us very little – only that A and B are related, but not *how* they are related. To do this we must specify the form of the function. *But the specification of a functional form depends upon the level of measurement of the constituent variables.* So it is useful to look at the problems of specification at different levels of measurement.

6.5 Specifying Functions at the Ratio and Interval (*Cardinal*) Level

The form of the relationship between X_1 and X_2 is specified explicitly as an algebraic equation. The simplest possible relationship is a linear one

$$X_1 = a + \beta X_2 \tag{6.1}$$

where α and β are constants. This function, if plotted in a graphical manner is a straight line with gradient β and an intercept of α on the X_1 axes. Although the straight line relationship is the simplest, it is perhaps rather rare in sociology; we frequently expect more complex non-linear relationships. The problems of specifying functions will be considered in detail in Chapter 8.

It is worth emphasising that one of the most suitable ways of depicting functional relationships between cardinal variables is by the use of simple graphs (not graphs in the sense of Chapter 2). This is, in fact, often helpful even when the variables concerned are not strictly cardinal. In fact, sociologists make little use of graphical representations for they rarely consider the *form* of functional relationships, remaining content with statements to the effect that variables are related. The model building perspective tends, however, to emphasise the form of relationships and we shall continually emphasise this aspect.

An example from sociology of a cardinal variable relationship is that between 'time in formal education' and 'terminal income'. We may suspect that terminal income is a function of time spent in formal education, go on to postulate a linear relationship and test this using standard regression techniques.

In general, when testing propositions relating two cardinal variables there are four types of parameter which interest us:

(i) Parameters describing the *form* of the function (e.g. α and β in expression (6.1)).

(ii) Tests of significance and confidence intervals for the parameters in (i).

(iii) Parameters describing the *strength* of the relationship (e.g. the product-moment correlation coefficient derivable from the regression of one variable on the other).[2] This coefficient squared also gives an indication of the *completeness* of the analysis it is equal to the variance in the explained variable explained by the explanatory variable.

(iv) Tests of significance and confidence intervals for the parameter in (iii).

6.6 Specifying Functions at the Ordinal Level
The characteristic form of a relationship where the variables are ordinal is '*A* increases or decreases with *B*'. For example, 'intra-class consciousness increases with inter-class conflict'. Such a relationship can be represented by a graph but it must be remembered that the distance along the axes has no meaning, it is only the direction of the curve (i.e. increasing or decreasing) that matters. But the most common and practical way of representing the covariation of ordinal variables is by a contingency table where the categories are ranked. For example, we might obtain ordinal variables of intra-class consciousness and inter-class conflict with three categories – High, Medium and Low. The contingency table would then be of the form depicted in Figure 6.2.

Figure 6.2 An Ordinal Contingency Table

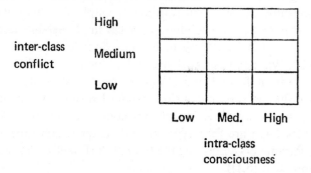

Note that it is possible to view this '9-cell space' as overlying a metric space. Whether or not this is meaningful will depend on whether it is possible to think in terms of underlying metric which, because of measurement difficulties, cannot be directly apprehended. But it is a good idea to adopt the convention of labelling the sides (axes) of contingency tables running from the low categories at the bottom left-hand corner to the high categories at the top right-hand corner.

Sociologists have become familiar with numerous non-parametric techniques for measuring the degree of association between two ordinal variables. They have, however, shown a marked reluctance to speak of the form of the relationship. This is not surprising as the concept of form, applicable at the cardinal level, is not directly appropriate since the distance property does not hold down the 'axes' of an ordinal contingency table and so the ideas of a linear and curvilinear relationship are not strictly appropriate. We may speak, nevertheless, of the *trend* in a table, for example, '*increases* in class-conflict lead to *increases* in inter-class consciousness'. This will, of course, be reflected in the sign of the measure of association. But there is an analogy to curvilinearity in the idea of a non-smooth monotonic relationship. So once again, with an ordinal proposition, we are interested in the following four types of parameters:

(i) parameters describing the *trend* of the ordinal function;
(ii) tests of significance for the parameters in (i);
(iii) parameters describing the strength and completeness of the relationship;
(iv) tests of significance for the parameters in (iii).

It is possible, of course, to make the appropriate assumptions and use parametric methods of analysis, strictly appropriate at the cardinal level, with ordinal propositions. The question then arises as to whether parametric or non-parametric techniques should be utilised in the analysis of ordinal propositions. There is no easy answer to this question. The advantages of parametric techniques (e.g. regression analysis) are perhaps three-fold. Firstly, there are well-established techniques for estimating the above four types of parameters. The properties of these estimates, and the assumptions upon which they are based, are also well known. Secondly, the techniques have a measure of statistical completion (R^2 in regression analysis) enabling us to say how much of the variance in the explained variable has been explained by the explanatory variable. Thirdly, the techniques normally rest upon an explicit mathematic form which becomes a more important consideration with multivariate models. The disadvantage, on the other hand, is that the assumptions of the techniques are normally very demanding, particularly in respect to the measurement properties of the variables and the properties of their distributions. The often suggested disadvantage of parametric techniques – their lack of flexibility in the hands of the analyst (Galtung, 1967) – was perhaps correct a few years ago, but with the advent of high-speed computing and highly flexible program packages this is perhaps no longer true.

The advantage of non-parametric techniques is, of course, that they do not make unwarranted assumptions about the distributions of the variables concerned. But what is the advantage of this in practice? If the variables concerned are *naturally* ordinal, that is the categories and ranking of the categories is *sociologically fixed and meaningful*, then it is perhaps best to use non-parametric techniques. For instance, a measure of association with a proportional reduction in error (Costner, 1965) property should be used. Then one can say that a set of sociologically fixed and meaningful categories provides certain predictive powers for another set of categories. The idea of trend is, however, not explicitly catered for by such techniques. Non-smooth increases or decreases of one variable with another can be detected by inspection, but there is no 'built in' technique for estimating this or whether it is significant or not. Maxwell (1961) has reviewed techniques where the χ^2 test is adapted to test for trends but, in so doing, assumptions must be made about the distances between categories.

If the categories are not sociologically fixed and meaningful but arbitrarily derived, it is often analytically useful to assume underlying cardinal variables, score the categories using numbers, and use parametric techniques like regression analysis. The idea of the shape of the trend can be introduced by using different scoring techniques. For instance, rather than scoring the categories in a linear manner, 1, 2, 3, etc., they may be scored in a non-linear way, 1, 2, 4, 16, etc. The computer permits relatively inexpensive and fast tests of different scoring techniques. We will return to these issues in the context of multivariate models in Chapter 8.

6.7 Specifying Functions at the Nominal Level

The problems here are similar to those encountered with ordinal variables, except that the order of the categories in the contingency table does not matter. The most important case is where the variables are dichotomies, since variables with more than two categories are more often than not of an ordinal variety. Again the dilemma relating to the selection of parametric as against non-parametric techniques arises; traditionally sociologists have used non-parametric techniques but in Chapter 8 the use of dummy variable[3] techniques will be emphasised.

6.8 Theoretical Contingent Connectives

It was observed earlier that propositions can be theoretical in one or both of two ways: the constituent concepts/variables can be theoretical as well as the connectives. Connectives between concepts or variables may be either logical (in analytical propositions) or contingent (in synthetic propositions). In this section theoretical contingent connectives and their underlying logic in sociological propositions will be considered. The problems of inferring from observational connectives (e.g. correlation, covariation, etc.) to theoretical connectives will not, however, be considered here but in Chapter 9.

Even after a cursory review of the sociological literature one cannot but be dismayed by the multitude of contingent connectives in use. One encounters, for example, 'to reflect', 'to influence', 'to legitimise', 'to sail close to', and so on. Perhaps the wide use of terms like these, which appear to be merely surrogates for the idea of causality, represents a hesitancy to go the full way and use the word 'cause'. If so, this is a well-founded hesitancy, for, after all, the idea of cause implies determination and we are loath to admit that human behaviour is determined. Are not the ideas of social choice, decision and innovation which lie at the very foundations of our major theoretical perspectives completely inimical to the idea of causation? Do we not believe that human behaviour is voluntaristic or intentional and how can this be so if behaviour is caused? But whether or not all

Hypo thetico dductive.

these are well-founded objections, in using a wide vocabulary of rather vague words in an attempt to avoid the issue we just multiply our difficulties. Many of the concepts like 'reflect' are surely special uses of the word 'cause'. So perhaps it is best first of all to gain a footing in this area by analysing what we *might* mean when we use the concept of cause in sociology.

The other major contingent connective in sociology is 'social function'. I use the adjective 'social' so as to avoid confusion with the idea of mathematical function already introduced. We will consider the problems of causation first and then drawing on our deliberations move onto consider social functions.

The reader should recognise that we are entering a very extensive philosophical thicket. The debate about the place of causality in human affairs is almost as old as philosophy itself and we cannot hope to do full justice to it here nor raise all the relevant issues. What we can do is to erect a rather relaxed notion of causality which is pertinent and adequate for our subsequent discussions. The reader interested in details of the philosophical problems is invited to look elsewhere. (Nagel, 1961, Hempel, 1966.)

We are therefore concerned to elaborate the minimal logical requirements for the use of causal propositions of the form '*B* causes *A*'. Let us assume, for the moment, that *A* and *B* are simple dichotomies so that the distinction between concept and variable falls away. The following points should then be noted about the use of the term cause.

(i) Cause is a T-concept. Causal connectives are not observed between variables, they are inferred from observations or, rather more precisely, certain sets of observations are compatible with a particular causal account. We are therefore concerned with the conditions under which this compatibility can be established. The logic is relatively straightforward when the proposition relating *A* and *B* is deterministic for, as we shall see below, the notions of necessity and sufficiency can be quite naturally deployed. If, however, the proposition is only probabilistic, the causal inference is rather more difficult.

(ii) If we say *B* causes *A* then there must be distinct ways of detecting or observing instances of *A* and *B*. That is, *A* and *B* must be separable events in the real world. They can, of course, refer to T-concepts but they must be *defined* or *operationalised* independently; the sets of items or indicators so involved must be mutually exclusive. The contingent separability of *A* and *B* excludes the possibility of a logical or analytical relationship between them.

(iii) If *B* causes *A* then we require that *B* be temporally prior to *A* (problems of reciprocal causality will be considered later).

(iv) We cannot necessarily infer a causal link from a correlation or covariation between *A* and *B*, even if it has a value of ± 1.

(v) We cannot necessarily infer from a 'known' causal link between *A* and *B* to a correlation or covariation between them. This point is not often recognised and it will be taken up a little later on.

(vi) We should be careful to distinguish between a logical statement of the conditions under which we entertain the notion of causality between *A* and *B* and the causal link itself. Causal links are *contingent connectives* and not logical relations but we can attempt to express the logical conditions necessary for the idea of causality to hold.

(vii) There are three possible *logical* interpretations of a causal link between *A* and *B* (i.e. $B \rightarrow A$).

(a) ($B \Leftrightarrow A$): *B* is a *necessary* and *sufficient* condition for *A*;

(b) ($B \Rightarrow A$): *B* is a *sufficient* but *not necessary* condition for *A*;

(c) ($B \Leftarrow A$): *B* is a *necessary* though *not sufficient* condition for *A*.

(viii) It is often claimed that to assert a causal connection between two events is to assert that there is a general proposition (law) relating them. This proposition is, of course, circumscribed by a set of initial conditions. This view will be adopted and, furthermore, the assumption made that a statement of the form '*A* is a necessary condition for *B*' implies a universal proposition of the form 'All *B*s are *A*' and a statement of the form '*A* is a sufficient condition for B' implies a universal proposition of the form 'all As are B'.

Causal accounts of phenomena are usually regarded as explanations so we will now examine each of the three logical conditions in the light of the other points and the hypothetico-deductive model of explanation.

Cause as a Necessary and Sufficient Condition If a causal link $(B \to A)$ is given the *logical* interpretation $(B \Leftrightarrow A)$ and we assume that this *entails* the universal proposition $(x)\,[Bx \Leftrightarrow Ax]$ then the hypothetico-deductive model of explanation has the form

$$\frac{(x)\,[Bx \Leftrightarrow Ax]}{x \in (c_1 \cdot c_2 \cdot c_3 \ldots c_n)} \tag{6.2}$$
$$(Bx \Leftrightarrow Ax)$$

where $c_1, c_2 \ldots c_n$ is a set of initial conditions.

Remembering that we are treating A and B as dichotomous variables it is interesting to note what (6.2) implies for the appropriate 2×2 Table; it would have the form

	$\widetilde{B}$	B	
A	$a = 0$	b	$\widetilde{A}$ = absence of A
$\widetilde{A}$	c	$d = 0$	$\widetilde{B}$ = absence of B

The $(A\widetilde{B})$ (i.e. cases of A that are not B) and $(\widetilde{A}B)$ (i.e. cases of B that are not A) entries are zero. Notice also that under these conditions the cross-product term $(bc - ad) = bc$ and this correlation measures like

$$Q = \frac{(bc - ad)}{(bc + ad)} = 1.$$

But our common experience is that distributions of this sort are rarely, if ever, obtained. So we must have some initial misgivings about adopting the criteria of necessity and sufficiency for causality. Furthermore, even if a table with the $(A\widetilde{B})$

and $(\tilde{A}B)$ entries equal zero is obtained, this does not guarantee $(A \Leftrightarrow B)$ for it may be that the zeros appear merely as a consequence of our sampling; that is, even if the *population* contains some As that are not Bs and Bs that are not As, this is quite compatible with a sample where none of these cases appear. B being a necessary and sufficient condition for A implies that $(A\tilde{B}) = (\tilde{A}B) = 0$ but on the basis of a sample where $(A\tilde{B}) = (\tilde{A}B) = 0$ we *cannot* imply that A is a necessary and sufficient condition for B.

So it appears that we are on very shaky ground if we wish to impose the logical criteria of necessity and sufficiency onto our concept of causality. It would, on the face of it, be to impose restrictions that could never be met except perhaps when we study total populations.

One way of attacking the problem is to suggest that cases of $(\tilde{A}B)$ appear because the set of initial conditions has not been correctly specified. So the examples of $(\tilde{A}B)$ one encounters are not ABs as they 'should' be (according to our model) since, either,

(a) the unit of analysis which is a B is not also a C_i as it should be. In other words, both variables C_i and B have to be present to cause A and in the cases of Bs that are not As, C_i was not present. We might call C_i a *positive catalyst*; technically it is an *interaction* condition with B for explaining variance in A. So the general proposition takes the form: $(x) [(C_i \cdot B)x \Leftrightarrow Ax]$; or

(b) a variable, say C_j, is present that should not be. In other words, variable C_j has to be *absent* for B to cause A and in the cases of Bs that are not As C_j was present. We might call C_j a *negative* catalyst. So the general proposition takes the form $(x) [(\tilde{C}_j \cdot B)x \Leftrightarrow Ax]$.

The full logic of positive and negative catalysts will be examined in the next section.

The cases of $(A\tilde{B})$ cannot be dealt with in this manner. They, in effect, deny the *necessity* of the causal relationship between B and A since there are some As that are not Bs. *The only way in which these can be accounted for is by postulating additional variables over and above* B (*say* Z) *which are sufficient* (*though not necessary since* A *is sufficient also*) *for causing* A. So *B* is not a necessary condition for *B*. The general proposition in the hypothetico-deductive model now assumes the form

$$(x)\,[(Bx \lor Zx) \Leftrightarrow Ax]. \qquad (6.3)$$

And, of course, the initial conditions under which *Z* and *B* are separately sufficient for *A* may well be different.

Thus, when encountering cases of *A*s that are not *B*s we must surrender the notion of necessity in causality. It will subsequently be argued that the criterion of simple necessity of the sort under investigation is not a characteristic of any useful conception of causality in sociology.

Cases of $(\tilde{A}B)$ can also be attributed to additional sufficient variables where $(Z \Leftrightarrow \tilde{A})$. In the simple dichotomous case we have to view *Z* as acting 'after' *B* and destroying *A*. In the case of scaled variables we can think in terms of concurrent causes but *Z* is a stronger cause nullifying the effects of *B*.

Cause as a Sufficient Condition Only If a causal link $(B \rightarrow A)$ is given the logical interpretation $(B \Rightarrow A)$ and we assume this entails a universal proposition then the hypothetico-deductive model of explanation has the form

$$(x)\,[Bx \Rightarrow Ax]$$
$$\frac{x \in (c_1 \cdot c_2 \cdot c_3 \ldots c_n)}{(Bx \Rightarrow Ax)} \qquad (6.4)$$

where as usual, $c_1, c_2, \ldots, c_n$ is a set of initial conditions. The corresponding 2×2 Table would then be as follows:

	$\tilde{B}$	B
A	a	b
$\tilde{A}$	c	$d = 0$

where the $(\tilde{A}B)$ entry is zero. The cross-product term $(bc - ad)$ $= bc$ so measures of correlation like $Q = 1$. We do not thus require a necessary relationship for a correlation coefficient (based on a cross-product) to be unity.

In practice, of course, such distributions are rarely obtained. But we can still utilise the idea of B being a sufficient condition for A by adopting the strategy outlined above of searching for appropriate initial conditions, i.e. interaction conditions.

Cause as a Necessary Condition Only If a causal link $(B \to A)$ is given the logical interpretation $(B \leftarrow A)$ and the assumption is made that this entails a universal proposition then the hypothetico-deductive model of explanation has the form

$$(x)\,[Ax \Rightarrow Bx]$$
$$\frac{x \in (c_1 \cdot c_2 \cdot c_3 \ldots c_n)}{(Ax \Rightarrow Bx)} \tag{6.5}$$

The corresponding 2×2 Table is as follows:

A	$a = 0$	b
$\tilde{A}$	c	d
	$\tilde{B}$	B

where the $(A\tilde{B})$ entry is zero. The cross-product term $(bc - ad)$ $= bc$ so measures of correlations like $Q = 1$. Thus we do not require a sufficient relationship between B and A for a correlation coefficient of this sort to be unity; all that we require is that the relationship between the variables be *either* necessary *or* sufficient. That is, either $(\tilde{A}B) = 0$ or $(A\tilde{B}) = 0$. It was noted earlier that cases of $(A\tilde{B})$ can only be 'explained' by invoking additional conditions sufficient for B so we may expect sufficiency to play a major role in a satisfactory formulation of causation in sociology. We now turn to a formulation of causality suitable for the actual practice of sociological model building.

6.9 *The Logical Features of Causation in Sociology*
The view will be adopted that, when asking for a causal explana-

tion of an event A, it will characteristically have the following logical features:

(i) The event A will be *over-determined* in the sense that there will be more than one set of *conjoined conditions* sufficient but *not* necessary for A.

(ii) The sets of conjoined conditions, as the name suggests, comprise the logical conjunction of a set of variables.

Any one constituent variable of such a set will be described as an *open necessary* condition for the other constituent variables in the set to be sufficient for the event A.

The conception of open necessity calls for some clarification. In general, a constituent variable of a set of conjoined conditions will only be a *sufficient condition* to render the conjunction of the variables, in turn, sufficient for the caused variable. This is so since there will normally be other 'equivalent' variables that could take the place of the given constituent variable and still provide the causal sufficiency of the set. *But the point is that at least one of these equivalent variables must be present and this is how the necessity is involved.* It should be noted that to say that one variable is sufficient to make another sufficient for a third variable is equal to saying the *conjoin* of the first two variables is sufficient for the third

$$[B \Rightarrow (C \Rightarrow A)] \Leftrightarrow [(B \cdot C) \Rightarrow A] \qquad (6.6)$$

is a tautology.

The idea of open necessity dictates that the set of conjoined conditions will not be sufficient for the effect in the absence of any one of the constituent variables (or their equivalents). Of course, we do not usually know the full range of equivalents for any given constituent variable. So each constituent variable in a set of conjoined conditions can be depicted as an open set of alternants one of which must be present (in logical terms, take truth-value true) for the total set to be a sufficiency for the caused variable.

We do not, in general, know the full extent of the set of component variables and so we must leave this, open, too.

Furthermore, we are not normally in a position to specify all the alternative sets of conjoined conditions, each of which is sufficient for the event A. So this set of alternants must also be represented as open.

The general logical format of our scheme is thus

$$\left[[(B_1 \vee B_1^1 \ldots) \cdot (B_2 \vee B_2^1 \ldots) \ldots] \vee [(C_1 \vee C^1 \ldots) \cdot (C_2 \vee C_2^1 \ldots)\right.$$
$$\left. \ldots] \vee \ldots\right] \Rightarrow \left[A\right] \qquad (6.7)$$

where, for example, B_1^1 and B_1 are alternative (equivalent) variables, the presence of one of which is necessary to render the set $\{B_1 \, B_2 \ldots\}$ a sufficient condition for A.

The reader should note the 'nested' nature of formulation (6.7); it consists of sets of disjunctions which are internally conjoined sets of variables but each of these variables can be broken into a set of disjuncts. The formulation could be extended indefinitely 'downwards' so that, for instance, B_1^1 and B_1^2 would be broken down into sets of conjoined variables. This characteristic seems eminently desirable as it, in effect, permits a finer and finer 'grid' to be placed on causal models; variables can be broken down into less general ones. Some capital will be made out of this point when we come to consider problems of theoretical elaboration in model building.

For present purposes the formulation (6.7) is over-elaborate and it can be replaced by the general form

$$[(B_1 \cdot B_2 \ldots) \vee (C_1 \cdot C_2 \ldots) \vee \ldots] \Rightarrow [A] \qquad (6.8)$$

remembering that B_1, B_2, C_1, C_2 etc. will normally have equivalent alternatives. In any one set of conditions one variable is selected as *a* cause of B and the other variables as the conditions (cf. initial conditions) under which this variable will effect the causation. From a logical standpoint it is immaterial which variable is selected as a cause and which as conditions. It is often one that can be manipulated in some way or is important in terms of some theoretical ideas.

So far, apart from the conception of open necessity, all mention of necessity has been avoided. Presumably if we could select the *complete* set of disjuncts for the left-hand side of (6.8) then we would be willing to replace the material implication by logical equivalence and thus render the set of disjuncts both a necessary and sufficient condition for A. The objection to this is that we might never be certain that we have obtained a full list of disjunctive conditions – there might always be a further set, of as yet undiscovered conditions, that would be sufficient for A. The way to get around this objection is to include as one of the disjuncts a condition characterising the 'all the other possible causes'. Let us call it u. So (6.8) may now be recast as

$$[(B_1 \cdot B_2 \ldots) \vee (C_1 \cdot C_2 \ldots) \vee \ldots \vee (u)] \Leftrightarrow [A] \qquad (6.9)$$

where the expression on the left-hand side is now a necessary and sufficient condition for A.

Turning now to an algebraic representation rather than a strictly logical one (6.9) may be written, without loss of generality, as

$$A = (B_1 \times B_2 \ldots) + (C_1 \times C_2 \ldots) \ldots + u \qquad (6.10)$$

which is immediately recognisable as a straightforward linear additive equation with multiplicative *interaction conditions* in each term. If the variables concerned were cardinal ones, we might treat (6.10) as a linear regression problem with interaction. Then u would be the well-known stochastic error term resulting from excluded variables and measurement error in A.

But the causal logic of (6.10) can best be appreciated if it is assumed that all the variables involved are dichotomous, taking on scores of 1 and 0. Then A will be 1 if *any* one of the terms in the right-hand side of (6.10) is 1, i.e. any one is sufficient to 'switch on' A. But note also that, since each term is a product, if any constituent variable of a term is 0 then the total term is zero. It is in this sense that the constituents of the terms are necessary for the whole term to be causally effective. In terms of (6.9) rather than (6.10) we may pursue an entirely analogous argument using truth-values throughout the expression. For A to be true (occur!) it is sufficient for any one of the disjuncts to be true but, for a disjunct to be true, *all* its constituent variables must also be true.

Formulations (6.9) and (6.10) also enable us to be more precise about what were earlier termed positive and negative catalytic effects. If in any one of the terms of the form $(B_1 \cdot B_2 \cdot B_3 \ldots)$, B_1 is regarded as the causal variable, then $B_2 \cdot B_3 \ldots$, etc., are positive catalysts, i.e. they or some equivalent alternatives must be present to make B_1 causally effective. But it is also possible to have a term in which the absence of a variable is specified, e.g. $(B_1 \cdot \tilde{B}_2 \ldots)$. In this case, the absence of B_2 or some equivalent is necessary for B_1 to be a sufficient cause. Situations like this are, of course, not normally catered for in an algebraic expression of functional relationships like (6.10).[4] For there is no difference drawn, in this sort of formulation, between variables that have no effect whether they are present or absent and variables that must necessarily be absent. The logical formulation (6.9), however, does – for a negative catalyst B_2 would appear in a term as $(B_1 \cdot \tilde{B}_2)$ so that for the conjoin to be true, $\tilde{B}_2$ must be true.

An important point alluded to earlier may be brought out here. It is perfectly possible, because a negative catalytic variable C masks the relationship, for B to be a cause of A but for there to be no correlation between them. And since it is also possible to have a correlation between two variables without a causal link, a correlation is neither a necessary nor a sufficient condition for causation.

6.10 Cause and Anthropomorphic Concepts

Before we can go on to consider some general issues about the place of causal propositions in sociological model building, there is one further class of problems that must be considered briefly.

It is commonplace to attempt an explanation of human behaviour in terms of 'reasons', 'purposes', 'intentions', 'volitions', 'motives', etc.; the question arises, can these conceptions in any way be fitted into causal explanations or do they completely defy causal treatment?

The first basic distinction we have to make is between *behaviour* and *action*. When I say, 'my eye winked', I am describing a piece of my behaviour; I observe that my eye winked, but as far as I am aware (problems of the unconscious aside), *I* did not wink my eye. That is, I, as a conscious agent, did not intend to wink my eye. When I say, 'I winked my eye', then I am describing my agency over the behaviour – it is an intentional or purposeful entity. This type of entity we call *action*. So being rather simplistic to start with: in some sense, action is intentional behaviour. Sociologists are usually interested in explaining human actions. Action clearly has a behavioural component – the actual movement of the eyelids – but we have to go on and ask what is the relationship between the intention and this component.

But first let us note that at the level of common-sense understanding, we give very different explanations of human actions and behaviour. When asked to explain a 'wink' (which is, shall we say, a tic of the eye) the explanation sought for would be in terms of physiological or perhaps psycho-physiological determinants. But when asked to explain a 'wink' as an action we usually seek the intention, perhaps the purpose, and even more remotely, the reasons why the actor had the intentions or purposes he in fact had.

There are two current views about the relationship between intentions or reasons and actions.

(i) The logical view maintains that the relationship between intentions, or reasons, and actions is a conceptual or logical one, and that consequently the notion of causal link between the two (a contingent connective) is entirely inappropriate.

(ii) The causal view maintains that it is essentially correct to assert a causal link between intentions, or reasons, and actions.

It is helpful in sorting out the relative merits of these two positions to remind ourselves of two of the conditions under which we are willing to say *B* causes *A*.

(i) *B* must be temporally prior to *A*.

(ii) *B* must be independently recognisable from *A*, or it must not be solely an analytical question to ask for the relationship between *A* and *B*.

The logical viewpoint on the relationship between intentions, reasons, etc., and action rests upon the assumption that (b) does not hold. That is, intentions and actions are not contingently but logically related. For, the argument runs, it would be a logical contradiction to deny an action and affirm an intention – the relationship between intention, action is one of logical necessity. So part of what we mean when we describe something as an action is that it is intentional. Intentions are not recognisable independently of their actions. We should note that the philosophers that ascribe to this position are not using the word 'intention' in a *deliberative sense*. Clearly one can, at a particular time, intend (in the sense of resolve) to do something at a later time and then not carry it out. Intention in this sense is clearly contingently related to the action (if it is carried out). Rather they are concerned with what we might term the non-deliberative use of intention; for instance, the intention whereby we *distinguish* a wink of the eye from a tic of the eye.

So, for this school of philosophers, intentions and actions are logically related and it would be mistaken to seek for a causal connection between the two. *But note that this interpretation is still open to a causal explanation of why people have the intentions they do. So we could ask for a causal explanation of their action in the sense that action means intended behaviour.*

The alternative view posits a causal link between the actual intention and the behavioural component of action. The claim is this: intentions (in the non-deliberative sense) are physical events independently recognisable from, and temporally prior to, the behavioural component of action. Furthermore, it is not a conceptual absurdity to deny the behavioural component of action and assert a non-deliberative intention. So we must, if we adopt this viewpoint, embrace the idea that somebody can intend (i.e. 'really intend') and not behave accordingly. So it appears, at least at first sight, that the word 'intend' is being used in a deliberative sense, but the actor does not carry out his intentions because perhaps he has 'changed his mind' or even been physically frustrated. Also, of course, just as with the non-causal viewpoint, we can ask why people have the intentions they do. We can represent the differences in the two standpoints as follows:

(structure) → (action = intentional behaviour)

(structure) → (intention) → (behavioural component of action) where (structure) is used to represent some variable causally 'determining', in one case, the action and in the other, the intention as an intervening variable which, in turn, causally determines the behavioural component of action.

What are we to make of these two viewpoints? Perhaps the first thing that might be observed is that highly competent philosophers are in disagreement on the topic, which should, I think, give us some grounds for caution. Nevertheless, we have, as practising sociologists, to outline some provisional strategy. We might well ask what difference it would make to the model building perspective in sociology if we adopted one viewpoint rather than the other.

A query that favours the non-causal interpretation is that, if we rejected this interpretation, how would we distinguish between behaviour and action? For instance, how would we distinguish between a wink of the eye (which, shall we say, is intended to signal something or other) and a tic of the eye? According to the logical viewpoint, there is no difficulty, action is intentional and is therefore a different *category of event* from behaviour.

But how could a person who believes in a causal connection between intention and action make the distinction between action and behaviour? How could he say one event is a wink and another a tic? It is imperative, at this point, to distinguish clearly between the behavioural component of action and the action itself. The logical and causal viewpoints agree that there are, in the case of both behaviour and action, movements in the real world – movement of the eyelids in our example. The causal viewpoint ascribes these movements to the category of action (a wink) by determining the category of the cause of the movement.

It uses the concept action to name a causal process. It distinguishes a wink from a tic by searching for the nature of the causal agency of the physical movements. In one case the cause is intentional, in another, physiological. So in one sense the causal viewpoint accepts a logical (definitional) relationship between intention and action – action is that behaviour which is intended but a contingent (causal) relationship holds between any particular intention and the behavioural consequence. Thus it appears quite compatible to say:

(i) action and intention are logically related; action *means* intended behaviour; and

(ii) the behavioural component of action and an intention are contingently related.

The scheme may be depicted as follows:

$$(\text{structure}) \rightarrow \left[\frac{(\text{intention}) \rightarrow (\text{behavioural component of action})}{=\text{action.}} \right]$$

We might note that the behaviour in our example – the movement of the eyelids – is normally *over-determined* in the sense that there is more than one causal route to it: at least one via intentions (i.e. action) and also at least one via physiological causes. So, if we can assume that sets of interaction variables must be conjoined with the 'variables' structure and intention, this scheme fits the logical features of causality outlined in the previous section.

6.11 The Place of Causality in Sociology

In the rest of this book the idea of cause will be used very extensively. In fact, the problem of inferring from correlational propositions to causal propositions (and models) will be the central concern.

Although it is quite natural to have reservations about using the idea of a causal link $B \rightarrow A$ when some Bs are not As and vice versa, we have seen that such situations are perfectly compatible with the idea of causality if further variables are postulated as either additional initial conditions or further variables sufficient to produce A. But perhaps we should raise again certain of the common objections made against the use of 'cause' and show how, given our rather relaxed idea of causality, they are seriously misleading.

(i) *Causality implies determinism:* Surely if we can say an individual's action is caused, we imply it is determined and thereby restrict the notions of freedom and rational decision in human affairs; the individual concerned could not have done otherwise! But to show that an action is caused does not imply that the actor could not have done otherwise. What it does show is that given a set of initial conditions (usually beliefs, values, etc.) the actor *does*, as a matter of fact, adopt certain purposes, frame intentions which he implements in behaviour. Indeed, if we recognise our behaviour as caused in this way, then it enables us to alter it; it enhances the idea of freedom and rational decision (see point ii).

(ii) *One cannot use the concept of cause where the problem of self-falsifying propositions occur:* This is clearly related to the last point. If one establishes a correlation between a certain social situation and an action and construes it as a causal link, e.g., if condition (C) then action (A) (i.e. $C \rightarrow A$) – then if the nature of this regularity is made available to the actor, he might well (for any number of 'reasons') cease doing A in condition C. Surely this is incompatible with the link $C \rightarrow A$? But what we should have included in the original set of initial conditions accompanying $C \rightarrow A$ is a statement like – 'the actor having no knowledge of the effect of C on his A'. Clearly when we make this information available to him, this initial condition is now false and therefore we do not expect to find confirmatory evidence for $C \rightarrow A$. This is a rather crude device, what we really need are theories indicating 'why' actors react in certain ways.

In cases like this we may see the elaboration of causal links and the relation of these to the actors concerned as an ongoing dialectical process. It clearly extends the bounds of 'rational' social action by bringing to the critical attention of the actors the nature of the influence under which they labour. It is, of course, possible to become involved in an infinite regress in connection with this problem. Actors may, from the social analyst's point of view, be 'awkward' and continually falsify his predictions. *But it would perhaps be wise in sociological investigation to distinguish between causal propositions that are likely to be invariant to knowledge of this sort and those that are not.*

If we concentrate on causal propositions of the form $A \to C$, i.e. action has consequences (causes) C (given a set of initial conditions), then the problem does not occur at all. For even if the actor is initially unaware of the consequences of his action and we make him aware of them, and he finds C uncongenial, so ceases A; it still holds that if he did commit act A then C would follow. The counterfactual proposition therefore holds.

So once again, our knowledge of causal connections involving human action *extends* the idea of freedom and rational decision making by pointing out the consequences of action. It is worth noting that in one sense social causation is a type of Chinese box – it is based upon a possible infinite regress of causal accounts. If we explain human action/behaviour A in terms of a causally antecedent variable B, it is still quite legitimate to ask for an explanation of why B influences A in this manner. In doing so, we appear to ask for a meta-causal account of the causal link between A and B. And one can, of course, go on to ask the meta-meta-question. This sort of enterprise should not be confused with the query as to the cause of B itself, i.e. the variables that bring about B which in turn causes A. The problem applies also to causal accounts of the physical world – why are the causal laws of physics the way they are? If pressed the physicist will dismiss such deliberations as metaphysical. For instance, he is not 'normally' interested in what gravity *is* but in the fact that it causes interacting bodies to move in certain ways. The social scientist, however, cannot dismiss such questions in the same way; whereas the physicist can remain content with kinematics the social scientist is much more impelled in the direction of not social kinematics, but social dynamics. This is because causal links in the social domain are *made* by man. A failure to recognise this is a sort of reification. So it seems a far more pressing problem to answer the question why causal links are the way they are when they involve conscious human beings. Note that when a man admits that something influences (causes) his behaviour, he also often has an account of why this is so. So if we start with internal causal variables the first order meta-account might well be forthcoming from the actor himself. With external variables this cannot be the case. But the view we have adopted of social causation – whereby the sociologists' causal accounts often render the nature of their determination transparent to actors, allows the meta-question to become one of rational and critical assessment, thus, once again, extending the domain of rational social action. Logically one can argue that the higher order meta-question – 'why does he believe that he is influenced in that way?' – will eventually exhaust the intellectual resources of the actor, but this is a logical point of little practical implication.

(iii) *Non-Perceived Antecedents:* Sociologists often try to explain human behaviour/action in terms of social structural antecedents that are not perceived by the actors themselves. That is, in terms of our earlier distinction, they use an external variable as an explanatory one. An example of this is the explanation of 'political liberality' in terms of 'status disequilibrium'. The latter variable is not normally part of the so-called cognitive map of the actor, he does not use the concept of status disequilibrium. But the concept/variable is a description of a state of affairs of which the individual components are, in all probability, perceived by the actor. That is, he recognises and evaluates his relative position on the dimensions, but he does not constitute these into the formal conception of disequilibrium.

In cases like this we earlier spoke of *constructivist concepts.*

A constructivist concept is in some way aggregated out of internal concepts. This definition is perhaps not an easy one to establish on logical grounds, since aggregation is a very loose term. But it is, in practice, helpful. If we consider the general conception of status inconsistency, i.e. the class of all inconsistent profiles in a multi-dimensional ranking system, then we are, as sociologists, creating an equivalence class out of all these different possible profiles. And if we relate the concept to some other variable there is the implicit assumption that they all have the same type of effect. In fact, we know that they do not. And the problem becomes – how many and which equivalence classes can be meaningfully established? This is, of course, an empirical question which cannot be settled *a priori* but only in the context of a particular proposition or model where the constructivist variable appears as an explanatory one. The meaningfulness of the equivalence classes created is thus a function of the problem in hand and a particular class may be appropriate for one problem and not for another.

In connection with this problem it is useful to distinguish between the following situations:

(a) Where the actor perceives (cognises and evaluates) a particular variable as *the* or *a* cause of his behaviour/action. There are no problems as the external and internal account are identical.

(b) Where the actor perceives (cognises and evaluates) a particular variable as causing his behaviour/action. But the (external) social analyst views the actor's perception (definition of the situation) as faulty. From the analyst's point of view the causal structure would often look something like

$$S \to Sp \to B$$

where S is the objective situation, Sp the actor's perception of the situation and B the actor's behaviour. So Sp becomes an intervening variable between S and B. One would still want to go on and ask why Sp is not identical to S. A way of answering this question is to suggest a further series of variables (most probably psychologically characterising the individual) which, along with S, are sufficient for Sp (i.e. they interact with S in its effect on Sp). Pictorially this would look like

$$(S \cdot C_1 \cdot C_2 \ldots) \to Sp \to B$$

where the series of additional variables C_i has been left open. In this manner 'perceived variables' and 'definitions of the situation' can be brought into causal models. This, needless to say, is likely to be a complicated matter and even more complex causal structures can be countenanced when cognitions and evaluations are broken out into separate variables.

6.12 Social Functional Propositions
The characteristic form of a social functional proposition is

X has (social) function Y in system S.

There are thus three entities involved:
  (i) the function serving variable (X)
 (ii) the served function variable (Y)
(iii) the system S which is normally a set of variables of type (i) and (ii) referred to as a functional system.

Social functional propositions make stronger claims about the relationship between X and Y than mere covariation. To say that X bears a social functional relationship to Y is normally taken to imply that X 'maintains' Y in the sense that if Y is disturbed from an equilibrium value then X will adjust its value such that Y is restored to its equilibrium value. From this it should not necessarily be concluded that functional analysis is static; the equilibrium state of Y may be a 'rate of change' or even a 'rate of rate of change'. But the essential idea is one of *maintenance* of values of Y. Furthermore, it is usually assumed that the equilibrium state of Y is necessary for the maintenance of the system S in the sense that, if for some reason Y is not maintained at equilibrium (or perhaps more realistically within certain limits of equilibrium), then the system will be fundamentally altered – or even terminated. Thus in a social functional system S with $y_1 \ldots y_n$ served function variables it is *necessary* that each one be maintained in an equilibrium state for the system to 'continue functioning'. It is possible that one served functional variable is a function serving variable for another variable.

But to start with let us forget about the system S and abstract from it the social functional link – X has (social) function Y. How does this relate to our previous ideas on causality? If a causal account of a functional relationship of this sort can be provided it must account for the equilibration of variable Y.

The negative feedback causal diagram in Figure 6.3 has this property.

Figure 6.3 A Negative Feedback Social Functional Causal Structure

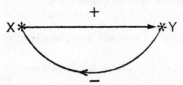

In this diagram, $X \xrightarrow{(+)} Y$ means increases in X cause increases in Y and decreases in X cause decreases in Y, and $Y \xrightarrow{(-)} X$ means increases in Y cause decreases in X and decreases in Y cause increases in X. For assume Y has an equilibrium value and is moved above it (by some exogenous factor) then this will cause a decrease in X (via $X \xrightarrow{(-)} Y$) but the decrease in X will, in turn, cause a decrease in Y (via $X \xrightarrow{(+)} Y$) which, if the parameters relating X and Y are of suitable magnitudes, lead to a re-establishment of the equilibrium value of Y. In addition, if Y is moved below its equilibrium value this will cause an increase in X (via $Y \xrightarrow{(-)} X$) but the increase in X will, in its turn, cause an increase in Y. There appears, therefore, to be a built in equilibrating process in such a system. We may note, however, that the function serving and served function variable are not distinguishable on formal grounds. For if X is changed upwards in value, this will cause an increase in Y which will cause a decrease in X, etc. So variable X will also appear to return to an equilibrium value. This raises, in a rather novel way, a classical problem of functionalism in social science – how are the served functions in a system to be located? On purely formal grounds (if the previous analysis is accepted) the answer is that they cannot. So we have to look for non-formal answers to this question. One is where the model involves intentionality. Assume an individual or a collectivity of individuals are intentionally maintaining a particular goal state (e.g. government maintaining relatively fixed rate of unemployment) then he/they will respond to changes in the goal state induced by factors beyond his/their immediate control (exogenous factors) by altering his/their behaviour in order to re-establish the original state. The causal diagram for such a process may look something like that in Figure 6.4.

Figure 6.4 A Negative Feedback Structure Involving Intention

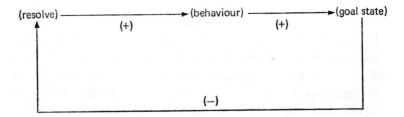

If, however, there is no way of studying the functional process in terms of intention (or a surrogate concept) then it seems impossible to distinguish between the function serving variable and function served variables (see Section 7.9). In cases like this, we may view a set of variables as interrelated into a system of dependencies when it may be asked under what conditions the system as a whole is stable. Blalock (1969) has recently considered these problems in a revealing way and we will also return to them briefly in Chapter 9.

6.13 Structural Propositions
In Chapter 4 the distinction was drawn between pure and structural measurement, the latter leading to what we might term structural variables. A proposition relating two structural variables may be called a *structural proposition*. Such propositions occur fairly frequently in sociological contexts. The idea

that one 'structure' exerts a determining influence (causal influence!) over another is very central to much social theory. For example, the theoretical tenet of Marx to the effect that the economic structure exerts some determinancy over the cultural structure might be construed in this way.

Some way of analysing contingent relations between structures is therefore required. The easiest way of doing this is to think in terms of two graphs (see Chapter 2) defined over the same point set. Let the two relations be R_1 and R_2; then there are logically four types of associated pairs:

   (i) pairs related by R_1 and R_2;

   (ii) pairs related by R_1 but not by R_2;

   (iii) pairs related by R_2 but not by R_1;

   (iv) pairs ordered by neither R_1 nor R_2.

So the joint distribution of associated pairs over relations R_1 and R_2 may be depicted as a simple 2×2 Table where the total number of entries will be $n(n-1)/2$ if the relations are symmetric and $n(n-1)$ if they are directed. The observation that we can reduce the system of two structures to a contingency relation between associated pairs enables us to use standard contingency statistics or adaptations of parametric techniques to examine relationships between structures.

If the relationship between the points in the structure are of an ordinal variety (i.e. ordinal structures) then the same type of analysis can be accomplished but the appropriate contingency Table will have $l \times m$ cells, where l and m are the number of ranked categories in the linear order defined on each relation.

We can thus speak of contingent relations between structures, obtain appropriate summary statistics, and ultimately attempt to erect causal models relating them.

6.14 Structural-Property Propositions

It is also possible to relate the properties of a unit of analysis to its relationships with other units. We then speak of a *structural-property proposition*. Sociological examples abound – for example, the properties that an individual has as a consequence of his socio-structural environment. There are two analytically distinct types of analysis:

(a) relating a property of a unit to its in-degree, and
(b) relating a property of a unit to its out-degree.

In both cases the type of analysis appropriate will depend on the measurement properties of the unit and the relationship. If the unit is characterised by a nominal or ordinal property and the relationship is simple binary or ordinal then the problem reduces to one of classical contingency. If, on the other hand, the property and relationship are measured at the cardinal level the total out-degree or in-degree can be calculated (i.e. the sum of the values on all the appropriate arcs) and classical parametric techniques can be employed.

It is possible to engage in more ambitious structural-property analysis; for instance, relating the property of a unit to the degree to which it is *connected* in a structure (i.e. the number of units that can be reached from the unit in question by following paths of arcs). There has been very little effort to use structural-property analysis in a creative way in sociological research.

7. Interrelated Propositions

7.1 Introduction

So far we have seen how to convert concepts into variables and variables into propositions; we now pass on to the next level, interrelated propositions.

Most propositions in sociology are non-deterministic, for example, Cor (AB), but it is helpful to start by looking at deterministic relations between propositions, for we have adopted the perspective that it is often intellectually convenient to assume an underlying deterministic relation between variables, even when we know that only correlational measures departing from unity will, in practice, be obtained.

The power of deterministic relations is that they are *transitive* (Chapter 4, p. 43) and the full complexity of deterministic theoretical structures rests very centrally upon this property. Unfortunately, however, non-deterministic relations are not in general, transitive – correlations for instance, are only transitive under very special circumstances. Statistical independence is not a transitive relation either, so we must anticipate some rather acute problems.

7.2 Interrelated Deterministic Propositions

Consider three dichotomous variables:

    inter-group conflict (A)
    group consciousness (B)
    group cohesion (C).

Next consider the three propositions:

    inter-group conflict (leads to) group consciousness.
    group consciousness (leads to) group cohesion.
    inter-group conflict (leads to) group cohesion.

These three propositions could be expressed in terms of changes (either increases or decreases) of the variables concerned, e.g. 'increases in inter-group conflict (lead to) increases in group cohesion'. The logic of the following paragraphs would, however, not be materially altered; the As, Bs and Cs would stand for expression of increase or decrease and the terms ΔA, ΔB and ΔC may be substituted for A, B and C respectively. We will, however, return to statements of change in the closing section of this chapter.

Formally, if 'leads to' is interpreted as $\Rightarrow$ (i.e. material implication) then from the first two propositions may be written:

$A \Rightarrow B$ (A is a sufficient condition for B) and
$B \Rightarrow C$ (B is a sufficient condition for C)

but the following expression may also be written:

$$[(A \Rightarrow B) \cdot (B \Rightarrow C)] \Rightarrow [(A \Rightarrow C)] \qquad (7.1)$$

which is a tautology. In other words, material implication is transitive. So in a deterministic system, the proposition ($A \Rightarrow C$) can be deduced from the conjoin of the propositions ($A \Rightarrow B$) and ($B \Rightarrow C$), i.e. the proposition to the effect that 'inter-group conflict leads to group cohesion' can be deduced from the conjunction of the two propositions – 'inter-group conflict leads to group consciousness' and 'group consciousness leads to group cohesion'. This deduction enables us, if we so wish, to regard the propositions ($A \Rightarrow B$) and ($B \Rightarrow C$) as axioms in an axiomatised system where ($A \Rightarrow C$) is a theorem. Of course, in the case of three propositions like this, the axiomatisation carries with it little in the way of simplification. We can deductively unpack only one further proposition from two 'axioms'. There is not, therefore, much intellectual efficiency gained in the exercise of axiomatisation. If a measure of *axiomatic reduction* is adopted as follows:

$$\left[1 - \frac{\text{number of axiom propositions}}{\text{total number of propositions}} \right]$$

then, in the case under consideration, it is one-third. Clearly the measure is zero when the number of axioms equals the total number of propositions in the system.

The above example states that, if A is a sufficient condition for B, and B is a sufficient condition for C, then A is a sufficient condition for C. *Sufficiency is transitive.* If a *causal link* is interpreted as a simple sufficient condition in this manner then causal links are likewise transitive. Of course, it is also true that if B is a necessary condition for A and C a necessary condition for B then C is a necessary condition for A. But since our ultimate aim is to relate logical deductions of this sort to causal linkages and we have argued that sufficiency is the important logical concept in this respect we concentrate upon it rather than necessity.

Caution must be exercised here since some possible ambiguities arise in the use of the word 'cause' as a sufficient condition. It was suggested in the last chapter that, when we speak of a causal event A as a sufficient condition for an event B, we construe this as *contextual sufficiency* – we say that A is a sufficient condition for B in the context of further conditions (the set of initial conditions or interaction conditions).

So the general form of the argument would be:

If inter-group conflict in situations $k_1 \cdot k_2 \ldots$ etc. (leads to) group consciousness

and group consciousness in conditions $d_1 \cdot d_2 \ldots$ etc. (leads to) group cohesion

then inter-group conflict in situations $k_1 \cdot k_2 \ldots$ *and* $d_1 \cdot d_2 \ldots$ leads to group cohesion.

Formally:

$$\left[[(k_1 \cdot k_2 \ldots) \cdot (A \Rightarrow B)] \cdot [(d_1 \cdot d_2 \ldots)(B \Rightarrow C)] \right] \Rightarrow$$
$$\left[(k_1 \cdot k_2 \ldots) \cdot (d_1 \cdot d_2 \ldots) \cdot (A \Rightarrow C) \right]. \tag{7.2}$$

A special case of this is when the two sets of interaction conditions (i.e. the ks and ds) are the same. But in general it is imperative to recognise that both sets of interaction conditions must hold for the transitivity to be established. In the following discussions we will not make explicit reference to the attendant interaction conditions for chains of deduction unless some special feature of the argument warrants it. The reader should therefore assume that the conditions have been fully specified.

Now, if we consider the *causal* structure,

$$A \rightarrow B \rightarrow C \text{ (}A \text{ causes } B \text{ and } B \text{ causes } C\text{),} \qquad (7.3)$$

if *B* is an intervening variable between *A* and *C*, we would expect changes in *A* to lead to changes in *C* 'through' *B*.

Contrast this with the causal structure

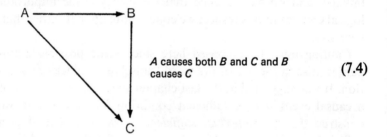

A causes both *B* and *C* and *B* causes *C*   (7.4)

Here, there is an additional *direct* causal link between *A* and *C*. So there is a *direct* and *indirect* causal connection between *A* and *C*.

In causal structure (7.3), *A* is only a sufficient condition for *C* if *B* (*and its appropriate interaction conditions*) are present. But in (7.4) *A* is a sufficient condition for *C*, even in the absence of *B* (and the appropriate interaction conditions).

In both cases, of course, *B* must result from the presence of *A* and its interaction conditions. In (7.3), however, *C* will result only if the conditions under which *B* causes *C* hold, whereas in (7.4) *C* will result whether this is the case or not. If the interaction conditions for the causal sufficiency of *A* and *B* are identical then the occurrence of *A* can guarantee the presence of *C* unless the causal process consumes time and the conditions only hold whilst *A* becomes *B*s but not after this.

Some caution must therefore be exercised in interpreting arguments consisting of chains of propositions of the form 'if *A* then *B*', 'if *B* then *C*', etc. The argument, 'if *A* causes *B* directly and *B* causes *C* directly then *A* causes *C* directly', is not necessarily correct.

Direct causality is not generally transitive. But causal influence (indirect causal connection) is transitive if the initial conditions are fully specified. We can say: 'if *A* causally influences *B* and *B* causally influences *C* then *A* causally influences *C*'.

The upshot of what has been said in the last few paragraphs is that care must be exercised in interpreting social causality as a contextual sufficient condition. The map of logical relationships (structures) onto causal structures is not one to one. In general there is more than one causal structure compatible with strings of statements of sufficiency.

Transitivity extends down a chain of material implications of any length. If we introduce a fourth nominal variable, collective behaviour (*D*), then we may write:

$$[(A \Rightarrow B) \cdot (B \Rightarrow C) \cdot (C \Rightarrow D)] \Rightarrow [(A \Rightarrow D)]$$
$$\text{for since } [(A \Rightarrow B) \cdot (B \Rightarrow C)] \Rightarrow [(A \Rightarrow C)] \qquad (7.5)$$
$$[(A \Rightarrow C) \cdot (C \Rightarrow D)] \Rightarrow [(A \Rightarrow D)].$$

This process can clearly be reiterated down a chain of any number of deductions.

As earlier suggested, chains of this sort may be regarded as rather primitive axiomatised systems. With *n* 'variables' there will be (*n*–1) 'axioms' and a total of *n*(*n*–1)/2 propositions. So the effective axiomatic reduction is given by

$$1 - \frac{2}{n}. \qquad (7.6)$$

Thus, as *n* increases, the intellectual efficiency of stating the system in axiomatic form also increases.

7.3 Some Limitations on Inference Chains
It is perhaps helpful, at this juncture, to take note of some illegitimate inferences which constrain the structure of deductive systems.

1. If A is a sufficient condition for B and B a sufficient condition for C then C is *not* a sufficient condition for A. In terms of our example, if we interpret 'leads to' as a sufficient condition, then if inter-group conflict leads to group consciousness and group consciousness leads to group cohesion then it does *not* follow that group cohesion leads to inter-group conflict. Though, of course, we can say *only if* group cohesion then inter-group conflict, i.e. group cohesion is a necessary condition for inter-group conflict. This indicates how important it is to keep the logical notions of necessity and sufficiency distinct from those of causality. The inference that 'only if group cohesion then inter-group conflict' must not be construed to imply that group cohesion is *causally or temporally prior* to inter-group conflict. In fact, according to our above formulations, the temporal ordering is precisely the reverse. The possible ambiguity arises because, whenever we interpret the *logical* component of $(A \rightarrow B)$ as A is sufficient for B, then B is a necessary condition for A.

2. No relationship can be inferred between two conditions that are separately sufficient for a third condition. For example, if inter-group conflict and group consciousness are separately sufficient for group cohesion, we cannot infer any relationship between inter-group conflict and group consciousness. That is,

from $\quad(A \Rightarrow C) \cdot (B \Rightarrow C)$ nothing follows relating A and B
for $\quad [(A \Rightarrow C) \cdot (B \Rightarrow C)] \Rightarrow [(A \Rightarrow B)]$ is not a tautology (7.7)
nor is $[(A \Rightarrow C) \cdot (B \Rightarrow C)] \Rightarrow [(B \Rightarrow A)]$.

3. No relationship can be inferred between two conditions that have a common sufficient condition. For example, if inter-group conflict is a sufficient condition for group consciousness and group cohesion then we cannot infer anything about the relationship between group consciousness and group cohesion. That is:

from $\quad(A \Rightarrow B) \cdot (A \Rightarrow C)$ nothing follows relating B and C
for $\quad [(A \Rightarrow B) \cdot (A \Rightarrow C)] \Rightarrow [(B \Rightarrow C)]$ is not a tautology (7.8)
nor is $[(A \Rightarrow B) \cdot (A \Rightarrow C)] \Rightarrow [(C \Rightarrow B)]$.

Building upon these three points, a general rule of thumb may be stated about deduction in chains of deductions.

Rule (a) Deductions cannot be made when the structure thereby becomes *intransitive*. This follows from point (1) above. Material implication is transitive. We will adopt a shorthand way of depicting deductive chains so that:

$$(A \Rightarrow B) \cdot (B \Rightarrow C) \cdot (C \Rightarrow D) \qquad (7.9)$$

becomes $\qquad (A) \Rightarrow (B) \Rightarrow (C) \Rightarrow (D).$ $\qquad (7.10)$

Thus, in *deductive structures* of the form:

$$(A) \Rightarrow (B) \Rightarrow (C) \Rightarrow (D) \dots \text{etc.} \qquad (7.11)$$

If additional implications between variables are deduced then the structure so produced must be transitive.

Rule (b) Deductions cannot be made when the material implication can be entered into a structure 'both ways round', still preserving transitivity. For example, from the structure (7.12),

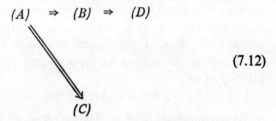

$$(7.12)$$

either of the propositions $(B \Rightarrow C)$ *or* $(C \Rightarrow B)$ could be entered, still preserving transitivity, but both are ruled out as valid deductions by rule (b); likewise any relationship between C and D. The proposition $(A \Rightarrow D)$ can, however, be deduced.

7.4 Deductive Structures as Linear and Partial Orders
Our discussion of implicational systems enables us to view deductive structures as linear or partial orders (Chapter 4, p. 45); this is often very helpful in handling complicated theoretical structures, so we will consider some elementary examples. They

should, however, be interpreted as examples only; no claims are made for their sociological validity.

Consider the following variables (as before, we assumed these are nominal though they could be regarded as standing for statements of increase or decrease):

A = status disequilibrium
B = strain
C = reforming aspirations
D = social protest
E = mobilisation of opposition
F = collective action in protest
G = collective action in opposition
H = élite intervention

The simplest possible model involving these variables might be:

$$(A) \Rightarrow (B) \Rightarrow (C) \Rightarrow (D) \Rightarrow (E) \Rightarrow (F) \Rightarrow (G) \Rightarrow (H),$$

with the bracketed terms having the same significance as before. It is important at this stage not to interpret these links as causal ones – it is, of course, tempting to do so; but we have, at the moment, no reason to suppose any pattern of temporal priority at all.

The model is a *linear order*, for the '$\Rightarrow$' relation is:

(i) asymmetric; if $(A \Rightarrow B)$ then $(B \Rightarrow A)$, and
(ii) transitive; if $(A \Rightarrow B) \cdot (B \Rightarrow A)$ then $(A \Rightarrow C)$.

Linear orders can be depicted as matrices so, from the original seven propositions, we can, according to the transitivity law, deduce a further 21 propositions leading to the matrix representation of the structure defined in Figure 7.1.

In this matrix a cell entry is given the value 'a' if the proposition relating the row variable to the column variable is an 'axiom', the value 1 if the proposition can be deduced from the axioms and 0 if it cannot.

If, however, *incomparability* (Chapter 4) is introduced into the structure, a partial order (without equivalence classes) will result, for the structure will then be asymmetric and transitive, with incomparability between at least one pair of elements. Our previous rule of thumb enables us to see how this can come about. If two variables are either both sufficient conditions for a third variable or one variable sufficient for two other variables then in both cases we can infer nothing about the two variables.

For example, a possible deductive structure relating the above named variables is

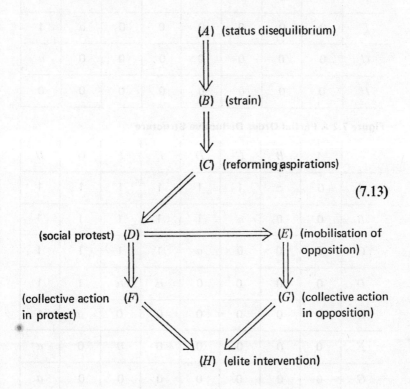

(7.13)

Figure 7.1 A Linear Order Deductive Structure

	A	B	C	D	E	F	G	H
A	0	a	1	1	1	1	1	1
B	0	0	a	1	1	1	1	1
C	0	0	0	a	1	1	1	1
D	0	0	0	0	a	1	1	1
E	0	0	0	0	0	a	1	1
F	0	0	0	0	0	0	a	1
G	0	0	0	0	0	0	0	a
H	0	0	0	0	0	0	0	0

Figure 7.2 A Partial Order Deductive Structure

	A	B	C	D	E	F	G	H
A	0	a	1	1	1	1	1	1
B	0	0	a	1	1	1	1	1
C	0	0	0	a	1	1	1	1
D	0	0	0	0	a	a	1	1
E	0	0	0	0	0	0	a	1
F	0	0	0	0	0	0	0	a
G	0	0	0	0	0	0	0	a
H	0	0	0	0	0	0	0	0

where F and G are 'incomparable'; the implication between F and G cannot be inserted as it could be either $F \Rightarrow G$ or $G \Rightarrow F$ while preserving transitivity. The implication $C \Rightarrow E$ can, however, be made. The matrix representing the structure is depicted in Figure 7.2.

Note that with this matrix some zeros appear above the main diagonal, indicating deductions that cannot be made. In general; deductive structures which can be depicted as partial orders will have some zeros in this position.

The deductive structure under consideration has a feature worth noting. The 'lowest' element H is a necessary condition for either F or G. That is, H is over-determined as two 'arms' of the deductive chain converge at this point, and it should be contrasted with the following structure:

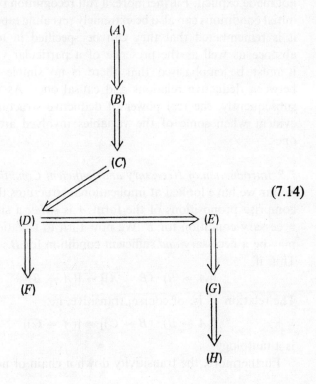

(7.14)

Here H is not over-determined. On the face of it the theoretical implications of structure (7.14) are no different from those of (7.13). But if it is recalled that normally each deductive link is circumscribed by a set of initial conditions, it is possible in (7.14) to obtain F (collective action in protest) without H when the interaction conditions for either E to be sufficient for G or G to be sufficient for H are not present. When any variable like D in (7.14) is a sufficient condition for two other variables (E and F) then it is, of course, possible that the initial conditions will not be identical for both processes.

In conclusion then, it is often very useful to try to construct deductive structures when interpreting complex theoretical writings. Such an exercise often indicates ambiguities in the theory and ultimately how propositions can be deduced that are not made explicit. Furthermore, a full recognition of the role of initial conditions can also be extremely revealing especially when it is remembered that they can be specified in terms of the absence as well as the presence of a particular variable. But it must be emphasised that there is no simple relationship between deductive relations and causal ones. As we shall see subsequently, the real power of deductive structures becomes evident when some of the variables involved are theoretical ones.

7.5 Introduction of Necessary and Sufficient Conditions

So far we have looked at implicational structures that typically comprise propositions of the form A is *either* a sufficient *or* a necessary condition for B. We now turn to situations where A may be a necessary *and* sufficient condition for B.
Thus if

$$[(A \Rightarrow B) \cdot (B \Rightarrow A)] \Rightarrow [(A \Leftrightarrow B)] \qquad (7.15)$$

The relation $\Leftrightarrow$ is, of course, transitive, i.e.

$$[(A \Leftrightarrow B) \cdot (B \Leftrightarrow C)] \Leftrightarrow [(A \Leftrightarrow C)] \qquad (7.16)$$

is a tautology.

Furthermore, the transitivity down a chain of necessary and

sufficient conditions holds, for example, using our shorthand notation once again,

if $(A) \Leftrightarrow (B) \Leftrightarrow (C) \Leftrightarrow (D)$,
then $A \Leftrightarrow C, A \Leftrightarrow D, B \Leftrightarrow D$.   (7.17)

The addition of the '$\Leftrightarrow$' relation to implicational structures makes possible weak orders and partial orders with 'equivalence' classes.

The '$\Leftrightarrow$' relation is an equivalence relation, i.e.

(i) it is symmetric; if $A \Leftrightarrow B$ then $B \Leftrightarrow A$;

(ii) it is reflexive; $A \Leftrightarrow A$ (Logically there is nothing to prevent us stating this although it is, of course, normally regarded as trivial.);

(iii) it is transitive (above).

An example of a weak order structure might be

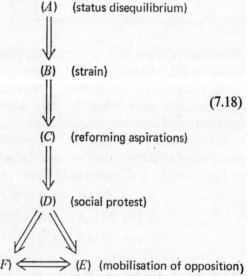

(7.18)

where E and F constitute an equivalence class: collective action in protest is a necessary and sufficient condition for mobilisation of opposition and vice versa.

The matrix representation of the structure is then as depicted in Figure 7.3.

Figure 7.3 A Weak Order Deductive Structure

	A	B	C	D	E	F
A	0	a	1	1	1	1
B	0	0	a	1	. 1	1
C	0	0	0	. a	1	1
D	0	0	0	0	a	a
E	0	0	0	0	a	a
F	0	0	0	0	a	a

Note that 'a' is put down the main diagonal for rows E and F to allow for the reflexivity needed for the definition of equivalence. These entries are trivial axioms. The other feature of interest is, of course, the entry below the main diagonal corresponding to necessary and sufficient relationships.

It should be noted that the '$\Leftrightarrow$' relation allows much more freedom of inference than '$\Rightarrow$' in a deductive structure.

For example, the following inferences can be made:

$$[(A \Leftrightarrow B) \cdot (B \Leftrightarrow C)] \Rightarrow [(A \Leftrightarrow C)] \qquad (7.19)$$
$$[(A \Leftrightarrow B) \cdot (A \Leftrightarrow C)] \Rightarrow [(B \Leftrightarrow C)]$$
$$[(A \Leftrightarrow C) \cdot (B \Leftrightarrow C)] \Rightarrow [(A \Leftrightarrow B)].$$

That is, the closure of a triad of variables into an 'equivalence class' can always be established.

7.6 Deductive Structures and Theory Building

The intellectual appeal of deductive structures like those discussed in the previous section rests upon their axiomatised form.

Given a set of axioms, as a consequence of the transitivity law, one can deduce further propositions. If the axioms are true then the deduced propositions are also true. There is thus an undeniable intellectual efficiency in stating 'theories' in this sort of axiomatised form. In the case of the '$\Rightarrow$' relation, as long as the matrix representing the theory has at least one axiom in each row then the structure is connected (Chapter 2, p. 17), and, in the case of the '$\Leftrightarrow$' relation, strongly connected (Chapter 2, p. 18).

But the question obviously arises as to what practical purpose such structures can play in sociological investigation. On the face of it, if we know the axioms are true (i.e. suppose we have made empirical tests and found them to be so), then the deductions are also true. However, this statement is rather deceptive. Consider the following deductive structure:

$$(A) \Rightarrow (B) \Rightarrow (C) \Rightarrow (D). \qquad (7.20)$$

From this we can deduce $(A \Rightarrow C)$, $(A \Rightarrow D)$ and $(B \Rightarrow D)$. But remember that in general the 'axioms' will be circumscribed by a set of initial conditions, so the deductive structure is better depicted as

$$(A.a) \Rightarrow (B.b) \Rightarrow (C.c) \Rightarrow (D) \qquad (7.21)$$

where a, b and c stand for appropriate conjoined initial conditions. Thus the deduction of $(A \Rightarrow C)$ will only be effected under conditions a and b; and the deduction of $(A \Rightarrow D)$ only under conditions a, b and c. Thus we have to know the truth of the full sets of initial conditions to know the truth of the axioms. This is not normally an easy task.

But, furthermore, if we can test the 'truth' of the axioms directly, clearly we can also test the deduced relationships directly. So there appears to be very little to be gained in practice by using deductive structures of this sort. The reason for this is that all the variables A, B, C and D and their appropriate initial conditions have been construed as directly observable, i.e. as O-variables or concepts. If we introduce T-variables the practical purpose as well as intellectual appeal becomes clearer.

Consider the structure

$$(O_1) \Rightarrow (T_1) \Rightarrow (O_2) \Rightarrow (O_3) \qquad (7.22)$$

where T_1 is a theoretical variable, and O_1, O_2 and O_3 are observational variables.

From this structure, the following propositions can be deduced

$$(O_1 \Rightarrow O_2), (O_1 \Rightarrow O_3) \text{ and } (T_1 \Rightarrow O_3).$$

But the only propositions of which the 'truth' can be directly empirically established are $(O_2 \Rightarrow O_3)$, $(O_1 \Rightarrow O_2)$, $(O_1 \Rightarrow O_3)$, the latter two being deduced from axioms. So empirically testing these two propositions provides an indirect test of the propositions that are *not directly testable*. And, of course, if they are established as correct, this provides some confirmation of the theoretical structure (not proof, of course). If either $(O_1 \Rightarrow O_2)$ or $(O_1 \Rightarrow O_3)$ is false then this necessarily means that either one or both of $(O_1 \Rightarrow T_1)$ and $(T_1 \Rightarrow O_2)$ are false. (We assume $(O_2 \Rightarrow O_3)$ is true, for one would not consider an axiom comprised solely of O-variables that was false.)

So it appears that deductive structures really come into their own when theoretical variables are involved. They enable us to provide indirect tests for propositions that are not subject to direct empirical investigation.

7.7 Interrelated Non-Deterministic Propositions

So far our attention has been solely directed towards deterministic propositions and deductive structures. Although such propositions are rarely attained in sociology, a detailed discussion of them is warranted as it is entirely consonant with our earlier statement suggesting that sociological proposition and explanation rest upon an assumption of underlying deterministic relations. Empirically ascertained probabilistic relations are in some sense an approximation to these underlying relations. But we must now go on to study the problems of relating non-deterministic propositions.

The most common form of proposition in sociology is of the

form Cor (AB). The question arises therefore, as to whether the following argument is valid:

if there exists a Cor (AB)
and a Cor (BC)
then there exists a Cor (AC).

That is, are correlations transitive in a manner analogous with deductive implications? The first thing to recognise is that correlation measures lie between -1 through 0 to $+1$, so we must expect some complications because of this.

Zetterberg (1965) made popular a form of argument which has been developed somewhat by Costner and Leik (1964) and has become known as the *sign rule* which considers the following arguments:

1.   Cor $(AB) > 0$
and   Cor $(BC) > 0$
then Cor $(AC) > 0$

2.   Cor $(AB) > 0$ Cor $(AB) < 0$
and   Cor $(BC) < 0$ and   Cor $(BC) > 0$ (7.23)
then Cor $(AC) < 0$ then Cor $(AC) < 0$

3.   Cor $(AB) < 0$
and   Cor $(BC) < 0$
then Cor $(AC) > 0$

If we write '$+$' for Cor $(AB) > 0$ and '$-$' Cor $(AB) < 0$, then the arguments in (7.23) may be summarised in the 'multiplication' Table depicted in Figure 7.4.

Figure 7.4 The Sign Rule Multiplication Table

Cor (BC)

Cor (AB)	+	−
+	+	−
−	−	+

cell entries represent the sign of Cor (AC)

But do arguments (7.23) apply in general? Let us concentrate first of all upon the product moment correlation coefficient, as its properties are well known.

From elementary correlation theory the following relationship is familiar:

$$r_{AC} = r_{AB} \times r_{BC} + r_{AC\cdot B} (1 - r^2{}_{AB})^{\frac{1}{2}} (1 - r^2{}_{BC})^{\frac{1}{2}}. \qquad (7.24)$$

The first thing to be noted about this expression is that r_{AC} (the 'deduced' relationship) is not merely a function of r_{AB} and r_{AC}, since the partial correlation coefficient $r_{AC\cdot B}$ also enters into the picture.

Using this relationship five conditions can be specified under which the sign rule holds:

(i) If $r_{AC\cdot B} = 0$ then expression (7.24) reduces to $r_{AC} = r_{AB} \times r_{BC}$ (assuming neither r_{AB} nor r_{BC} are zero). So the sign rule clearly holds, since if r_{AB} and r_{AC} are either both positive or both negative then r_{AC} is positive and if they have different signs r_{AC} is negative. But when is $r_{AC\cdot B}$ zero? In the ideal case (i.e. when errors are ignored) under two *causal* conditions:

(a) when B is an intervening variable between A and C, and there is no direct causal link between A and C, i.e.

$$A \rightarrow B \rightarrow C \text{ or } A \leftarrow B \leftarrow C, \text{ and} \qquad (7.25)$$

(b) when B is a common causal antecedent to A and C and there is no direct causal link between A and C.

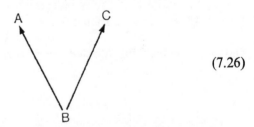

$$(7.26)$$

We may conclude, therefore, that a *sufficient* condition for the sign rule to hold is that either of the causal models (7.25) or (7.26) holds between the variables.

(ii) If $r_{AC \cdot B}$ has the same sign as $r_{AB} \times r_{AC}$ then r_{AC} will also have the same sign as this product and so the sign rule will hold. However, there are no clear causal structural criteria corresponding to the situation, so it is perhaps of little practical value.

(iii) If $r_{AC \cdot B}$ has a different sign from the product $r_{AB} \times r_{AC}$ but is *less* in absolute value than

$$\frac{r_{AB} \times r_{BC}}{(1 - r_{AB})^{\frac{1}{2}} (1 - r_{BC})^{\frac{1}{2}}} \tag{7.27}$$

then the sign rule will hold. But once again this condition does not correspond to any causal criteria and is therefore only of marginal interest.

(iv) If either r_{AB} or $r_{BC} = 1$ or -1 then $r_{AC} = r_{AB} \times r_{AC}$ so the sign rule will hold. (The argument will apply if both are unity, but then, apart from sampling fluctuation, we are dealing with a deterministic structure.) This means, in effect, that arguments containing one deterministic and one correlational proposition of the following form are always valid:

$$A \Rightarrow B \qquad\qquad \text{Cor } (AB) > 0$$
$$\text{and } \frac{\text{Cor } (BC) > 0}{\text{Cor } (AC) > 0} \qquad \text{and } \frac{B \Rightarrow C}{\text{Cor } (AC) > 0}.$$

Likewise, $\tag{7.28}$

$$A \Rightarrow B \qquad\qquad \text{Cor } (AB) < 0$$
$$\text{and } \frac{\text{Cor } (BC) < 0}{\text{Cor } (AC) < 0} \qquad \text{and } \frac{B \Rightarrow C}{\text{Cor } (AC) < 0}.$$

Arguments with $A \Leftrightarrow B$ (i.e. A as a necessary and sufficient condition for B) as constituent premise would also be valid. So deterministic and probabilistic propositions can be linked as 'premises' which allow deduction by transitive closure.

This observation seems fairly useful in sociology since we frequently wish to say that some variable is sufficient for another and then go on to relate this second variable to a third one in a probabilistic manner. For example, we may wish to say: 'If status disequilibrium then strain', and strain shows a positive correlation with political liberality, therefore status disequilibrium shows a positive correlation with political liberality.

(v) Finally, if the correlations r_{AB} and r_{BC} are sufficiently high then the sign rule holds irrespective of the value of the partial coefficient (for a proof of this point see Costner and Leik's paper, 1964).

Of course, our above example when one or both of r_{AB} and $r_{BC} = 1$ or -1 is a special case of this general relationship.

A similar argument to the one above can also be applied to regression coefficients as well as correlation coefficients. For

$$b_{AC.B} = \frac{b_{AC} - (b_{AB})(b_{BC})}{1 - (b_{CB})(b_{BC})}. \qquad (7.29)$$

The important causal condition occurs when $b_{AC.B} = 0$ so then

$$b_{AC} = (b_{AB})(b_{BC}). \qquad (7.30)$$

The product moment correlation coefficient is, of course, derived from a postulated linear relationship between the variables concerned. Furthermore, it also assumes no interaction between the variables. A natural development of the above argument is in the direction of correlational propositions involving more than three variables. But since the interesting interpretations involve causal models it is perhaps best to postpone its argument until Chapter 9.

Reasoning very similar to the above may be applied to the situations where the variables related are not cardinal but either ordinal or nominal.

Consider, for instance, the relationship between three dichotomous variables A, B and C. Lazarsfeld has made popular the analysis of relationships of this sort: he was interested in the effect of a test variable, say B, on the relationship between A and C. A 2×2 Table of the joint distribution of A and C can be decomposed into two further tables, all the entries in one being Bs and in the other not-Bs.

Figure 7.5 A Stratified Contingency Table

$$\begin{array}{c|c|c|} A & a & b \\ \hline \tilde{A} & c & d \\ \hline & \tilde{C} & C \end{array}\; N \;=\; \underbrace{\begin{array}{c|c|c|} A & a_1 & b_1 \\ \hline \tilde{A} & c_1 & \cdot d_2 \\ \hline & \tilde{C} & C \end{array}\; N_1}_{B} \;+\; \underbrace{\begin{array}{c|c|c|} A & a_2 & b_2 \\ \hline \tilde{A} & c_2 & d_2 \\ \hline & \tilde{C} & C \end{array}\; N_2}_{\tilde{B}}$$

Then, if there are N units of analysis with N_1 *B*s and N_2 not-*B*s, and we concentrated upon the normed cross product terms,

$$\frac{bc - ad}{N} = \delta_{AC}, \quad \frac{b_1c_1 - a_1d_1}{N_1} = \delta_{AC\cdot B} \text{ and } \frac{b_2c_2 - a_2d_2}{N_2} = \delta_{AC\cdot \tilde{B}}.$$

It is a matter of elementary algebra to show that

$$\delta_{AC} = \frac{N}{N_1 + N_2}\, \delta_{AB}\, \delta_{BC} + \delta_{AC\cdot B} + \delta_{AC\cdot \tilde{B}}.$$

where δ_{AB} and δ_{BC} are the cross product terms for the Tables giving the covariations of *A* and *B*, and *B* and *C* respectively.

This expression is not, on the face of it, entirely analogous to that for the product moment correlation coefficient. The apparent difference is that the partials $\delta_{AC\cdot B}$ and $\delta_{AC\cdot \tilde{B}}$ appear as summed terms and, in order to obtain an expression:

$$\delta_{AC} = \frac{N}{N_1\, N_2}\, \delta_{AB}\, \delta_{BC}, \tag{7.32}$$

both these terms must go to zero. But unless there is an interaction effect of *B* on the relationship between *A* and *C*, then if $\delta_{AC\cdot B}$ is zero so is $\delta_{AC\cdot \tilde{B}}$ and vice versa. The product moment coefficient $r_{AC.B}$ is, of course, computed assuming no interaction effects (i.e. the regression equation of *A* onto *C* and *B* would contain *C* and *B* as additive terms). The slope of the curve relating *A* and *C* is independent of the value of *B*. Thus, in the absence of interaction effects, the expressions for δ_{AC} and r_{AC} are analogous. In line with our above arguments, the *important* condition under which the sign rule holds is when $\delta_{AC\cdot B} = \delta_{AC\cdot \tilde{B}}$

$= 0$. That is, in causal terms, B is either an intervening or common antecedent to A and C. Most measures of correlation in a 2×2 Table are based upon the cross product term; the percentage difference measure $\dfrac{bc - ad}{(a + c)(b + d)}$, for example, and this measure is analogous to the regression coefficient for a 2×2 Table (see Chapter 8).

Correlations between sociological variables are ubiquitous. It has often been remarked that 'everything correlates with everything else'. If this is at all true, one might expect that statistical independence between variables would be of some theoretical significance, providing, as it were, dislocations in a system of intercorrelations. But if A and B and B and C are statistically independent then $r_{AB} = r_{BC} = 0$, so

$$r_{AC} = r_{AC \cdot B}. \tag{7.33}$$

In other words, statistical independence is not transitive either.

7.8 The Relationship between Deductive and Non-Deductive Structures
The deductive structure

$$(A) \Rightarrow (B) \Rightarrow (C) \tag{7.34}$$

between three dichotomous variables A, B and C would have joint distributions as follows:

A	0	X
$\tilde{A}$	X	X
	$\tilde{B}$	B

B	0	X
$\tilde{B}$	X	X
	$\tilde{C}$	C

A	0	X
$\tilde{A}$	X	X
	$\tilde{C}$	C

where X indicates a non-zero entry. Of course, the correlations (based upon the cross product) Cor (AB), Cor (BC) and Cor (AC) would be $+ 1$. So we may write:

Cor $(AB) = 1$ and Cor $(BC) = 1$ therefore, Cor $(AC) = 1$.

But in practice, the cell entries $(A\tilde{B})$ $(B\tilde{C})$ and $(A\tilde{C})$ will not be zero so the correlations will depart from unity. It is still useful to think in terms of an 'underlying' deductive structure, however, and adopt our previously suggested strategy of viewing the original statement of the deductive structure as under-specified. There are further initial conditions needed for A to be sufficient for B, and B for C. The cases of $(A\tilde{B})$, $(B\tilde{C})$ and $(A\tilde{C})$ are those that do not fulfil these conditions. So we can accept correlations of less than unity and still retain as an organising intellectual device the idea of an underlying deductive structure.

Since there are cases of $(\tilde{A}B)$ there must also be some other variables (other than A) sufficient for B. A similar argument also applies to the entry $(\tilde{B}C)$. The entries $(A\tilde{B})$, $(B\tilde{C})$ and $(A\tilde{C})$ can also be accounted for in terms of additional variables sufficient for $\tilde{B}$ and $\tilde{C}$. In fact statistical analysis, as we shall see, normally assumes this.

Thus if we were tempted to view in causal terms the joint distributions between A, B and C with no entries equal to zero, our causal picture would look somewhat as in Figure 7.6.

Figure 7.6 A Three-Variable Causal Process

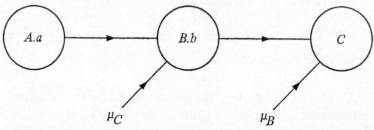

where a and b are initial conditions to account for the entries $(A\tilde{B})$, $(B\tilde{C})$ and $(A\tilde{C})$ and μ_B and μ_C are additional causal variables accounting for the $(\tilde{A}B)$ and $(\tilde{B}C)$ entries. The conditions 'b' should not be construed as being caused by the conjoin A and a but as having to be present when Bs come about for C to follow. The initial conditions in causal processes of this sort may be viewed as components of a 'situational mix', very often comprising norms, beliefs and values. There is also the further problem concerning a possible direct causal link between A and C but we leave any consideration of this to Chapter 9.

7.9 Deductive Structures, Statements of Change and Social Functional Equilibrium

In the opening paragraphs of this chapter we considered a deductive structure comprising three dichotomous variables, A, B and C. We now consider the case where A, B and C are ordinal variables so that propositions of the form: 'increases/decreases in A lead to increases/decreases in B' are appropriate.

We will adopt the following symbolism:

$\triangle A$ = increases in A and $\triangledown A$ = decreases in A
$\triangle B$ = increases in B and $\triangledown B$ = decreases in B
$\triangle C$ = increases in C and $\triangledown C$ = decreases in C.

Now consider the axioms

$$\text{(a) } \triangle A \Rightarrow \triangle B$$
$$\text{(b) } \triangle B \Rightarrow \triangle C \qquad (7.35)$$

from which we can deduce

$$\triangle A \Rightarrow \triangle C \qquad (7.36)$$

(i.e. increases in A 'lead to' increases in C).

Two further possible axioms are

$$\text{(a) } \triangledown A \Rightarrow \triangledown B$$
$$\text{(b) } \triangledown B \Rightarrow \triangledown C \qquad (7.37)$$

from which we can deduce

$$\triangledown A \Rightarrow \triangledown C. \qquad (7.38)$$

It should be noted that the non-deterministic (correlational) counterpart of the above arguments implicitly involves axioms 7.35 *and* 7.37. For example, if Cor $(AB) = +1$ then $\triangle A \Rightarrow \triangle B$ *and* $\triangledown A \Rightarrow \triangledown B$ giving a joint equilibrium distribution of A and B. So we have the following situation.

Correlational Form	Underlying Deterministic Structure
Cor $(AB) > 0$	$(\triangle A \Rightarrow \triangle B) \cdot (\triangledown A \Rightarrow \triangledown B)$
Cor $(BC) > 0$	$(\triangle B \Rightarrow \triangle C) \cdot (\triangledown B \Rightarrow \triangledown C)$ (7.39)
Cor $(AC) > 0$	$(\triangle A \Rightarrow \triangle C) \cdot (\triangledown A \Rightarrow \triangledown C)$

Thinking now in terms of causality: when we entertain the causal link $A \rightarrow B$ we usually imply that increases in A cause increases in B *and* decreases in A cause decreases in B. So in a cross-sectional survey we hope to observe A and B in aggregate equilibrium where 'high' As go with 'high' Bs and 'low' As go with 'low' Bs. I should like to call causal structures of this sort *maintenance causality* since, for the value of the effect to remain high, the causal variable must maintain its value. It is this sort of causal thinking that dominates the physical sciences and is highly susceptible to experimental investigation. It requires both 7.35 (a) *and* 7.37 (a) to hold to axiomatically catch its structure. And, analogously (7.39) represents a maintenance system of the form $A \rightarrow B \rightarrow C$.

Causality of the maintenance variety should be contrasted with what I will term *productive causality*. An example of this would be where 'increases in A lead to increases in B' but 'decreases in A do *not* lead to decreases in B'. So once B has attained a 'high' value it will not decrease if A does. It seems to me that productive causality is of very frequent occurrence in sociology and failure to recognise this has sometimes led to misrepresentation of data. In a productive causal sequence increases in A cause increases in B but it is possible to have cases of 'low' A (not A in the dichotomous case) which are 'high' B (B in the dichotomous case). This can come about since an increase in A will cause B to increase and B will stay at this value even if some exogenous factor eventually decreases A. It is, therefore, possible to confound over-determined causal structures with productive causality for both allow for cases of 'low' As that are 'high' Bs (not As that are Bs).

A productive causal link $A \rightarrow B$ will *not* require both 7.35 (a) and 7.37 (a) for its axiomatisation, but only one or the other. And deductive structures representing productive causality will likewise not require the full system 7.39. It is, therefore, essential, when postulating systems of interrelated propositions, to deal with increasing and decreasing values of the variables independently.

The symbols we have adopted enable us to be rather explicit about social functional propositions also. In Chapter 6 we construed a social functional proposition as a negative feedback process. Expressing the system depicted in Figure 6.4, for instance, we obtain using the notation:

$\triangle I$ and $\triangledown I$ = increases and decreases in framed intentions (resolve)

$\triangle B$ and $\triangledown B$ = increases and decreases in behaviour

$\triangle G$ and $\triangledown G$ = increases and decreases in goal state,

that:

1. $(\triangle G \Rightarrow \triangledown I) \cdot (\triangledown G \Rightarrow \triangle I)$
2. $(\triangledown I \Rightarrow \triangledown B) \cdot (\triangle I \Rightarrow \triangle B)$ (7.40)
3. $(\triangledown B \Rightarrow \triangledown G) \cdot (\triangle B \Rightarrow \triangle G)$

from which we can deduce

4. $(\triangle G \Rightarrow \triangledown G) \cdot (\triangledown G \Rightarrow \triangle G)$ (7.41)

which is, in effect, a statement of social functional equilibration of the goal state. It should be noted that to obtain *full* equilibration (i.e. increases of G 'leading to' decreases of G *and* decreases of G leading to increases of G) we require the full set of axioms corresponding to maintenance causality. A further point mentioned before can also be brought into focus by concentrating upon the above sort of axiomatisation. We could equally well axiomatise Figure 6.4 by the statements:

5. $(\triangle I \Rightarrow \triangle B) \cdot (\triangledown I \Rightarrow \triangledown B)$
6. $(\triangle B \Rightarrow \triangle G) \cdot (\triangledown G \Rightarrow \triangledown G)$ (7.42)
7. $(\triangle G \Rightarrow \triangledown I) \cdot (\triangledown G \Rightarrow \triangle I)$

from which we can deduce:

8. $(\triangle I \Rightarrow \triangledown I) \cdot (\triangledown I \Rightarrow \triangle I)$.

In other words we obtain the equilibration of intention (resolve). This strengthens the point made in Chapter 6 that it is impossible on formal grounds to separate the function serving (intention) and served function (goal state) variables – both exhibit a pattern of equilibration.

8. Some Salient Features of Sociological Covariation and Model Building

8.1 Functions

The most abstract way of stating a proposition is in functional form. A simple two-variable proposition, relating X_1 and X_2, is expressed in *implicit* form as $\phi(X_1X_2) = 0$; there are two[1] *explicit* forms corresponding to this, $X_1 = f(X_2)$ and the *inverse* function $X_2 = f(X_1)$. The distinction between implicit and explicit forms is one of convenience or emphasis. The implicit form postulates an interrelatedness, whereas the explicit form emphasises one variable as the explained (dependent) one and the other as the explanatory (independent) one. Normally functions in explicit form are adopted, since the typical exercise in sociology is to explain the variation in a given explained variable – we have a clear idea of what we want to explain and what we want to use to do the explaining. So from now on the explicit notation will be used.

Mathematically, we are used to thinking in terms of continuous, real valued functions (i.e. where we have continuous cardinal measures) but this conception of functions is not always useful in sociology. We should note, however, that a function is nothing more than a *mapping rule* (Chapter 3, p. 38) – a rule for transforming values of the explanatory variable into values of the explained variable. It may be single-valued, i.e. where there is only one value of the explained variable for each value of the explanatory variable, or *n*-valued where there are *n* values of the explained variable for each value of the explanatory variable.

In practice, sociological functions are almost invariably multivariate, i.e. they involve more than two variables. If, for example, the problem is to explain the variation in occupational status in a given population, it is unlikely that this can be completely accomplished in terms of just one explanatory variable, say 'years of formal education'. Other variables such as 'nature of home background' and 'social class' would also have to be involved as explanatory variables. So, in general, we deal not with simple functions of the form $X_1 = f(X_2)$, but with multivariate functions of the form

$$X_1 = f(X_2, X_3, X_4, \ldots, X_n) \tag{8.1}$$

(read: X_1 is a function of X_2 X_3 X_4, etc.). Although functions like this may be referred to as multivariate propositions, we will refer to them as *functional models*, for in effect, they allow us to state n propositions like X_1 and X_2 covary, X_1 and X_3 covary, and so on.

Just as the dependent and independent variables can be switched in a simple bivariate proposition, so they can in a multivariate functional model. With n variables $(X_1, X_2, \ldots, X_n)$, n functions can be written of the form:

$$X_1 = f(X_2, X_3, \ldots, X_n)$$
$$X_2 = f(X_1, X_3, \ldots, X_n)$$
$$.$$
$$. \tag{8.2}$$
$$.$$
$$X_n = f(X_1, X_2, \ldots, X_{(n-1)})$$

That is, where each variable is in turn expressed as a function of all the other $(n-1)$ variables.[2] A system of functions of this sort may be referred to as a *complete functional system*. Their most important feature is that all the variables appear as both explained and explanatory variables. So we can view the variables as 'being determined' and as 'determining' at the same time. The functions are not, therefore, to be viewed as independent but as *simultaneous* and all the variables are referred to as *endogenous*.

For example, one may entertain the model where group cohesion (X_1) is a function of inter-group conflict (X_2) and intra-group conflict (X_3); and where inter-group conflict is a function of group cohesion and intra-group conflict; and finally where intra-group conflict is a function of group cohesion and inter-group conflict. A formal statement of all this would be the following three simultaneous functions:

$$X_1 = f(X_2, X_3)$$
$$X_2 = f(X_1, X_3)$$
$$X_3 = f(X_1, X_2).$$
(8.3)

In fact, for technical reasons which will be discussed later, complete systems like this are rarely used in model building. Much more often attention is concentrated either upon one function, where the problem is to 'explain' the variance in a given explained variable, or on a system where not *all* the 'other' variables appear as explanatory variables in a given function.

Simultaneous systems of functions should be clearly distinguished from functions where more than one explained variable are functions of the same set of explanatory variables. An example of such a model is:

$$X_1 = f(Z_1, Z_2, \ldots Z_n)$$
$$X_2 = f(Z_1, Z_2, \ldots Z_n).$$
(8.4)

So far, it has been implicitly assumed that the functions are deterministic; that is, the function enables us, given values of the explanatory variables, to assign an exact value to the explained variable. In social science contexts however this is very rarely, if ever, found to be the case. If we take the above example once again and try to express a given explained variable X_1 (group cohesion) as a function of X_2 (intra-group conflict) then in practice it would almost always be found that, for a given value of X_2, we would obtain not a single value for X_1 but a *distribution of values for X_1*.

This is not quite the same as saying that the function is many-valued since we cannot, given a value of the explanatory variable, *fix* a series of values of the explained variable; all we can obtain is a distribution with certain characteristics. So in practice the value of X_1 is the result of a random selection from a one-dimensional probability distribution, which varies according to the value of X_2. Hence it is necessary to explicitly introduce a factor into functional models to account for this. A simple two-variable function then takes the *stochastic form*

$$X_1 = f(X_2, u_1) \tag{8.5}$$

where u_1 is a so-called disturbance (or stochastic) variable that comprises other variables which account for variation in X_1 but which have not been explicitly brought into the function.[3] The disturbance variable can thus be thought of as producing the distribution of the explained variable about the 'true' relationship with the explanatory variable. Since it is normally assumed that many additional but unimportant variables are involved, pulling values of the explained variable both up and down, we expect small values of u to be more frequent than large ones. So it is reasonable to think of u as a variable with a probability distribution with a mean of zero and a finite variance.

A single multivariate function in sociology is best expressed in the stochastic form:

$$X_1 = f(X_2, X_3, \ldots X_n, u_1). \tag{8.6}$$

The more explanatory variables that are incorporated into the function, the less important u will be (i.e. the smaller the amount of variance in X_1 left unexplained). The philosophy underlying a function of this form is to the effect that there are a great many variables that determine X_1 but for practical reasons (e.g. availability of data, very small amount of additional variance explained) not all are included, so u is taken to represent these excluded variables.

A system of simultaneous stochastic functions will now have the general form:

$$X_1 = (X_2, X_3, \ldots, X_n, u_1)$$
$$X_2 = (X_1, X_3, \ldots, X_n, u_2)$$
$$\cdot$$
$$\cdot \tag{8.7}$$
$$\cdot$$
$$X_n = (X_1, X_2, \ldots, X_{(n-1)} u_n).$$

Although, strictly speaking, a functional expression bears no direct relationship to causal terminology, it is often useful to think in terms of the explanatory variables exerting a causal influence on the explained ones. If we do this, then the disturbance terms can be conveniently conceptualised as 'other causes' of the explained variable which have been left out of the function. In a system like (8.7) the variables will be both 'causes' and 'effects'; X_1, for instance, is an 'effect' in the first function and a 'cause' in all the others.

In model building it is important to set out in functional form the types of relationships that are going to be studied. The idea behind a model is to explain the variance in one or a set of explained variables. Although the notion of functions derives largely from situations where we can obtain cardinal measures it will be argued subsequently that it is important, even with nominal and ordinal variables, to set out functional relationships.

Meanwhile, following Kish (1959), it is worth emphasising five types of explanatory variables that are potential causes of a given explained variable.

(i) The explanatory (causal) variables that have been explicitly introduced in the functional model ($X_2 \ldots X_n$ in (8.6)).

(ii) Potential explanatory (causal) variables that do not happen to vary in the situation where the data is collected (a survey or experiment).

(iii) Potential explanatory (causal) variables that have been explicitly controlled.

(iv) Variables that vary in the experimental situation and cause changes in the explained variable but which have not been controlled. These can be of two types:

(a) variables unrelated to any other explanatory variables in the model, and

(b) variables systematically related to some or all of the other explanatory variables in the model. For example, a confounding variable that is a cause of both the explained and an explanatory variable.

The aim of the model builder is to bring as many variables as possible into (i) and (iii). The stochastic term will account for (iv)(a) but not (iv)(b). In the face of variables of this sort it is best to elaborate the model in order to explicitly include them; this will normally mean moving to a simultaneous system of functions whereby the confounding variable is construed as a cause of both the original explained and the explanatory variable.

8.2 Specifying Functions

Propositions or models in simple functional form tell us only that the variables in question are related; they covary. One must go on to ask what *form* the function has, that is, *how* they are related. The answer to this question depends upon the level of measurement of the variables involved. We have already seen that a simple proposition where the variables are cardinal can be expressed graphically and when ordinal or nominal by a contingency table. But for the moment we will concentrate upon cardinal variables and later consider complications introduced by other types of variables.

There are two major problems involved in specifying the form of a function like (8.6):

(i) How do the explanatory variables *combine* in producing the effect (explaining the variation) of the explained variable?[4] Are they additive or do they interact multiplicatively or both?

(ii) What *power* of the explanatory variable is operative? (e.g. first-power (linear form) or second-power (quadratic form), etc.).

Furthermore, if the function is a stochastic one, then additional assumptions have to be made about the disturbance term also. Since it is normally assumed that the disturbance term is a random variable these assumptions involve its expected value and variance and, in addition, how it relates to the explanatory variable(s).

The idea of deterministic functions will not be pursued any further, but it should be borne in mind that by adopting stochastic models we are *not* necessarily implying that the phenomena under investigation are 'intrinsically probabilistic'.

The stochastic term appears because of a multitude of variables determining the explained variable, many of which are not brought into the model; but the implicit assumption is of an underlying deterministic relationship. Measurement errors also come into the picture but we may note that a characteristic difference between the physical sciences and social sciences is that in the former, disturbances are normally attributable to measurement error, but in social science *errors of specification* (i.e. excluded relevant variables) are normally on equally important factor.

Furthermore, by introducing a stochastic term into a function we do, in one sense, render a functional relationship 'determinate' if not deterministic (the use of the equals sign signifies this); the explanatory variables and the disturbance term together account for all the variation in the explained variable. But, of course, we like the disturbance term to be responsible for as little of this variation as possible.

8.3 Types of Sociological Model
If it is allowed that variables can be either cardinal, ordinal or nominal, then some fairly typical analytical situations can be distinguished.

(1) *Where all the variables in the model are cardinal:* Classical parametric statistical techniques are appropriate.

(2) *Where all the variables in the model are ordinal:* Non-parametric statistical techniques are directly applicable. But it is also possible to make assumptions about underlying cardinal variables and use parametric techniques.

(3) *Where all the variables are nominal:* Non-parametric techniques are again directly applicable. But techniques like the use of *dummy regression* are also possible.

(4) *Models with variables at different levels of measurement:* Various techniques are available (e.g. tetrachoric correlations) but adaptations of parametric techniques are also a possibility and will be emphasised in a later section.

We will now consider the problem of model building in each

of these situations. The techniques mentioned will only be given in outline since their details are readily available in introductory texts on statistics.

8.4 Models with Two Cardinal Variables

The simplest stochastic function is a two-variable one of the form $(X_1, X_2, u) = \phi$ and the simplest way of specifying this is in the *linear* form; there are then two possible models, either:

$$X_1 = a_1 + \beta_{12} X_2 + u_1 \tag{8.8}$$

where X_2 is the explanatory variable and X_1 the explained variable, or

$$X_2 = a_2 + \beta_{21} X_1 + u_2 \tag{8.9}$$

where X_2 is the explained variable and X_1 the explanatory variable. In both cases, the parameters a and β can take any value: positive, negative or zero.[5] Which of these two models one concentrates upon depends solely on whether one wishes to explain the variation in X_1 or X_2. It is important to recognise that (8.8) and (8.9) are *postulated* as holding in a given *population* and the problem is to estimate values of a and β on the basis of observations in a *sample* on X_1 and X_2.

The justification for an *additive* disturbance term is that for any given value of the explanatory variable (X_2) there will be a distribution of the explained variable (X_1) such that the expected values are $a + \beta X_2$ but the actual values of the observations on the explained variables will correspond to $a + \beta X_2$ plus or minus a number u_i indicating the amount by which the value of the explained variable falls short or exceeds the expected value. If the error term is random then so is the explained variable. So, in effect, the model specifies a conditional distribution of the explained variable for each value of the explanatory variable. The path of the expected values of these distributions is, as is well known, the regression curve.

The ordinary least square estimation techniques will give estimates of a and β values (under the appropriate assumptions)[6]; these are denoted a_1 and b_{12} for (8.8) and a_2 and b_{21} for (8.9).[7]

The simple two-variable model gives:

(i) The *parameters of the form of* the relationship, a_1 or b_{12} or a_2 and b_{21}. The values of a give an estimate of the expected value of the explained variable when the explanatory variable is zero and the values of b an estimate of the value of the slope of the line relating the two variables.

(ii) Tests of significance for the a and b values using either the student t or F distributions.[8] Normally one tests whether or not the b value is significantly different from zero (see below, Section 8).

(iii) The product moment correlation coefficient r which gives an estimate of the *strength of the relationship*.

(iv) r^2 which gives an *estimate of the efficacy or completeness* of the model; it gives the proportion of variance in the explained variable explained by the explanatory variable. If it is high, say above 0·9 then there is perhaps no need to introduce additional explanatory variables. But this is a relative matter.

(v) Test of significance for r using the Z-distribution.

It is normal practice, unless some theoretical ideas suggest otherwise, to initially test the linear model as a fit to the data. It is worth noting at this stage the way in which the results of regression analysis are normally presented in computer print-out, and reported. The standard errors of the estimates of a and b are usually placed in parentheses underneath the actual estimates. For example, results may be reported in the form:

$$X_1 = 20 + 40\,X_2.$$
$$(15)\quad (10)$$

This is convenient because when one is testing the hypotheses $a = 0$ and $\beta = 0$ then t is distributed according to:

$$\frac{b_{12}}{\text{standard error of } b_{12}} \quad \text{and} \quad \frac{a_1}{\text{standard error of } a_1}$$

and at the 95 per cent probability level the value of t varies between 2·3 (sample size $N = 10$) to 1·96 (N is ∞). Thus a quick test for significance is to check that the estimate is at least twice the value of the standard error. In the above example a_1 is not significant, but b_{12} is.

So far we have considered models where only the first power of the explanatory variable enters the equation. It is often (perhaps more often than not) the case that the covariation between sociological variables is not linear. For example, the relationship between 'group cohesion' and the incidence of 'inter-group conflict' may well have a covariation pattern something like that in Figure 8.1.

Figure 8.1 A Non-Linear Accumulation Effect

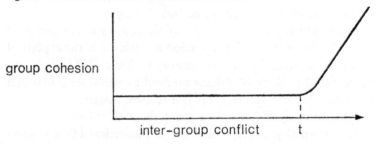

There is little or no increase in group cohesion for moderate increases in inter-group conflict but, when the inter-group conflict reaches the value t, group cohesion begins to increase rapidly.

In terms of causality this means that inter-group conflict can increase to t without *causing* any change in group cohesion but, beyond this point, increases in inter-group conflict cause increases in group cohesion.

This might be termed the *accumulation effect in sociological covariation*. There is a certain range of variation of the causal explanatory variable which exerts no, or very little, causal agency over the explained variable, but beyond which there is a very marked effect. Common sense dictates that human behaviour is often rather like this. We 'tolerate' some feature in our social structural environment as long as it is at a relatively low intensity; it has no influence on our behaviour, then at a certain 'point' (or perhaps more realistically, within a certain range) we 'do something about it'. In situations of this sort, where behaviour is related to some socio-structural variable, curves of the general form in Figure 8.1 will more often than not be appropriate.

A similar situation is as depicted in Figure 8.2, where for low

Figure 8.2 A Non-Linear Saturation Effect

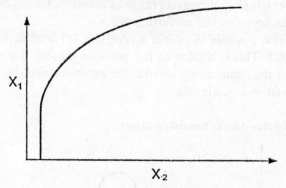

values the causal explanatory variable X_2 exerts a marked influence on X_1 but then the effect tails off. This might be termed the *saturation effect in sociological covariation.*

Both accumulation and saturation effects can be obtained in the same model; the curve would then look somewhat as in Figure 8.3.

Figure 8.3 Non-Linear Accumulation and Saturation Effects

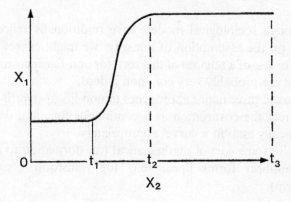

Common experience tells us that behaviour is often influenced in this way; initially there is little or no effect of the explanatory causal variable $(0-t_1)$, then a marked effect (t_1-t_2), finally little or no effect once again (t_2-t_3). Perhaps many 'influence relationships' are of this sort. An influence stimulus of low intensity has no effect, above a certain threshold it has a marked effect but only over a limited increasing range of intensity, for beyond that range the stimulus has no further effect.

It is also possible to obtain a *reversion effect* as depicted in Figure 8.4. This is similar to the previous pattern but at high values of the explanatory variable the explained variable begins to drop from a maximum.

Figure 8.4 Non-Linear Reversion Effect

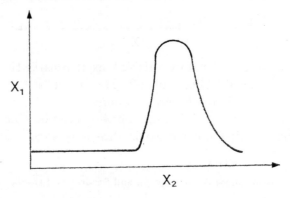

Although sociological models have traditionally relied very heavily on the assumption of linearity, we might expect in the future for less of a reliance of this sort, for non-linear covariation patterns are probably very common indeed.

There are three major approaches to non-linear covariation:

(i) Treat the covariation as a continuous function, define it algebraically and 'fit a curve' appropriately.

(ii) Use some sort of mathematical transformation to render the non-linear forms linear (e.g. log transform, reciprocal transform).

(iii) Treat the covariation as discontinuous and use linear approximations over different ranges of the explanatory variable.

We will now briefly consider each of these.

8.5 Fitting Non-Linear Functions

Inspection of the scatter diagram or some *a priori* theoretical ideas might suggest that a non-linear relationship between variables is more appropriate than a linear one.

The most general two-variable non-linear stochastic model is

$$X_1 = a_1 + \beta_{12} X_2 + u_1 \qquad (8.10)$$

where a, β and n are unknown constants. There is, however, no simple way of solving this type of expression. Of course, if we have some theoretical ideas about the value of n these can be used to test the model directly, by regressing X_1 onto X_2^n. However, there are rarely any reasons in sociological investigations to postulate a particular value of n; although an inspection of the scatter diagram may enable us to make a guess at it. But there is a more systematic technique available, using polynomials which we will now consider.

The simplest way of proceeding is to fit the data to a simple polynomial in X_2. Two points can, of course, be fitted perfectly by a straight line, three points by a second-degree function and n points by a $(n-1)$ degree function. So in general, use can be made of the polynomial

$$X_1 = a_1 + \beta_{12} X_2 + \gamma_{12} X_2^2 + \delta_{12} X_2^3 + \ldots + \eta_{12} X_2^n + u_1$$
$$(8.11)$$

where β_{12}, γ_{12}, etc., are constants and u_1 is a disturbance term. If a $(n-1)$ degree polynomial is used, a perfect fit can always be obtained for n observations. To do this, however, would be to surrender a generalising perspective; in practice, only the second and perhaps third powers are used. Regression is then carried out in the standard manner, the values of X_1 are regressed onto X_2, X_2^2 and X_2^3, etc.; so analytically this is similar to having

more than one explanatory variable and the estimation technique
reduces to that appropriate to the many variable linear model
discussed below. If the fitting of polynomials is carried out
'blind' then different models can be fitted to the data and the
value of R^2 (the multiple correlation coefficient) taken as a guide
to the best model.[9]

What I have termed the reversion effect (Figure 8.4) may well
be fitted by an inverted parabola by using the second-power
polynomial:

$$X_1 = a_1 + \beta_{12} X_2 + \gamma_{12} X_2^2 + u. \qquad (8.12)$$

Some idea of how many terms to include in the model can be
obtained by inspecting the scatter diagram. It will usually give
some indication of the number of turning points; if there is one
then a second-degree equation is required; if there are two a
third-degree equation and if three a fourth-degree equation and
so on. The major drawback of this technique is that it is not easy
to construe the equations as representing any underlying causal
mechanism.

8.6 Using Mathematical Transformations

If it can be assumed that X_1, X_2 and the disturbance term u_1, are
related by an expression of the form

$$X_1 = \beta X_2^n u_1 \qquad (8.13)$$

where β and n are constants, then a log-transform will give

$$\text{Log } X_1 = \text{Log } \beta + n \text{ Log } X_2 + \text{Log } u \qquad (8.14)$$

which has the general form of the two-variable linear model and
thus ordinary least squares estimation techniques can be
utilised. It is unlikely, however, that most sociological examples
will conform to this model – it implies that when X_2 is zero the
expected value is X_1 and that the disturbance term is proportional
to X_1. There are other possible transformations but they are at
present of little practical value in sociological investigation. The
interested reader is referred to Johnston (1963) or Malinvaud
(1966).

8.7 Treating Covariations as Discontinuous

Consider the accumulation effect between X_1 and X_2 as depicted in Figure 8.5.

Figure 8.5 Two Linear Regression Lines Fitted to an Accumulation Effect

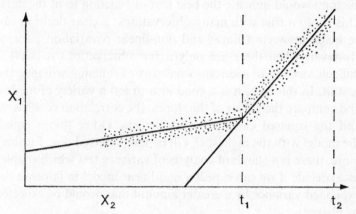

Here two linear regression lines are fitted, the first over the range of X_2, 0 to t_1 the second over the range t_1 to t_2. The logic of this sort of fitting is as follows:

(i) Inspect the scatter diagram and decide on point t_1. (This is rather arbitrary but, given the fairly crude nature of most sociological data, is no handicap.)

(ii) Use linear regression techniques on the two ranges of the explanatory variable $(0–t_1)$ and $(t_1–t_2)$.

(iii) Consequently compute

$$b_{12}\,(0–t_1) \text{ and } r_{12}\,(0–t_1)$$
$$b_{12}\,(t_1–t_2) \text{ and } r_{12}\,(t_1–t_2)$$

(iv) Test the significance (departure from zero values) of these parameters. In particular, one might find that $b_{12}\,(0–t_1)$ does not depart significantly from zero.

Intelligently used, the technique of fitting linear models over specified ranges of variation of the explanatory variable can be extremely helpful. This is especially so when we come to interpret covariation in a causal manner since emergent covariation (as Figure 8.5) then corresponds to emergent causality. The technique is, however, cumbersome with multivariate models.

It might be thought that a simple inspection of the scatter diagram would indicate the best sort of function to fit the data. This is often true with many observations; a clear decision can be made between a linear and non-linear covariation pattern. However, when there are only a few observations it is often difficult visually to ascertain what sort of function will give the best fit. In this case, it is a good idea to test a variety of models and compare the values of the slopes, the correlation coefficients and the squared correlation coefficients. Other things equal, the model with the highest r^2 will be the preferred one. Furthermore, there is a standard analysis of variance test which enables us to decide if we can expect a non-linear model to improve the explained variance by a greater amount than would be expected by chance.

8.8 Three-Variable Cardinal Models

Turning now to a three-variable function $(X_1, X_2, X_3, u) = \phi$. There are three possible explained variables. But let us assume that the problem in hand is to explain the variation in X_1; so this is the explained variable. The simplest model is then a *linear additive* one of the form

$$X_1 = \alpha_1 + \beta_{12} X_2 + \beta_{13} X_3 + u_1 \qquad (8.15)$$

where α_1, β_{12} and β_{13} are unknown constants which may normally take on any value positive, negative or zero. It is important to recognise the implications of the assumption of additivity of the two explanatory variables. Thinking causally, changes in X_2 are sufficient to cause changes in X_1 independent of X_3 and X_3 independent of X_2. And when u_1 is interpreted as 'all the other causes' of X_1, this equation logically corresponds to the over-determined causal model introduced in Chapter 6.[10]

The least squares estimates equation corresponding to (8.15) indicates the independence of the 'effects' of X_2 and X_3 on X_1; it has the form:[11]

$$X_1 = a_1 + b_{12 \cdot 3} X_2 + b_{13 \cdot 2} X_3 + u_1 \qquad (8.16)$$

where $b_{12 \cdot 3}$ gives the slope of the curve of X_1 on X_2 with the 'linear' effect of X_3 held constant. It means that the gradient of the curve of X_1 on X_2 is identical for all values of X_3. Similarly the gradient of the curve of X_1 on X_3 ($b_{13 \cdot 2}$) is identical for all values of X_2.

In geometrical terms the relationship between X_1, X_2 and X_3 would be represented by a plane in three-dimensional space. The assumption of the additive model is that the gradient of this plane in the X_1, X_2 axes is the same for all values of X_3 and the gradient in the X_1, X_3 axes is the same for all values of X_2. The relationship between the explained variable and a particular explanatory variable is not altered by the other explanatory variables. Ordinary least squares estimation gives the following estimates:

(i) estimates of the *form* parameters a_1, $b_{12 \cdot 3}$ and $b_{13 \cdot 2}$,

(ii) tests of significance for these parameters,

(iii) estimates of strength of the individual relationships: the partial correlation coefficients $r_{12 \cdot 3}$ and $r_{13 \cdot 2}$ ($r^2_{12 \cdot 3}$ gives the proportion of the variance in X_1 not explained by X_3 accounted for by X_2, and $r_{13 \cdot 2}$ has a similar interpretation),

(iv) tests of significance of these parameters,

(v) estimate of the multiple correlation coefficient $R_{1 \cdot 23}$ and $R^2_{1 \cdot 23}$ (sometimes called the coefficient of determination) gives the proportion of the variance in X_1 explained by X_2 and X_3. In fact R^2 is not an unbiased estimator and the so-called adjusted coefficient of determination ($\bar{R}^2$) is usually used. It takes the value,

$$\bar{R}^2 = 1 - (1 - R^2) \frac{(n-1)}{(n-k-1)}$$

with n observations and k explanatory variables.

R^2 will, in general, increase as more explanatory variables are brought into the model. $\bar{R}^2$ may, however, decrease if an increase in R^2 is small as the addition of variables reduces the degrees of freedom.

The three-variable linear additive model must be sharply contrasted with:

$$X_1 = a + IX_2 X_3 + u \qquad (8.17)$$

where I is a constant that can take on any value, positive, negative or zero. Then note (thinking, for the sake of convenience, in causal terms):

(i) that if $X_2 = 0$ then X_3 will *not* lead to changes in X_1 and if $X_3 = 0$, X_2 will not lead to change in X_1 either.

(ii) that, in general, the effect X_2 has on X_1 is a function of X_3 and the effect X_3 has on X_1 is a function of X_2.

X_2 and X_3 are said to exhibit multiplicative *interaction* in their effect on X_1; changes in X_2 and X_3 are both necessary, and together sufficient to produce effects in X_1.

Let us assume for the sake of exposition that X_3 is an ordinal variable taking on three values, 'zero', 'medium' and 'high', then three curves would be obtained relating X_1 and X_2 for the different values of X_3. An example may look like Figure 8.6.

Figure 8.6 Interaction Effects

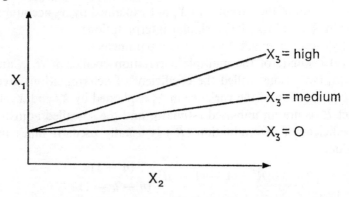

So the gradient of the curve relating X_1 and X_2 is dependent on the value of X_3. This is entirely different from the additive model where the analogous gradient is independent of the value of X_3.

It was argued in an earlier chapter that interaction is a characteristic feature of sociological covariation.

A more complex model that involves both direct *and* multiplicative interaction effects is given by the expression

$$X_1 = a_1 + \beta_{12} X_2 + \beta_{13} X_3 + I X_1 X_2 + u_1 \qquad (8.18)$$

where $a_1, \beta_{12}, \beta_{13}$ and I are constants.

So far it has been assumed that the explanatory variables enter the model in a linear fashion. There is no reason, of course, why non-linear forms should not be used. Either or both of the explanatory variables may be non-linear. The general additive model is given by the expression

$$X_1 = a_1 + \beta_{12} X_2^n + \beta_{13} X_3^m + u_1 \qquad (8.19)$$

where n and m are constants. An even more complex model, but perhaps of rather limited practical application, is where X_2 and/or X_3 enter the expression as polynomials similar to those encountered above. So the general expression becomes

$$X_1 = a_1 + (\beta_{12} X_1 + \gamma_{12} X_1^2 \ldots) + (\beta_{13} X_3 + \gamma_{13} X_3^2 \ldots) + u_1. \qquad (8.20)$$

Furthermore, non-linear terms can be introduced into the multiplicative interaction model giving a general expression of the form:

$$X_1 = a_1 + \beta X_1^n X_2^m + u \qquad (8.21)$$

where n and m are constants. Little use has been made of such models in sociology.

8.9 Many Variable Single Equation Cardinal Models

Most sociological models are multivariate in the sense that to explain the variation in any one variable it will involve not one or two but many explanatory variables. Let us therefore concentrate upon the explicit functional form:

$$X_1 = f(X_2, X_3, X_4, \ldots X_n, u_1). \qquad (8.22)$$

Then once again the simplest possible specification is a linear additive expression of the form:

$$X_1 = a_1 + \beta_{12} X_2 + \beta_{13} X_3 + \beta_{14} X_4 \ldots + \beta_{1n} X_n + u_1 \qquad (8.23)$$

G

Standard multiple regression techniques permit estimation of the parameters of such models giving:

$$X_1 = a_1 + b_{12\cdot34} \ldots {}_nX_2 + b_{13\cdot24} \ldots {}_nX_3 \ldots + b_{1n\cdot23} \ldots {}_{(n-1)} X_n + u_1. \tag{8.24}$$

The value of $R^2_{1\cdot23} \ldots {}_n$ gives the proportion of variance of X_1 explained by $X_1, X_2 \ldots X_n$ and corresponding to each partial regression coefficient a partial product moment correlation coefficient can be estimated, e.g. $r_{12\cdot34} \ldots {}_n$.

The logic of a model of this sort is very close to that introduced in Chapter 6. In causal terms, each explanatory variable is *sufficient* to produce effects in the explained variable independently of the other explanatory variables. It depicts an *over-determined situation*.

Just as we encountered interaction effects for the three-variable model, so more complex interaction situations can occur in multivariate functions. Consider, for example, the function $X_1 = f(X_2, X_3, X_4, u_1)$. An extreme case of interaction would be a model of the form

$$X_1 = a_1 + I X_2 X_3 X_4 + u_1 \tag{8.25}$$

where all three explanatory variables interact in their effect on X_1. It is also possible to have direct effects and an indirect interaction effect leading to the model

$$X_1 = a_1 + \beta_{12} X_2 + \beta_{13} X_3 + B_{14} X_4 + I_{234} (X_2 X_3 X_4) + u_1. \tag{8.26}$$

The most general model involving both direct and interaction effects has the form

$$X_1 = a_1 + \beta_{12} X_2 + \beta_{13} X_3 + \beta_{14} X_4 + I_{23} X_2 X_3 + I_{24} X_4 + I_{34} X_3 X_4 + I_{234} X_2 X_3 X_4 + u_1 \tag{8.27}$$

with three *first order* interactions between pairs of explanatory variables and one *second order* interaction between all three.

Given a large set of explanatory variables, there are clearly very many models available. And, in the absence of *a priori* theoretical or empirical reasons to favour one particular model rather than another, many models have often to be tested against the data. Given the speed of the modern computer, this is not as laborious as it might sound.

The many variable additive model may be non-linear in some or all of its explanatory variables.

$$X_1 = a_1 + \beta_{12} X_1^m + \beta_{13} X_2^n \ldots + \beta_{1n} X_n^t + u_1 \quad (8.28)$$

where m, n and t are constants.

Fitting many non-linear terms in a multivariate model is messy but initial inspection of scatter diagrams often gives clues. In the absence of this, one normally tries the second power first, which has the intellectual rationale of *self-interaction*.

We are now in a position to formulate a general model of sociological covariance corresponding to the basic conception of causality introduced in Chapter 6.

Each major explanatory variable will have a set of interaction conditions attached to it. So we obtain

$$X_1 = a_1 + \beta_{12} (X_2 \, C_1 \, C_2 \ldots) + \beta_{13} (X_3 \, D_1 \, D_2 \ldots) \ldots + \\ \beta_{1n} (X_n \, Z_1 \, Z_2 \ldots) + u_1 \quad (8.29)$$

where $(C_1 \, C_2 \ldots)$, $(D_1 \, D_2 \ldots)$ and $(Z_1 \, Z_2 \ldots)$ are multiplicative interaction variables.

An expression of this form is extremely complex and usually the sets of interaction variables are not brought explicitly into the model; they are the conditions that intensionally define the population to which the model pertains. They are the initial conditions under which the explanatory variables $X_2, X_3, \ldots X_n$ are related to X_1. In practice they are often regarded as dichotomous variables. It is important to recognise how a failure to specify interaction conditions can lead to faulty conclusions. Let us assume that variables X_1, X_2 and C are related as follows

$$X_1 = a_1 + \beta_{12} X_2 \, C + \mu_1 \quad (8.30)$$

where C is a dichotomous variable and X_1 and X_2 are continuous. If it is not known that C enters the equation in this way, one may regress X_1 onto X_2 when some of the cases are Cs and some are not. The results may lead us to conclude that there is a very low relationship or no relationship between X_1 and X_2. But if the role of C is explicitly recognised, and X_1 regressed onto X_2, only for those cases that are Cs, then a significant relationship will emerge. It is not difficult to appreciate the likelihood of errors of this sort arising in complex multivariate models with many interaction variables in each term. The uncritical use of regression analysis without careful theoretical thought and much testing of alternative models can only lead to superficial and faulty conclusions. However, there are now emerging automatic interaction-seeking computer programs which promise to be extremely valuable in the future (Sanquist and Morgan, 1969).

8.10 The Assumptions of Regression Models
At this stage it is worth reviewing the limiting assumptions upon which ordinary least squares estimates are based. These are technical statistical matters and the intention here is only to alert the reader to the problems. For a full statistical consideration see, for instance, Malinvaud (1966) and Johnston (1963).

Measurement Error in the Variables The ordinary least squares technique can accommodate *random* measurement errors in the explained variable since they automatically merge with the disturbance term. In general, they will increase the spread around the regression line (plane) and thus attenuate the correlation coefficient (r), but the value of the regression coefficient (b) will not be affected. This is one argument for placing more reliance on regression coefficients rather than correlation coefficients (see Section 8.13). It is nevertheless important to realise that regression coefficients are only invariant to *random* measurement error in the explained variable. If the error is *non-random* then the coefficient will be affected. Sociological variables based upon verbal testament are often subject to non-random error, if the variable in question is subject to negative evaluation; as the objective value of the variable increases then there is a systematic increasing tendency to understate its value. This will tend to decrease the value of the regression coefficient. A constant source of error (one acting in an identical manner for all values of the explained variable) will not affect the slope of the regression line but will alter the value of the intercept term (*a*), pushing its value up or down depending on the direction of the error. Non-random measurement errors, if present, normally have to be dealt with *ad hoc*. If there are reasons for believing that high values of the variable have been under-reported and the slope of the relationship under investigation is low, perhaps even zero, then it is possible that the error is masking a significant relationship. The reverse situation is also possible – non-random measurement error can generate a significant slope when there is no relationship between the variables under investigation. Blalock (1964) has developed a rather revealing way of looking at measurement errors in terms of causal models whereby both the true value and measurement error causally determine the observed value of the variable. If one can predict that the non-random measurement error in the explained variable will move the slope value in the opposite direction to that predicted in the theory, then it is obviously legitimate to claim, in the face of confirmatory results, that they would have been even stronger without the errors.

Turning now to measurement error in the explanatory variables. Errors of this sort (random and non-random) will set up a relationship between the disturbance term and the variable in question, thus invalidating one of the major assumptions of the ordinary least squares model.[12] This will lead to:

(i) *biased* estimates of the slopes and intercept (i.e. the expected value of their sampling distributions are not equal to the parameter itself), and

(ii) the estimates will be *inconsistent* (i.e. the bias does not disappear as the sample size becomes infinitely large).

Various estimation techniques for models with measurement error in the explanatory variable are available and the reader is referred to standard statistical texts (e.g. Johnston, 1963, Chapter 6).

Autocorrelation An assumption of the ordinary least squares estimation technique is that the disturbance terms are serially independent. When this is not the case the variables are said to be autocorrelated. Although autocorrelation does not bias the estimates of the slopes it does lead to large sampling variances and, since the so-called Generalised Least Squares technique leads to estimates with lower sampling variances, ordinary least squares technique is *inefficient*.

Furthermore it can be shown that, if the autocorrelation is positive, the ordinary least squares estimates of the sampling variances are underestimated; this has the effect of distorting the tests of significance and may make results appear significant when in fact they are not.

There are various techniques for detecting autocorrelation like the Durbin-Watson *d* statistic. But the important question for us is how can autocorrelation be interpreted – if we encounter it what should our strategy be as model builders? There are two major ways in which autocorrelation can occur:

(i) An important explanatory variable(s) which enters into the disturbance term in a systematic way, has been omitted from the model. So the variable must be included in the model.

(ii) The model has been wrongly specified; for example, if the actual relationship between the variables is quadratic and one attempts to fit a linear relationship then one obtains auto-correlated disturbances.

So in the presence of marked autocorrelation one should examine the specification of the model and also (where data permits) see if additional variables reduce it.

Homoscedasticity An assumption of the ordinary least squares technique is that the error term has a constant variance. If it has not, the phenomena is referred to as heteroscedasticity. Hetero-scedasticity leads to large sampling variances. A common form of this problem is where the variance of the disturbance tends to increase or decrease proportionally with the explanatory variable (the scatter diagram is V-shaped). This can be overcome by expressing the explained variable as a proportion of the corresponding explanatory variable and regressing this trans-formed variable onto the original explanatory variable.

Multicollinearity If any of the explanatory variables are

themselves intercorrelated then they are said to exhibit multi-collinearity. Consider the model

$$X_1 = a_1 + \beta_{12} X_2 + \beta_{13} X_3 + \mu_1. \qquad (8.31)$$

Then if X_2 and X_3 intercorrelate we have multicollinearity which gives rise to large sampling variances for the estimates of the coefficients. If X_2 and X_3 intercorrelate perfectly there will be no scatter in the X_2/X_3 plane and the sampling variances become infinite.

It is instructive to see how perfect intercorrelation of two explanatory variables leads to complete indeterminacy of the regression coefficients. A perfect correlation may be taken to imply a perfect linear relationship between the explanatory variables of the form

$$X_2 = a' + \beta'_{21} X_3. \qquad (8.32)$$

Now (8.32) can be multiplied by any constant and added to (8.30) giving an expression that is mathematically equivalent to (8.30). This means that technically (8.30) is not *identifiable* (see next section).

Multicollinearity is pervasive in sociology; it is more often than not the case that explanatory variables are intercorrelated, often very highly. Since this introduces large sampling variances it becomes difficult to test hypotheses.

The operationalist approach to T-concepts introduced in an earlier chapter is, in effect, a way of getting around the problem of multicollinearity. An index is created out of many explanatory variables that exhibit high intercorrelations and the explained variable is then regressed onto the index. It is revealing to note how this practice relates to the problem of multicollinearity. When an index is constructed out of two potential explanatory variables such that they have 'equal weight' in the index, then this is the same as saying that they have equal effects on a given explained variable. In other words, one is implicitly equating the value of the two regression coefficients,[13] which can be construed as additional information for the regression model. So in one sense constructing indices does not circumnavigate the problem of multicollinearity for in deriving the index we must make *a priori* assumptions about the relative weightings of the variables (indicators) in the index. And this is entirely equivalent to making additional assumptions about the regression model.

It might be useful, therefore, to view index construction as a specific approach to the problem of multicollinearity. Curtis and Jackson (1963) have suggested that there are advantages in keeping individual indicators of a variable separate rather than combining them into an index. Measurement error is not likely to affect all indicators in the same way and therefore if all the separate indicators exhibit the same pattern of relationship with an explained variable, we can be more confident that the relationship is not a mere artefact of any measurement error.

8.11 Simultaneous Equation Cardinal Models

So far we have restricted our attention to situations where the model contains only *one* explained variable. It usually requires many explanatory variables to explain the variance in the one variable, but we now turn to more complicated situations where the distinction between the explained and explanatory variable is not clear cut.

Models of this sort are most easily introduced by considering the general multivariate functional model (8.2). If the functions in the model are all specified in a linear additive form, then the following *complete simultaneous linear additive system* is obtained:

$$X_1 = a_1 + \beta_{12} X_2 + \ldots + \beta_{1n} X_n + u_1$$
$$X_2 = a_2 + \beta_{21} X_1 + \ldots + \beta_{2n} X_n + u_2$$
$$\vdots \qquad\qquad\qquad\qquad\qquad (8.33)$$
$$X_n = a_n + \beta_{n1} X_1 + \ldots + \beta_{n(n-1)} X_{(n-1)} + u_n.$$

A system of this sort, as we shall see, is not of much use since, on the basis of observations on the n variables, the parameters of the system cannot be determined – technically they are not identifiable. This is an important observation, as sociologists are in the habit of speaking of systems where 'everything affects everything else'. But such systems are technically of little use; to enable them to be studied they must be embedded in a further set of determining variables which do not exhibit a pattern of mutual dependence.

Thus a more general set of simultaneous equations is analytically more useful. If it is allowed that not all the variables are simultaneously determined, then the distinction can be drawn between:

(a) *endogenous variables* – those variables whose values are determined within the model, and

(b) *exogenous variables* – those variables whose values are determined outside the model.

By convention the exogenous variables are designated Z_t. Then any explained (endogenous) variable is, in general, a function of some exogenous variables and some endogenous variables. So if the model is specified as linear and additive the following system of equation is obtained:

$$X_1 = a_1 + \beta_{12} X_2 + \ldots + \beta_{1n} X_n + [\gamma_{11} Z_1 + \ldots + \gamma_{1m} Z_m]$$
$$+ u_1$$
$$X_2 = a_2 + \beta_{21} X_1 + \ldots + \beta_{2n} X_n + [\gamma_{21} Z_1 + \ldots + \gamma_{2m} Z_m]$$
$$+ u_2$$
$$\cdot$$
$$\cdot \quad (8.34)$$
$$\cdot$$
$$X_n = a_n + \beta_{n1} X_n + \ldots + \beta_{n(n-1)} X_{n-1} + [\gamma_{n1} Z_1 + \ldots$$
$$\gamma_{nm} Z_m] + u_n$$

where x_t, $i = 1,2, \ldots n$ are the endogenous variables and Z_t, $i = 1,2, \ldots m$ are the exogenous variables.

Such a system is more conveniently expressed in matrix notation as:

$$BX + TZ = u \quad (8.35)$$

where B is an $n \times n$ matrix of coefficients of endogenous variables.

T is an $n \times m$ matrix of coefficients of exogenous variables, and X, Z and u are column vectors of n, m and n elements respectively. It must be emphasised that system (8.35) is regarded as comprising a set of simultaneous equations. Technically, there are two major problems with systems of equations of this sort.

(i) *The problem of identification*: Can the parameters of the system be uniquely determined from joint observations on the X and Z variables?[14]

(ii) *The problem of estimation*: Can unbiased estimates of the parameters be obtained? In particular, are the assumptions for least squares estimates likely to be met?

As there are many excellent introductory statistics texts on these problems (Johnston, 1963, Malinvaud, 1966), we will only consider them briefly. Identification is logically prior to estimation since one must make sure a model is identifiable before it is meaningful to search for an estimation technique. If a model is not identifiable then the parameters cannot be estimated.

Identification For any one equation in a system of linear equations to be identifiable, it is a *necessary condition* that the number of linear restrictions on the coefficients to be at least equal to the number of endogenous variables minus one in the system (i.e. $(n–1)$). The *sufficient condition* for identification is that at least one determinant of order $(n–1)$ can be defined from the columns of the matrix of the coefficients corresponding to the variables that have been *excluded* from the equation. In practice, the sufficient conditions are usually met when the necessary ones are met, so we concentrate upon the latter.

Identification of a system of linear equations can be effected in terms of restrictions on either:
  (i) the β coefficients (B matrix)
  (ii) the γ coefficients (T matrix), or
  (iii) the variance-covariance matrix of the disturbance terms.

The normal procedure is to set some β and/or γ parameters equal to zero ('zero restrictions'). We could, of course, set them at some predetermined value (one that is theoretically fixed), but in sociology it is extremely rare that this can be accomplished; theoretical sociology rarely, if ever, gives us reason to fix the values of parameters. As sociological model building becomes a cumulative enterprise, it might happen that the value of coefficients can be fixed on the basis of previous research, but at the moment we have to remain content with setting parameter values at zero. Another possibility is to assume that two or more coefficients are equal. But, again, we rarely have theoretical reasons for doing this. The most common form of restriction, on the variance-covariance matrix, is the assumption that the covariances of the disturbance terms are zero. This condition is sufficient to make recursive systems (see below) identifiable.

It has been emphasised that any system of equations must be tested for identifiability before any considerations about estimation can be made. It is only meaningful to make estimates of parameters in identifiable systems. If some theoretical ideas suggest a model in which all the equations are not identifiable then the system can be rendered identifiable by one of two strategies. Either some endogenous variable can be left out of certain equations (the appropriate β coefficient set at zero) or some additional exogenous variables must be brought *into the system* so that the number of variables excluded from a given unidentifiable equation is equal to $(n-1)$.

This, of course, introduces a statistical artefact into model building; for it appears that a linear system can always be *rendered* identifiable by suitably elaborating the set of exogenous variables. This is both helpful and embarrassing. It is helpful where interest is centred upon a particular system of endogenous variables for which there are good theoretical reasons for studying; we can then search around for variables exogenous to the system. But this should not be carried on completely indiscriminately, there should normally be some additional theoretical reason for bringing them into the model. The embarrassment arises since there are no restrictions on this search process at all; it allows altogether too much flexibility. So caution must be exercised.

Let us take an example; suppose we are interested in the interrelationship between the three variables:

$$X_1 = \text{group cohesion}$$
$$X_2 = \text{inter-group conflict}$$
and $\quad\quad X_3 = \text{intra-group conflict}$

and the following model holds theoretical interest:

$$
\begin{aligned}
X_1 &= a_1 + \beta_{12} X_2 - \beta_{13} X_3 + u_1 \\
X_2 &= a_2 + \beta_{21} X_1 \quad\quad\quad\; + u_2 \quad\quad (8.36)\\
X_3 &= a_3 - \beta_{31} X_1 \quad\quad\quad\; + u_3.
\end{aligned}
$$

So all three variables are endogenous to the system, and there are no exogenous variables at all. In the absence of any restrictions on the covariances of the disturbance terms, none of the equations is identifiable. *So as it stands, the theory is no use.* If, however, the following exogenous variables are also considered:

$Z_1 = $ presence of external enemies

$Z_2 = $ presence of specific authority structures in the group,

and added to the system in the following manner:

$$
\begin{aligned}
X_1 &= a_1 + \beta_{12} X_2 - \beta_{13} X_3 + u_1 \\
X_2 &= a_2 + \beta_{21} X_1 - \gamma_{21} Z_1 + u_2 \quad\quad (8.37)\\
X_3 &= a_3 - \beta_{31} X_1 - \gamma_{31} Z_2 + u_3
\end{aligned}
$$

then this system can be re-written rather more generally as:

$$
\begin{aligned}
X_1 &= a_1 + \beta_{12} X_2 - \beta_{13} X_3 + 0Z_1 + 0Z_2 + u_1 \\
X_2 &= a_2 + \beta_{21} X_1 + 0_1 X_3 + \gamma_{21} Z_1 + 0Z_2 + u_2 \quad (8.38)\\
X_3 &= a_3 + \beta_{31} X_1 + 0X_2 + 0Z_1 + \gamma_{32} Z_2 + u_3.
\end{aligned}
$$

The number of endogenous variables is three. So each equation in 8.37 is identifiable, since the number of linear restrictions (zero parameter values) is two in each equation.

When constructing models it is helpful to set up a coefficient Table like the one in Figure 8.7 where each equation can be checked for identifiability. The number of zeros in each row of this table must be *at least* equal to the number of rows in the table minus one. The final column being used to check-off whether each equation is or is not identifiable.

Figure 8.7 A Table for Detecting Identification

Equation	X_1	X_2	X_3	Z_1	Z_2	Identification
1	1	1	1	0	0	✓
2	1	1	0	1	0	✓
3	1	0	1	0	1	✓

A particular type of system of simultaneous linear equations which has special relevance to causal modelling, and therefore calls for special comment, is a so-called *recursive system*. A linear recursive system has the following general form:

$$X_1 = u_1$$
$$X_2 = a_2 + \beta_{21} X_1 + u_2$$
$$X_3 = a_3 + \beta_{31} X_1 + \beta_{32} X_2 + u_2$$
$$X_4 = a_4 + \beta_{41} X_1 + \beta_{42} X_2 + \beta_{43} X_3 + u_3 \qquad (8.39)$$
$$\cdot$$
$$\cdot$$
$$\cdot$$
$$X_n = a_n + \beta_{n1} X_1 + \ldots + \beta_{n(n-1)} X_{(n-1)} + u_n.$$

X_1 is exogenous to this system as its value is only determined by u_1 not by any other variables in the system. The coefficient table for a recursive system of four variables is depicted in Figure 8.8.

In matrix terminology the β matrix has a lower triangular form. But note, since the number of endogenous variables in the system is three,[15] equations 3 and 4 are *not* identifiable. However, if the assumption is made that the disturbance terms in all the equations do not covary, i.e. in general Cov $(u_i u_j) = 0$ then recursive systems are identifiable[16] and furthermore, as we shall

Figure 8.8 The Coefficient Table for a Four-Variable Recursive Model

Equation	X_1	X_2	X_3	X_4	Identification
1	1	0	0	0	✓
2	1	1	0	0	✓
3	1	1	1	0	✗
4	1	1	1	1	✗

see in the next section, simple least squares estimation techniques can be applied to each equation separately.

Estimation Consider the system of equations (8.40)

$$X_1 = a_1 + \beta_{12} X_2 + \gamma_{11} Z_1 + u_1$$
$$X_2 = a_2 + \beta_{21} X_1 + \gamma_{22} Z_2 + u_2. \tag{8.40}$$

Both equations are identifiable so the next question is how can their parameters be estimated? In particular, can ordinary least squares estimates be utilised?

If the first equation is substituted in the second we obtain

$$X_2 = a_1 + \beta_{21} (a_1 + \beta_{12} X_2 + \gamma_{11} Z + u_1) + \gamma_{22} Z_2 + u_2. \tag{8.41}$$

So X_2 is a function of u_1. Thus in the first equation of (8.40) the explanatory variable and disturbance term are correlated and consequently least squares estimates of the a and β coefficients will not be unbiased nor consistent. If bias is not particularly troublesome then least squares techniques can be used. But if not, different methods must be used. We will not pursue these here however as they are well reviewed elsewhere (Johnston, 1963, Malinvaud, 1966), but the reader should note that straightforward least squares estimates are not usually applicable with simultaneous equation models.

Ordinary least squares estimates can be used with recursive systems (assuming Cov $(u_i\, u_j) = 0$), as the explanatory variables are *not* correlated with the disturbance terms. A substitution of one equation into another along the above lines does not set up a dependency between the explanatory variable and the disturbance term. This follows, of course, from the structure of the system; variables *only* depend on variables appearing before them in the system.

It is instructive to set out the recursive system (8.39) in estimated form:

$$X_1 = \mu_1$$
$$X_2 = a_2 + b_{21} X_1 + \mu_2$$
$$X_3 = a_3 + b_{31\cdot2} X_1 + b_{32\cdot1} X_2 + \mu_3$$
$$X_4 = a_4 + b_{41\cdot23} X_1 + b_{42\cdot13} X_2 + b_{43\cdot12} + \mu_4 \qquad (8.42)$$
$$.$$
$$.$$
$$.$$
$$X_n = a_n + b_{n1\cdot23\,\cdots\,(n-1)} X_1 \cdots + b_{n(n-1)\,\cdot\,123\,\cdots\,(n-2)} X_{n-1}$$
$$+ u_n.$$

The coefficients then indicate the variables that are controlled. There is, of course, a partial correlation coefficient corresponding to each partial regression coefficient. These coefficients are of importance in causal modelling introduced in the next chapter.

8.12 Ordinal and Nominal Models

So far it has been explicitly assumed that all the variables entering into models are cardinal. But from what was said earlier it might be expected that such variables will be of relatively rare occurrence in sociology. One is much more likely to encounter the situation where nominal and ordinal variables are related. The appropriate joint distributions are then no longer depicted in graphical terms, but as contingency tables of one sort or another. The question naturally arises about the specification of functions when the variables are nominal and ordinal. Sociologists have not traditionally posed this question for they have not based their investigations on explicitly stated functions. Furthermore, usually only two or three variables have been considered at a time, but as we move towards complex multivariate models it is perhaps best even with nominal and ordinal variables to think in terms of functions and see whether any special problems arise.

Starting with the simplest case, how does one specify the function $X_1 = f(X_2, u_1)$ where X_1 and X_2 are simple dichotomies? The covariation of X_1 and X_2 is, of course, depicted by a simple 2×2 Table:

	$\widetilde{X}_2$	X_2	
X_1	a	b	$(a+b)$
$\widetilde{X}_1$	c	d	$(c+d)$
	$(a+c)$	$(b+d)$	N

Given a Table like this, there are many non-parametric techniques for measuring the association between X_1 and X_2 but their relative advantages and disadvantages will not be pursued here. The interested reader is referred to Galtung (1967). If it is recalled that a function is a mapping rule enabling one to compute values of an explained variable given the value of the explanatory variable, then in a 2×2 Table, where X_2 is taken as the explanatory variable, the mapping rule is normally of a stochastic nature; we cannot predict the category of X_1 knowing the category of X_2 (unless there is a perfect correlation) but we can think in terms of conditional probabilities of a unit of analysis being an X_1 given it is an X_2 or an $\widetilde{X}_2$. Such an emphasis would naturally lead us to concentrate upon the difference of proportions (i.e. difference in conditional probabilities) as a mapping rule or function relating X_1 and X_2. The difference in proportion for the above 2×2 Table is given by

$$d_{12} = \frac{b}{b+d} - \frac{a}{a+c}. \qquad (8.43)$$

Furthermore, if X_1 and X_2 are scored such that $X_1 = X_2 = 1$ and $\tilde{X}_1 = \tilde{X}_2 = 0$, d_{12} is entirely analogous to the regression coefficient of X_1 onto X_2. It can also be shown that

$$\phi = \sqrt{\frac{\chi^2}{N}} \qquad (8.44)$$

is equivalent to the product moment correlation coefficient.[17] Concentrating upon the difference in proportions parameters is thus consonant with our earlier plea (Chapter 6, p. 113) for the study of trends in contingency problems. It has become the established practice in sociological investigation, however, to concentrate upon measures of association between nominal and ordinal variables. This is because the idea of form has no simple meaning when we use such variables. But it would perhaps be useful if we started to think in terms of the trends in relationships – even if only in an approximate way. In many cases, we only adopt nominal and ordinal variables because of poor measuring techniques, believing there to be an underlying cardinal scale. So in this case, we are making an approximate effort to establish a relationship which underneath will definitely have some particular form.

Since there is a direct analogy between using traditional measures like proportional difference to estimate the relationship between dichotomous variables and *dummy regression*,[18] it is natural to search for similar techniques where more than one explanatory variable is involved in the model. The most severe limitation of traditional non-parametric techniques is that there is normally no way of deciding whether additional variables are required and actually bringing them into the model. In dummy regression, the value of R^2 gives us some idea of whether additional variables are required and, by basing the analysis on an explicitly formulated mathematic function, other variables can be brought in a systematic manner.

Consider the function $X_1 = f(X_2, X_3, u)$ where X_1, X_2 and X_3 are all still dichotomous.

In non-parametric terms the model may be depicted as a

dichotomous cube which can be broken down into the following
partial contingency Tables:

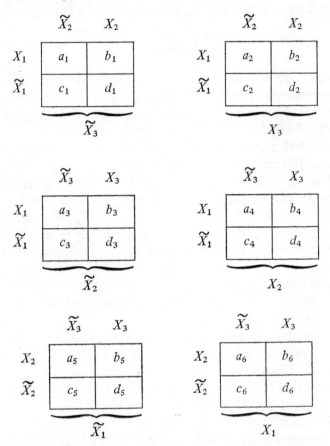

Difference of proportion parameters and measures of association
can be computed for each Table. For instance, the top left-hand
Table would give

$$d_{12 \cdot \bar{3}} = \frac{b_1}{c_1 + d_1} - \frac{a_1}{a_1 + c_1} \qquad (8.45)$$

$$\phi_{12 \cdot \bar{3}} = \sqrt{\frac{X^2}{a_1 + b_1 + c_1 + d_1}}.$$

It should be noted that $d_{12.\bar{3}}$ is the difference of proportions for the relationship between X_1 and X_2 for the cases which are not X_3, and similarly $d_{12.3}$ is the difference of proportions for the relationship between X_1 and X_2 for the cases which are X_3. Supposing our interest centres on the explicit function $X_1 = f(X_2, X_3, u)$, then the first problem of specification is how X_2 and X_3 combine in their effect upon X_1. If their effect is 'additive' then the shape of the relationship between X_1 and X_2 should be the same for both values of X_3. In other words, the value of $d_{12.3}$ should not be significantly different from $d_{12.\bar{3}}$. If, however, X_2 and X_3 interact in their effect upon X_1 then $d_{12.3}$ should be significantly different from $d_{12.\bar{3}}$. Looking at a three-variable function in this manner does, therefore, enable us to detect 'interaction' and 'additive' effects of two explanatory variables on a given explained variable. And this has traditionally been seen as one of the major advantages of non-parametric contingency techniques. Analysts have been able to break down tables according to third and fourth variables and 'get a feel' for the relationships. The familiar techniques of elaboration developed by Lazarsfeld and his school are based upon these ideas.

However, the dichotomous cube can also be treated directly as a multivariate dummy regression problem. The simplest model is the additive one given by the expression

$$X_1 = a + \beta_{12} X_2 + \beta_{13} X_3 + \beta_{14} X_4 + u_1 \qquad (8.46)$$

where the variables take on the values one or zero. The normal regression techniques may be applied and estimates of a and β coefficients accomplished.[19] The value of $R^2_{1.23}$ will give an estimate of statistical completion of the model. Furthermore, interaction terms could also be added to this model without difficulty along the lines indicated in Section 8.9.

The question naturally therefore arises as to which techniques are the 'best' – the traditional contingency analyses or dummy regression analyses. There is perhaps no simple all-embracing answer to this question and in cases of real doubt both should be pursued and the results compared. The dummy regression technique does have the very real advantage that parameter estimation is based on all the units of analysis and thus, in many variable problems, 'running out of cases' does not become as acute a problem as with the traditional approach. If we start breaking down a contingency table according to a third and then a fourth variable the entries in the cells rapidly dwindle. For instance, $d_{12\cdot3}$ is based upon only those units that are X_3 and $d_{12\cdot\bar{3}}$ only those that are not X_3. The least squares estimator of β_{12}, $d_{12\cdot3}$ is based upon all the cases and is in fact a weighted mean of the two previous parameters.

On the other hand, traditional techniques are in some ways more flexible; if $d_{12\cdot3} = d_{12\cdot\bar{3}}$ then we have interaction which can be discovered! However, with regression techniques a prior commitment must be made to a model involving an interaction term. But this is not as inconvenient as might be anticipated. Firstly, the computer enables us to adopt many different models and compute the parameters of each quickly and inexpensively. Secondly, contingency techniques can be used as an exploratory device to suggest models that can then be set up as regression models. So this author believes that much greater emphasis should be placed on dummy regression techniques. (For an alternative view, see Galtung, 1967.) Even when the variables entering a model are dichotomous, it is advisable initially to set out the model in functional form and then to specify the function in the same manner as for cardinal variables. Different models can, of course, be compared and the value of the multiple correlation coefficient will give an indication of the statistical completion of the 'explanation'.

So far we have confined attention to dichotomous variables; a rather more troublesome situation is where the nominal variables concerned are polytomies rather than dichotomies. Following Suits (1957), consider first of all a simple two-variable model $X_1 = f(X_2, u)$, where X_2 has three categories R_1, R_2 and R_3; X_1 may be dichotomous or cardinal. Then one can construct three vectors with entries of 1 and 0 corresponding to each category of X_2. But since R_1, R_2 and R_3 are categories of the same variable, if any element of the vector R_i $(i = 1, 2, 3)$ is 1 then the corresponding components of the two other vectors will be zero. So, if we adopt the model,

$$X_1 = a + \beta_{11} R_1 + \beta_{12} R_2 + \beta_{13} R_3 + u_1 \qquad (8.47)$$

then, in general, the a and β coefficients will be unidentifiable, since it is entirely analogous to the problem of perfect multi-collinearity. To obtain determinate estimates of the parameters some additional constraint must be imposed on the model. There are two possibilities: firstly one can set a equal to 0 or secondly the value of one of the β coefficients can be set at zero[20]. The former technique is perhaps the most useful. Dummy regression techniques can thus be used when the explanatory variable is nominal, with many categories.

If there are more than two explanatory variables in the model so that we have t nominal variables where the ith variable contains k_i mutually exclusive classes, then t sets of dummy variables R_{ij} $(i = 1, 2, \ldots t; j = 1, 2 \ldots k_i)$ can be defined. $R_{ij} = 1$ if the unit of analysis belongs to the jth class of the ith variable, otherwise $R_{ij} = 0$. Then the general linear additive model is

$$X_1 = a_1 + \sum_{i=1}^{i=t} \sum_{j=1}^{j=k_i} \beta_{ij} R_{ij} + u_1. \qquad (8.48)$$

Once again, constraints have to be made to render the parameters determinate. Suits suggests that this is most easily accomplished by dropping out one dummy variable from each nominal variable. It should also be possible to treat the explained variable in a similar manner so that each successive pair of adjacent categories of the variable is treated as a dummy variable.[21]

It appears, therefore, that nominal variables can be handled within the general framework of multiple regression. The next question is whether ordinal variables can be likewise included in this framework.

It will be recalled that with ordinal variables we can determine a ranking of the categories of the variable but know nothing of the distance between them. There are two ways of treating ordinal variables in the context of multiple regression.

(i) By ascribing numerical values to the categories.

(ii) By breaking the variable down into dummy variables in the same manner as for nominal variables.

When numerical values are ascribed to the categories of an ordinal variable, the assumption is made that the distance property of the numbers has meaning, and when they are translated into dummy variables the assumption is that the 'distance' between all adjacent categories is identical.

Let us first of all consider what sort of distortions can be introduced by ascribing numerical values to an ordinal scale. The typical case might be where we have a scale categorised as zero, very low, medium, high and very high, and these are scored 0, 1, 2, 3, 4 and 5 respectively. The first point to note is that different scorings can be adopted to try and reflect different types of *trend*. If a 'non-linear' trend is suspected then the categories may be scored appropriately. Different ascriptions of numbers can be compared and *ceteris paribus* the model giving the highest value of R^2 adopted.

But it is convenient to distinguish between two situations:

(i) where it is believed that there is a genuine underlying cardinal variable which, because of the crudity of our measuring technique, cannot be directly measured, and

(ii) where no assumptions can be made about underlying cardinality.

In the former situation we can view the measurement of the variable as a mapping rule from an *unknown* underlying variable to a set of category scores. If this rule were uniform then this is entirely equivalent to changing the units of measurement of the variable in question (e.g. converting yards to feet). But of course, since the underlying scale is not known, we cannot tell whether this is the case or not. In general, however, we might expect the mapping rule to be highly irregular – 'expanding' and 'contracting' different segments of the true scale. Although the nature of the mapping rule cannot, in principle, be established it is useful to consider what types of distortion are likely to be introduced in practice, and see how these produce distortions in the value of the regression coefficient.

We can approach the problem by asking two major questions; firstly, does the mapping rule increase or decrease the overall *range* of the scale? Secondly, what is the distribution of the 'condensations' and 'expansions' of the scale?

Let us start by assuming there are no distortions (or they are randomly distributed with respect to the true scale) in an ordinal explanatory variable. Then if the mapping increases the range of the scale it will decrease the slope of the curve and if it decreases the range it will increase the slope of the curve. If the variable in question is the explained one, increasing the range of the scale will increase the slope and vice versa.

In sociological contexts it is typically the case that the range of scales is reduced by ordering categorisation and we must anticipate differing effects on the slopes depending on whether the variable is the explained or the explanatory one. If both variables are ordinal and the induced increase or decrease in range is approximately the same for each variable, this will have little effect on the slope.

Turning now to distortions due to irregular condensation and expansion of the scale, let us assume that the overall range of the scale is not altered. The 'top' and 'bottom' of the measured scale correspond reasonably well with the true values. If the distortions are randomly distributed with respect to the true values of the variables then this will have no effect on the slope of the curve. This is the case for both explained and explanatory variables. The distortions will, however, usually increase the scatter around the curve and consequently attenuate the correlation coefficient.[22]

If the distortions bear a systematic relationship to the true values then the problem is not so straightforward. The slope of the curve will depend upon the location and type of distortion. Ordered metric variables are of obvious importance in this context. If the rank correlation between the ranking of the categories and the ranking of the first differences is low then this means that the 'distances' between categories are approximately randomly distributed with respect to the variable. If this is the case, we are perhaps on fairly safe ground in numerically scoring the ordinal variable.

If there is no question of an underlying cardinal variable then the idea of distortion of a true scale drops away and the way in which numbers are ascribed to the categories is entirely arbitrary. It is in situations like this that non-parametric techniques are traditionally at a premium. But this author believes that in complex multivariate models parametric techniques are still useful. After all, as long as the method whereby the ordinal categories are generated are clear and reproducible then, despite the inapplicability of the full assumptions of parametric models, little harm can be done in trying them out – where possible in parallel with non-parametric techniques. Parametric tests of significance on the derived parameters are not strictly applicable but, as long as the problems are recognised, there is perhaps more advantage in their use than disadvantage.

The reduction of ordinal variables to a series of dummy variables has the advantage that 'non-linear' trends can be *detected*. If the slopes of the regression lines on different dummy categories are significantly different then this is indicative of non-linear trends (assuming equal intervals between adjacent categories).

In conclusion, then, it appears that, with caution and a certain amount of creative activity, regression techniques can be extended to ordinal systems of variables. Though one must ever be aware of possible distortions, the use of non-cardinal variables in regression models is very much an open area of research.

8.13 Form, Strength of Relationship and Significance

It was noted in Chapter 6 that it is important, when studying patterns of covariation, to distinguish between the form of the relationship, the strength of the relationship, and the statistical significance of the parameters measuring these. To make these points clear, let us assume, for the moment, that we can obtain cardinal measures of the two variables X_1 and X_2 and establish a linear covariation between them represented by the familiar equation:

$$X_1 = a_1 + \beta_{12} X_2 + u_1. \tag{8.49}$$

And suppose least squares estimates of the slope (b_{12}), intercept (a_1) and the product moment correlation coefficient (r_{12}) are made.

Tests of significance (student t or F distributions) can, under appropriate assumptions, be attached to the estimates a_1 and b_{12}. It is normal to ask whether or not they depart significantly from zero. So we can establish, at a given probability level, our confidence that these parameters do or do not depart from zero. Of course, if we have *a priori* theoretical reasons to suppose either a_1 or b_{12} have particular values other than zero, we could use the tests of significance to compare a_1 and b_{12} with these values. In this case the appropriate question is not whether the estimated value departs significantly from the theoretical value but whether it is sufficiently close to it to enable us to place faith in the estimate. In sociology, however, this rarely happens – sociological theory does not normally dictate the values of parameters, all it says, is that X_1 and X_2 are related.

The value of r_{12} fixes the *strength of the relationship* between X_1 and X_2, the spread of the scatter around the regression line. The Z distribution can be used to test the significance of the value of r_{12}. Again it is usual to ask whether or not its value departs significantly from zero. It is important to establish the correct interpretations of this parameter and its test of significance. The test of significance on r_{12} gives a measure of our confidence in the strength of a relationship. The same value of r_{12} with a larger sample size will give us greater confidence than with a smaller sample size. *A very high value of* r_{12} *can be obtained but little confidence can be placed in it because of the small sample size.* It is, therefore, not strictly correct to speak of high, medium or low correlations without going on to ask the questions about significance of the value given a particular sample. In model building it is absolutely essential to use correlation measures in conjunction with their appropriate tests of significance.

We have, then, with the simple bivariate linear model, four types of parameters at our disposal:

   (i) measures of *form* a_1 and b_{12}
   (ii) tests of significance for a_1 and b_{12}
   (iii) a measure of the *strength of the relationship* r_{12}
   (iv) tests of significance for r_{12}.

The question as to their relative importance in model building naturally arises. The value a_1 is not normally of particular interest and indeed it is often the accepted practice to study the covariation of variables measured from their means when the curve goes through the origin. So the important parameters are b_{12} and r_{12}. We can distinguish four distinct possibilities:

   (i) neither b_{12} nor r_{12} is significant
   (ii) both b_{12} and r_{12} are significant
   (iii) b_{12} is significant and r_{12} is not significant
   (iv) b_{12} is not significant and r_{12} is significant.

If neither b_{12} nor r_{12} is significantly different from zero then the variable X_2 is not *linearly* related in a significant manner to X_1. So we must either drop X_2 altogether or use a higher power (e.g. X^2) as an explanation of the variance of X_1. Note that by algebraic definition if $b_{12} = 0$, then $r_{12} = 0$ also.

If both b_{12} and r_{12} are significantly different from zero then we can say that there is a significant relationship between X_1 and X_2. The value of r^2_{12} will give the proportion of variance in X_1 'explained' by X_2. If r^2_{12} is high (say above 0·9) then there is only 10 per cent of variance left to be explained. We might search for additional variables to explain this additional variance but a r^2_{12} value of 0·9 is usually regarded as a very 'good' explanation indeed. If r^2_{12} is low (but still significant, remember), then X_2 only explains a small amount of the variance in X_1 and we would naturally search for *additional* (not alternative) variables to explain the additional variance in X_1.

If b_{12} is significantly different from zero and r_{12} is not, then there is a significant linear relationship between X_1 and X_2, but the amount of variance in X_1 explained by X_2 is small. In other words, there is much additional variance in X_1 to be explained, *so we must* search for additional variables to explain this variance.

If b_{12} is not significantly different from zero and r_{12} is, this means that there is very little variance in X_1 over the range of X_2 studied in the sample. The slope of the curve in the X_1, X_2 space is almost horizontal, but the scatter around this line only very slight (remember if $b_{12} = 0$ then $r_{12} = 3$.

In multivariate models there are three types of parameter to concentrate upon, the partial bs and rs and R^2. Broadly speaking the overall aim of model building is to maximise R^2 with a minimum number of significant partial bs.

Since in the simple linear model relating two variables we have both b and r values to concentrate upon, the question arises as to which is the most important. We noted in an earlier chapter that sociologists have traditionally concentrated upon correlation measures. This is largely because sociological variables are characteristically not cardinal and the idea of functional form has consequently played a small role in most investigations. But we have argued that these concepts can be extended to lower levels of measurement and so the problem still arises.

Figure 8.9 indicates some of the relative advantages and disadvantages of b and r coefficients.

These issues have been studied in detail by Blalock (1964) so we will only give them a cursory review here.

The value of b will obviously depend on the measurement units of both X_1 and X_2. The slope of the curve can be altered by altering these units. But the value of r will not be so affected – the scatter around the regression line will be the same whatever the units of measurement. This property of the b coefficient is, however, not particularly detrimental as long as we recognise it. A low b value can always be increased by reducing the size of the measurement units in the explanatory variable and/or increasing

Figure 8.9 Analytical Advantages of Regression and Correlation Coefficients

	Regression coefficients	Correlation coefficients
Measurement units	value of b dependent on measurement units of X_1 and X_2	value of r not dependent on measurement units of X_1 and X_2
Variation in explained variable	value of b does not depend on variation in explained variable	value of r does depend on variation in explained variable
Variation in explanatory variable	value of b does not depend on the variation in the explanatory variable	value of r does depend on variation in the explanatory variable
Measurement error in the explained variable	value of b not affected	value of r attenuated

their size in the explained variable. Since regression coefficients depend upon the units of measurement, it is impossible to directly compare two coefficients for different variables if they are differently measured. So it is difficult to get comparative estimates of the effects of explanatory (causal) variables on a given explained variable. If, however, variables are standardised, by dividing them by their standard deviations, and the standardised variables are regressed, we obtain *standardised regression coefficients* which do enable direct comparisons of effects to be made. Standardised regression coefficients have become commonly used in causal analysis where comparative causal efficiency is sought. Standardised regression coefficients are, however, a function of the variances in the dependent and independent variables and thus have the disadvantages associated with correlation coefficients.

Turning to variation in the explained variable: the value of r in any particular investigation is dependent on this variation. For a given linear relationship and variation in the explanatory variable, the higher the variation in the explained variable the lower the value of r, and the lower the variation the higher the value of r. The value of b, however, is not affected in this way.

The slope of the regression line will be independent of the variation in the explained variable.

This clearly gives b coefficients an advantage over r coefficients in sociological analysis, for if we use r its value will be a function of the amount of variation we *happen* to obtain in the explained variable in our sample whereas the b value is invariant to this. This means r values may vary from sample to sample from the same population and from population to population with differing variation in the dependent variable.

Clearly one way in which we can introduce variation into the explained variable is by random measurement error. Such error does not involve special difficulties in least squares regression but the value of r will be affected by these errors whereas the b coefficients will not.

Turning finally to variation in the explanatory variable. Once again the b value is independent of its variation – the gradient of the curve is not affected by the amount of variation in the explanatory variable.

But, in general, for a given variation in the explained variable, the greater the variation in the explanatory variable, then the greater the proportion of variance in the explained variable will be accounted for. So r will increase with increasing variation in the explanatory variable. Algebraically this clearly follows from the expression

$$r_{12} = b_{12} \frac{s_2}{s_1} \tag{8.50}$$

where s_1 and s_2 are the standard deviations of X_1 and X_2 respectively. For a given value of b_{12} if s_2 is increased then r_{12} will increase. Standardised regression coefficients are likewise affected.

Since in taking samples we do not normally fix the variation in the explanatory variable, we might well expect different r values in different samples (even apart from sampling fluctuations) merely due to difference in variation in the explanatory variables. This is then a further argument for concentrating, in sociological analysis, on b values rather than values of r. In the next chapter therefore we will tend to emphasise b values rather than r values.

There is an important and related point concerning aggregation of units of analysis which was first systematically explored by Blalock (1964). If in an investigation the units of analysis are aggregated such that scores on individual units are replaced by mean scores for the aggregates then this will, in general, reduce the variation. If the aggregation reduces variation in both the explained and explanatory variable in proportional amounts then this will not alter the values of b or r. But if the variation of one or other of the variables is disproportionately altered as a consequence of aggregation then the values of r will be affected along the lines of the above argument. For further details the interested reader is referred to Blalock's book (1964).

9. Causal Models

9.1 Introduction

We will start this chapter by reminding the reader of some of the notational devices introduced in earlier chapters and will also establish some new ones.

1. X_2 X_1 X_2 causes X_1.

2. X_2 X_1

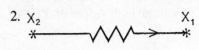

X_2 causes X_1 through a process of intervening variables. That is, we know the intervening variables 'exist' but for the purposes of the causal model (or as a consequence of inavailability of data) they are not made explicit; such a link provides a pivot for elaboration of a model. Of course, in one sense, all causal links can usually be further elaborated by specifying 'finer and finer' intervening variables. But the idea of this symbol is that, given the level of abstraction of the variables X_1 and X_2, those intervening variables that are missing must be inserted to make 'sociological sense'. For instance, if X_2 is 'status disequilibrium' and X_1 is 'political liberality', then there will be a series of intervening psychological 'strain' variables. If the causal link is considered in isolation these variables need not necessarily be specified. But if the causal link is embedded in a more elaborate causal structure where psychological variables appear elsewhere, then this form of link should be inserted if the strain variables are not also explicitly included. A causal link of this sort will, in general, consume time, so one will not necessarily observe equilibrium distributions of X_1 and X_2, for it will take time for X_1 to come to its appropriate equilibrium value after X_2 has changed its value.

3.

$$X_2 \quad\xrightarrow{\;+\;}\quad X_1$$

X_2 causes X_1 such that increases in X_2 lead to increases in X_1 and decreases in X_2 lead to decreases in X_1. *At aggregate equilibrium* high values of X_1 will be high values of X_2 and low values of X_1 will be low values of X_2. Cor $(AB) > 0$; $b_{12} > 0$.[1]

4.

$$X_2 \quad\xrightarrow{\;-\;}\quad X_1$$

X_2 causes X_1 such that increases in X_2 lead to decreases in X_1 and decreases in X_2 lead to increases in X_1. *At aggregate equilibrium* high values of X_1 will be low values of X_2 and low values of X_1 will be high values of X_2. Cor $(AB) < 0$; $b_{12} < 0$.

5.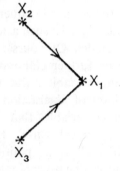

Either X_2 *or* X_3 causes X_1. Changes in X_2 or X_3 are *sufficient* to cause changes in X_1.

6.

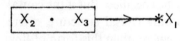

X_2 and X_3 together cause X_1. X_2 and X_3 *interact* in their effect on X_1. X_2 must be present for X_3 to cause X_1 and vice versa. X_2 and X_3 are jointly sufficient for X_1 and each is necessary to make this conjoin sufficient.[2]

7.

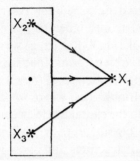

X_2 and X_3 have a direct causal effect on X_1 and an *interaction* causal effect. The direct effect is such that changes in X_2 or X_3 are sufficient for changes in X_1. The interaction effect is the same as in 6 above.

These are the basic constituents of complex causal structures. It remains to show what they correspond to in terms of models of covariation of the variables concerned. We will start with the simplest two-variable model, then move onto the three-variable model and finally, consider, very briefly, some multivariate models.

It is worth reminding ourselves at this juncture of the quasi-deductive nature of model building. We adopt a model which characteristically will have some definite implications (normally that certain coefficients will and will not be significantly different from zero), and these are tested against the data. So in causal model building there are three main steps.

(1) The adoption of a causal model and setting it out using the arrow structure symbolism outlined above.

(2) Constructing the algebraic model implied by the structure.

(3) Calculating the parameters of the model using the data and seeing whether they have the properties implied by the causal model.[3]

In this chapter it will be assumed that regression techniques are appropriate, that is, either the straightforward multiple regression models, or adaptations suitable for nominal and ordinal variables outlined in the previous chapter, are used.

9.2 Two-Variable Causality

In the absence of experimental techniques, whereby it is possible to study the change in one variable as another is manipulated,

it is always difficult to establish causal links between two variables. Indeed it is, in strict terms, a misnomer to speak of
establishing the presence of causal links at all. Rather, as we have
seen, we should say that certain observations (patterns of
covariation) are compatible with a particular causal model.

If attention is restricted to two variables (i.e. where we know
no other variables are involved)[4] then the causal models depicted
in Figure 9.1 exhaust the logical possibilities. We will now
consider each of these simple causal structures and show what
they imply in terms of the covariation of X_1 and X_2.

Figure 9.1 Two-Variable Causal Models

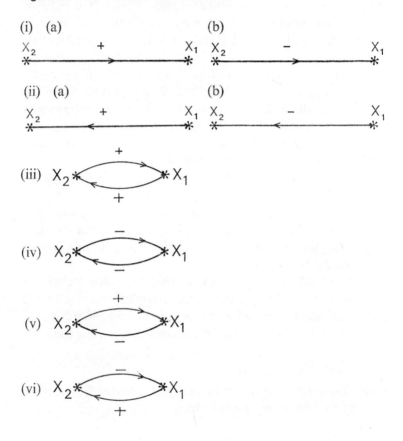

Cases (*i*) (*a*) *and* (*b*) Simple bivariate causality where X_2 causes X_1; the process may be depicted as a simple bivariate regression model. The equilibrium[5] linear model may then be put in the recursive form

$$X_2 = u_2$$
$$X_1 = a_1 + \beta_{12} X_2^n + u_1 \qquad (9.1)$$

where $n = 1$ if the relationship is linear and $n \neq 1$ if the covariation pattern shows an accumulation or saturation effect (Chapter 8).

If it is assumed that u_2 and u_1 are not correlated, which is the same as saying X_2 and u_1 are not correlated, then this implies there is no variable prior to X_1 and X_2 causing them both.[6] It must also be assumed that X_2 is temporally prior to X_1. Diagramatically this can be drawn as in Figure 9.2. The independence of X_2 and u_1 is implied by the absence of causal link between them. In so far as X_2 and u_1 do intercorrelate this suggests that a further variable(s) causing X_1 and X_2 should be explicitly brought into the model.[7]

Figure 9.2 A Simple Causal Model

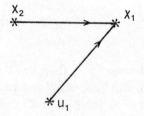

The predictions of this model are that

(i) b_{12} (the least squares estimate of β_{12}) departs significantly from zero. b_{12} will be positive for case (i)(a) and negative for case (i)(b).

(ii) The correlation will be significantly different from zero.[8] If r_{12}^2 is low this means that X_2 does not explain much of the variance in X_1 and so there must be either other causes of X_1 which are sufficient for X_1 (or changes in X_1) i.e. the system is over-determined. Or there is an unspecified interaction condition openly necessary for X_2 to cause X_1; some of the X_2 are under this condition and others not.

Cases (ii) (a) and (b) These are similar to the previous example, except that the direction of the causal link is reversed. Now X_1 causes X_2. We require therefore, a knowledge of the temporal priority of X_1 over X_2.

The equilibrium linear model for this causal structure is then

$$X_1 = u_1$$
$$X_2 = a_2 + \beta_{21} X_n^1 + u_2. \tag{9.2}$$

Case (iii) Sociologists have very frequently toyed with the idea of *reciprocal causality* so let us see, first of all, what this causal model implies. Assume the system is embedded in a *random environment* represented by u_1 and u_2 then the causal structure may be depicted as in Figure 9.3.

Figure 9.3 An Unstable Causal Model

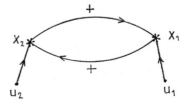

If u_2 causes an increase in X_2 then this will cause an increase in X_1 which, in turn, will 'feed back' and cause an increase in X_1 which again will cause an increase in X_2 and so on. The logic is, of course, entirely the same if the sequence is started by letting u_1 cause an increase in X_1.

Similarly, if u_2 causes a decrease in X_2 then X_1 will decrease and so, in turn, will X_2 once again. In the first situation X_1 and X_2 would constantly escalate in value and in the second, de-escalate to zero or, if negative values of X_1 and X_2 have meaning, constantly de-escalate. The process is clearly unstable though, in practice, it may have lower and upper bounds. The instability of this sort of structure is best illustrated in terms of two differential equations which may be assumed to represent the causal structure:

$$\frac{dX_1}{dt} = k_{11} X_1 + k_{12} X_2$$

$$\frac{dX_2}{dt} = k_{21} X_1 + k_{22} X_2.$$

(9.3)

These equations are more general than our causal structure as they allow for self effects (i.e. X_1 and X_2 causing themselves). In our case $k_{11} = k_{22} = 0$. Now for system (9.3) to be *stable* it is necessary that $k_{11} + k_{22} < 0$ and the determinant of the matrix of ks be positive.[9] Clearly this cannot be the case when $k_{11} = k_{22} = 0$. But it is worth while viewing reciprocal causal structures from this viewpoint for it indicates how self-effects can stabilise a structure. If k_{11} and k_{22} are sufficiently large to render the necessary conditions for stability good, then stability can be obtained. Self-effects are conceptually quite defensible in human behaviour as they often represent a sort of self-monitoring, when increased intensity in behaviour becomes increasingly costly. The classic example is Richardson's (1960) model of arms races, where expenditure on armaments has an inhibiting effect on increases in arms expenditure.

It is important at this juncture to distinguish between processes that take place instantaneously and those that consume time. In the former X_2 and X_1 will instantaneously accommodate to each other so that only the upper or lower bound or equilibrium distributions of X_1 and X_2 can be observed. And so it is impossible to distinguish this model from (i) (a) or (b). If, however, the process consumes time then it should be possible, with suitable observations over time, to study the actual process; the indirect causal symbolism depicted in Figure 9.4 is then more appropriate for time consumption will in general be indicative of intervening variables.

In order to study the dynamics of such a process let us now introduce a new type of diagram as depicted in Figure 9.5.

Figure 9.4 An Unstable Causal Model which Consumes Time

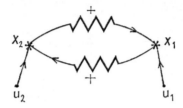

Figure 9.5 A Two-Variable Causal Process over Time

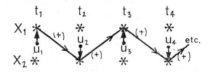

Here t_1, t_2, t_3 etc. represent an ordinal or metric time-scale. The diagram is self-evident and shows a causal process as follows:

$$X_1(t_1) \xrightarrow{\text{(+)}} X_2(t_2) \xrightarrow{\text{(+)}} X_1(t_3) \xrightarrow{\text{(+)}} X_2(t_4) \xrightarrow{\text{(+)}}$$

etc. $\hspace{10cm}$ (9.4)

Now this means, in terms of linear models,[10] that we are dealing with *lagged variables*. The values of X_1 and X_2 at different time periods are treated as variables in their own right. So the linear model will have a *recursive* form as follows:[11]

$$X_1(t_1) = u_1$$
$$X_2(t_2) = a_2 + \beta_{21} X_1(t_1) + u_2 \hspace{3cm} (9.5)$$
$$X_1(t_3) = a_3 + 0\, X_1(t_1) + B_{32} X_2(t_2) + \mu_3$$
$$X_2(t_4) = a_4 + 0\, X_1(t_1) + 0\, X_2(t_2) + \beta_{43} X_1(t_3) + \mu_4 \text{ etc.}$$

The model predicts, in terms of least square estimates, that $b_{31\cdot2} = b_{41\cdot23} = b_{42\cdot13}$ are not significantly different from zero. In effect, the causal structure is reduced to a sequential process. A consequence of explicitly viewing the causal structure as a recursive system should be emphasised. Looking at (9.4) one naturally predicts that the relationship between $X_2(t_4)$ and X_1 (t_1) will disappear if *either* $X_2(t_2)$ *or* $X_1(t_3)$ are held constant.

That is $b_{41 \cdot 2}$ and $b_{41 \cdot 3}$ will not be significantly different from zero. But if $b_{41 \cdot 2} = b_{31 \cdot 2} = 0$ then so does $b_{41 \cdot 23}$. For

$$b_{41 \cdot 23} = \frac{b_{41 \cdot 2} - b_{43 \cdot 2} - b_{31 \cdot 2}}{1 - b_{13 \cdot 2} \, b_{31 \cdot 2}}. \qquad (9.6)$$

So, in practice, recursive models over control but this does not matter. And it is always a good idea to base causal models on explicitly stated functional models to avoid possible attempted estimation of unidentifiable parameters.

In order to study a causal process of this nature, over time data is obviously required and also some *a priori* knowledge of the time periods. Unfortunately there has been little attempt to study processes of this sort and there is consequently little social theory about 'natural' time periods for such structures. It should be noted, however, that in using the symbol ———⌇⌇⌇—→ a series of intervening variables is assumed and assumptions about the nature of such variables might well provide clues about time lags but this is a problem that can only be settled in the context of individual empirical problems.

If the causal model under consideration is viewed as a positive feedback mechanism then it might be expected to have causal structure of the form depicted in Figure 9.6 where the feedback loop is rapid in comparison with the effect of X_2 on X_1.

Figure 9.6 A Causal Process with Rapid Positive Feedback

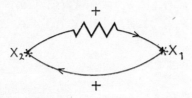

Diagramatically this process can be expressed by the time flow diagram in Figure 9.7.

The equilibrium model for this process can also be put in recursive form. This diagram facilitates an important observation; assume that, for some reason, observations cannot be

Figure 9.7 A Causal Model with Rapid Feedback

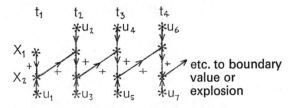

made on the values of the variables at the correct time intervals. For instance, if we have no way of distinguishing time intervals before t_3, so t_1 and t_2 are aggregated. The time-flow diagram would now be as depicted in Figure 9.8.

Figure 9.8 A Partially Aggregated Causal Structure

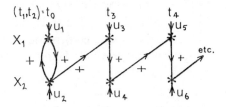

The appropriate equilibrium linear model is now:[12]

$$X_1(t_0) = a_1 + \beta_{12} X_2(t_0) + u_1$$
$$X_2(t_0) = a_2 + \beta_{21} X_1(t_0) + u_2$$
$$X_1(t_3) = a_3 + \beta_{32} X_2(t_0) + u_3$$
$$X_2(t_3) = a_4 + \beta_{43} X_1(t_3) + u_4 \qquad (9.7)$$

.
.
.

etc.

It should be observed that (9.7) is no longer recursive in form. Clearly if all the time periods are aggregated then the process is reduced to the structure depicted in Figure 9.9.

This is identical to the original 'instantaneous' model. If a time-flow diagram contains arrows going two ways between two variables in the same time period then the linear model will become *non-recursive*. On the other hand, if there are no two way arrows the linear model is recursive. *Non-recursive structures arise, therefore, for two-variable causation, when we cannot design suitably articulated measuring instruments to break down the time paths of the process. When such instruments can be found the causal process can be studied in terms of a recursive system.*

Figure 9.9 A Completely Aggregated Causal Structure

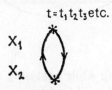

$t = t_1, t_2, t_3$ etc.

X_1

X_2

Case (iv) This is very similar to case (iii); for increases in X_2 cause decreases in X_1 which in turn cause increases in X_2. So X_2 will head off to a high value and X_1 to a low value. Again the process is unstably explosive unless some upper and lower bound constraints are applied.

Two-variable causal processes, with positive feedback, as we have seen, are unstable, they reflect a growth or decay process and the question obviously arises as to their utility in sociological analysis. Perhaps the most characteristic process of this sort is *planned growth* as depicted in Figure 9.10.

Figure 9.10 A Positive Feedback Process – Planned Growth

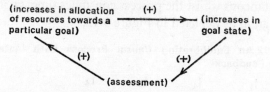

A planned growth process will continue (if the assessment is regarded as satisfactory) until an upper bound is reached – that is, an optimal amount of the goal state is obtained. This goal state may then be regarded as a 'desirable' state of affairs to maintain and the process whereby it is maintained will be

I

characterised by a negative feedback (a social functional process). So we now turn to consider these.

Case (v) This is sociologically much more interesting. If the causal structure is embedded in a random environment comprising u_1 and u_2 then it may be depicted as in Figure 9.11.

Figure 9.11 A Negative Feedback Causal Process

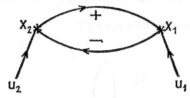

Once again it is worth while analysing the logic of this structure. If X_2 increases this will lead to an increase in X_1 which in turn will lead to a decrease in X_2 which will again lead to a decrease in X_1. If we start by considering an increase X_1, a similar logic is obtained, for an increase in X_1 will cause a decrease in X_2 which will, in turn, cause a decrease in X_1 which will cause an increase in X_2, etc. We encountered this sort of causal structure earlier when considering social functional propositions.

In the case where the process does not consume time only equilibrium values of X_2 and X_1 will be observed and there is no way of specifying the mechanism.

But a more interesting situation is where the negative feedback is instantaneous whilst the process consumes time, giving a time flow diagram as depicted in Figure 9.12.

Figure 9.12 An Equilibrating Causal Process with Instantaneous Negative Feedback

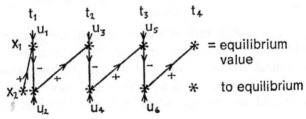

This diagram can be viewed as either a process whereby equilibrium is initially established or a repeated return to an equilibrium value of X_1 due to disturbances of its value.

The linear model will have a recursive form. But once again, if our observation technique is such that observations on the time dimension cannot be disaggregated, then the appropriate model will be non-recursive.

Case (vi) The logic of this structure is entirely analogous to case (v).

9.3 Three-Variable Causality

The most complex three-variable model one could encounter would be where all the six possible causal links hold between the variables as in Figure 9.13.

Figure 9.13 A Complete Three-Variable Causal Structure

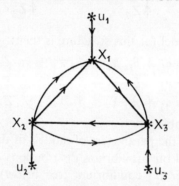

The equilibrium linear model would then be:

$$X_1 = a_1 + \beta_{12} X_2 + \beta_{13} X_3 + u_1$$
$$X_2 = a_2 + \beta_{21} X_1 + \beta_{23} X_3 + u_2 \qquad (9.8)$$
$$X_3 = a_3 + \beta_{31} X_1 + \beta_{32} X_2 + u_3$$

which is complete and non-recursive; it is, of course, not identifiable as it stands. In order to make a structure of this sort identifiable an additional exogenous variable must be brought into each equation. Figure 9.14 depicts a structure of this sort.

Figure 9.14 A Complete Three Endogenous Variable Causal Model with Three Exogenous Variables

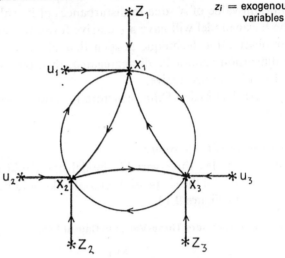

z_i = exogenous variables

The linear model for this structure is then:

$$X_1 = a_1 + \beta_{12} X_2 + \beta_{13} X_3 + \gamma_{11} Z_1 + u_1$$
$$X_2 = a_2 + \beta_{21} X_1 + \beta_{23} X_3 + \gamma_{22} Z_2 + u_2 \qquad (9.9)$$
$$X_3 = a_3 + \beta_{31} X_1 + \beta_{32} X_1 + \gamma_{33} Z_3 + u_3$$

which is identifiable.

Estimation of the parameters of models of this kind must, of course, be based on equilibrium distributions of the variables. If there is either no equilibrium (see below) or the process consumes time in coming to equilibrium, then it may be studied using lagged variable techniques similar to those outlined for the two-variable case. However, since complete causal structures in practice unlikely, we postpone such considerations until a little later when dealing with incomplete causal structures.

If the possibility of reciprocal causality is dropped then logically there are eight possible three-variable causal structures – two intransitive and therefore non-recursive and six transitive and therefore recursive.[13]

The transitive structures are set out in full detail in Figure

9.15. The variables have been expressed in terms of deviation from their means and so the a coefficients do not appear in the models. If uncorrelated disturbances are assumed all these six models are identifiable. That is, the correct number of co-efficients and covariations of the disturbances are set at zero to make the structure identifiable. So the predictions of the models are that the estimates of the coefficients are significantly greater than zero. If any of these coefficients turns out not to be significantly different from zero then it means that the model is incorrect since the appropriate causal link has to be removed from the structure. It is important to recognise that the causal models in Figure 9.15 can *all* be corroborated on the basis of observations on X_1 X_2 and X_3. In other words, given a set of data on these variables, estimation of the parameters for each model can be made. So we cannot choose between them except on *a priori* theoretical grounds and in terms of temporal ordering. In general, there will be a number of exactly identifiable models compatible with a given set of covariations. So in situations like this the logic of testing a model is rather weak. It is only when the causal structure has some of its links removed that direct tests of alternative models can be made. Figure 9.16 shows the effects of removing one causal link from a three causal link structure giving a two causal link structure.

Figure 9.15 Transitive Three-Variable Causal Models and their Linear Models

Structure *Equilibrium Linear Model*

(a)

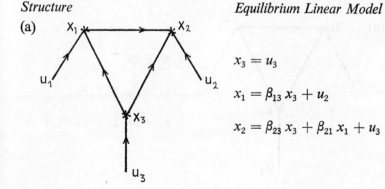

$$x_3 = u_3$$

$$x_1 = \beta_{13} x_3 + u_2$$

$$x_2 = \beta_{23} x_3 + \beta_{21} x_1 + u_3$$

Structure   *Equilibrium Linear Model*

(b)

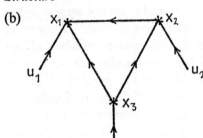

$$x_3 = u_3$$

$$x_2 = \beta_{23} x_3 + u_2$$

$$x_1 = \beta_{13} x_3 + \beta_{12} x_2 + u_3$$

(c)

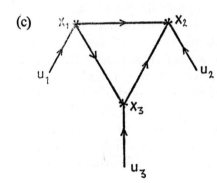

$$x_1 = u_1$$

$$x_3 = \beta_{31} x_1 + u_2$$

$$x_2 = \beta_{21} x_1 + \beta_{23} x_3 + u_3$$

(d)

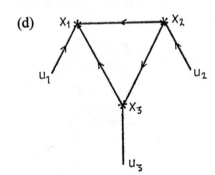

$$x_2 = u_2$$

$$x_3 = \beta_{32} x_2 + u_3$$

$$x_1 = \beta_{12} x_2 + \beta_{13} x_3 + u_1$$

Structure   *Equilibrium Linear Model*

(e)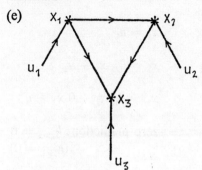

$$x_1 = u_1$$

$$x_2 = \beta_{21}\, x_1 + u_2$$

$$x_3 = \beta_{31}\, x_1 + \beta_{32}\, x_2 + u_3$$

(f)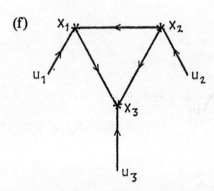

$$x_2 = u_2$$

$$x_1 = \beta_{12}\, x_2 + u_2$$

$$x_3 = \beta_{32}\, x_2 + \beta_{31}\, x_1 + u_3$$

Figure 9.16 Some Three-Variable, Two Causal Link Structures and their Linear Models

Structure   *Equilibrium Linear Model*

(a)

$$x_3 = u_3$$

$$x_2 = \beta_{23}\, x_3 + u_2$$

$$x_1 = \beta_{13}\, x_3 + 0_2\, x_2 + u_3$$

zero prediction: $b_{12\cdot3} = 0$

$(r_{12\cdot3} = 0)$

Structure   *Equilibrium Linear Model*

(b)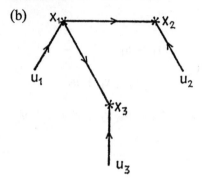

$$x_1 = u_1$$

$$x_2 = \beta_{21} x_1 + u_2$$

$$x_3 = \beta_{31} x_1 + 0 x_2 + u_3$$

zero prediction: $b_{23 \cdot 1} = 0$
$$(r_{23 \cdot 1} = 0)$$

(c)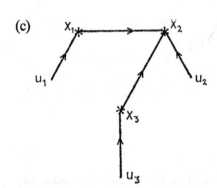

$$x_1 = u_1$$

$$x_2 = \beta_{21} x_1 + \beta_{23} x_3 + u_3$$

$$x_3 = u_3$$

(d)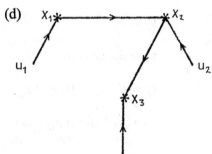

$$x_1 = u_1$$

$$x_2 = \beta_{21} x_1 + u_2$$

$$x_3 = 0 x_1 + \beta_{32} x_2 + u_3$$

zero prediction: $b_{31 \cdot 2} = 0$
$$(r_{13 \cdot 2} = 0)$$

also $r_{13} = r_{12} \cdot r_{23}$

In 9.16 (a), for instance, β_{12} (estimator $b_{12.3}$) will be zero. This is, of course, an example of spurious correlation. So is 9.16 (b) but in this case β_{32} (estimator $b_{32.1}$) is zero. Since both these linear systems are identifiable we can estimate whether or not the b estimates are significantly different from zero. 9.16 (d) is derived from 9.15 (e) and depicts a sequential model with X_2 intervening between X_1 and X_3. If one controls for the intervening variable then the relationship between the two terminal variables will disappear.

Where a model involves three variables, it is possible to have interaction effects; for example, the causal structure in Figure 9.17 would have the linear (interaction) model.

Figure 9.17 A Three-Variable Causal Structure with Interaction

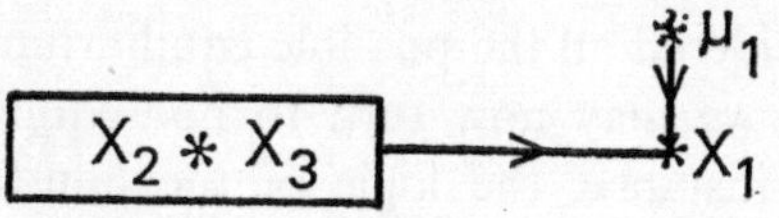

$$X_1 = a_1 + IX_2 X_3 + u_1. \qquad (9.10)$$

A specially important instance of this in sociology is where one of the variables X_1 or X_2 is a dichotomy such that the presence or absence of the variable is an openly necessary prerequisite for the causal process.

Of course, from what was said in an earlier chapter we expect that all the above three-variable models are circumscribed by interaction conditions (initial conditions). But this, of course, makes them more than three-variable models unless the conditions are used to define the population to which the model applies.

An even more complex three-variable causal model is where there is a direct causal effect and an independent interaction effect as in Figure 9.18.

Figure 9.18 A Causal Model with Direct and Interaction Effect

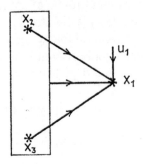

The structure has a linear model of the form

$$X_1 = a_1 + \beta_{12} X_2 + \beta_{13} X_3 + I_{12} X_1 X_2 + u_1 \qquad (9.11)$$

where I_{12} is the coefficient for the interaction effects of X_1 and X_2.

Having considered all the possible equilibrium three-variable causal models we may now turn to non-equilibrium models. Consider, for instance, the logic of the non-transitive three-variable structure; if there is a change in X_1 then this causes a change in X_2 which causes a change in X_3 which in turn causes a change in X_1. This gives the time-flow diagram in Figure 9.19.

Figure 9.19 A Non-Transitive Three-Variable Causal Process

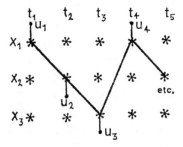

The linear model for this process (assuming measuring instruments are available) is

$$X_1 (t_1) = u_1$$
$$X_2 (t_2) = a_1 + \beta_{21} X_1 (t_1) + u_2$$

$$X_3\,(t_3) = a_2 + 0\,X_1\,(t_1) + \beta_{32}\,X_2\,(t_2) + u_3$$
$$X_1\,(t_4) = a_3 + 0\,X_1\,(t_1) + 0\,X_2\,(t_2) + \beta_{43}\,X_3\,(t_3) + u_4 \quad (9.12)$$

.
.
.

etc.

which has a recursive form. A rather different but perhaps more common sociological model is one closely related to our previous example of a social functional model – the causal process relating framed intention, action and consequence. In Figure 9.20 it is assumed that the causal process from intention to consequence is rapid in comparison with the feedback link which represents a period in which an assessment is made of the consequences of the action.

Figure 9.20 An Extension of the Social Functional Model

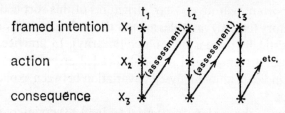

9.4 Many Variable Causality

The basic ideas of the previous sections of this chapter may be extended to models containing many variables. The most general causal structure will correspond to the linear model (8.31). One must, of course, ensure that the model is identifiable and suitable estimation techniques must also be employed. If the causal structure is transitive then the appropriate model will be recursive in form; if not, it will be non-recursive unless suitable time-lagged variables can be obtained.

The most straightforwad type of multivariate causal structure is where a single variable is caused by many alternative variables. Figure 9.21 depicts a situation where X_1 is caused by X_2, X_3, X_4 and X_5.

Figure 9.21 A Simple Over-Determined Causal Structure

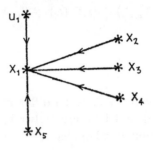

Thus X_1 is causally overdetermined in the sense that X_2, X_3, X_4 and X_5 are alternative causes, each sufficient for a change in X_1. The causal structure will have a linear model as follows:

$$X_1 = a_1 + \beta_{12} X_2 + \beta_{13} X_3 + \beta_{14} X_4 + \beta_{15} X_5 + u_1. \quad (9.13)$$

The important feature of 'star' structures of this sort is that the explanatory (causal) variables are not themselves causally related (i.e. statistically there is no multicollinearity). In practice, this is rarely found to hold and a double-headed arrow is sometimes used to indicate an unanalysed covariation between explanatory variables.[14]

If some of the explanatory variables in (9.13) do intercorrelate then the relationship should be explicitly brought into the model. For example, if X_2 and X_3 intercorrelate then this can mean one or a combination of three things:

    (i) X_2 causes X_3

    (ii) X_3 causes X_2

    (iii) X_2 and X_3 are spuriously related, i.e. they have a common causal antecedent.

Consider for example, the four-variable causal structure in Figure 9.22 where for convenience, the numbering of the variables has been slightly altered and the original variables X_4 and X_5 dropped.

Figure 9.22 A Four-Variable Causal Model

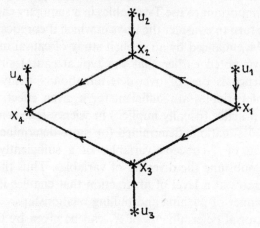

This will correspond to a linear recursive model of the form:

$$X_1 = a_1 + u_1$$
$$X_2 = a_2 + \beta_{21} X_1 + u_1$$
$$X_3 = a_3 + \beta_{31} X_1 + 0X_2 + u_3 \qquad (9.14)$$
$$X_4 = a_4 + 0X_1 + \beta_{42} X_2 + \beta_{43} X_3 + u_4.$$

The zero predictions are:

$$b_{32 \cdot 1} = b_{41 \cdot 23} = 0 \; (r_{23 \cdot 1} = r_{14 \cdot 23} = 0).$$

If, however, there was a direct causal link between X_1 and X_4, only $b_{32 \cdot 1}$ would go to zero; $b_{41 \cdot 23}$ would have a non-zero value.

If $X_3 X_4$ and X_5 in structure 9.21 were also intercorrelated then similar interpretations could be placed upon these relationships. It is thus possible to build up a complex causal network of interrelated variables and if the structure has some of the possible direct links missing then there will be appropriate zero predictions for the slopes or correlation coefficients.

The general picture should now be sufficiently clear for the reader to be able to translate easily between causal structures and the corresponding linear models and to appreciate the significance of zero predictions.

As the number of variables in the model increases, the number of alternative causal structures increases rapidly, and it therefore becomes important to use T-variables in a summary capacity; so finally we turn to consider the ways in which theoretical elaboration can be enhanced by an explicit study of causal models.

We have noted earlier that the typical causal situation in social science is one of over-determination – many different clusters of variables are sufficient for a given effect. Now the standard practice (usually implicit) in science is to render over-determined situations determined (or more determined) by the elaboration of T-concepts/variables of a sufficiently abstract nature to subsume the diversity of variables. Thus the concept *force* operates at a level of abstraction that enables it to stand for all manner of pushing and pulling relationships.

If the causal determinants of X_1 can be given by the model

$$X_1 = a_1 + \beta_{12} X_2 (C_1 C_2 \ldots) + \beta_{13} X_3 (D_1 D_2 \ldots) + \beta_{14} X_4$$
$$(E_1 E_2 \ldots) + u_1 \qquad (9.15)$$

then one may be able to find a variable T that 'stands for' X_2, X_3 and X_4. Note this is not difficult if the sets of interaction variables – the Cs, Ds and Es – are identical or nearly identical but, if they are not, T-elaboration is difficult because one would have to consider alternative conditions for the T-variable to be operative. The possibility of an abstract T becomes impossible if some of the interaction conditions are contradictory, e.g. $C_1 = \tilde{D}_1$. So it is therefore important in theoretical elaboration to study the interaction conditions under which different 'empirical' concepts operate before attempting theoretical subsumption.

Notes

1 The Model Building Perspective

1 The word model has been used in many different ways in sociology, which has given rise to an extended debate on the merits of various usages. This debate seems to this author largely a waste of time. The word is used here as a catch all – it means both the sets of relevant variables and the specified functional relationships between the variables.

2 The distinction between observational and theoretical concepts will be drawn in Chapter 2.

3 The most obvious form of entailment is logical deduction but, as we shall see, many propositions in sociology are of a statistical or probabilistic nature (e.g. group cohesion *correlates* with inter-group conflict) where the idea of entailment is less straight-forward (see Chapter 7, p. 154).

2 Units of Analysis

1 Lenski (1954) used the term 'status crystallisation' but following recent usage (see, for instance, Galtung, 1967), I will use the term 'status disequilibrium'. Status disequilibrium is the degree to which a unit of analysis has differing statuses on a set of ranking dimensions.

2 Perhaps one of the major problems facing contemporary sociology is the lack of any theory or meta-theory of 'significant' populations. See, for instance, Willer (1967).

3 Almost any elementary text-book on statistics will provide an introduction to these topics. See, for instance, Blalock (1960).

4 These properties may have differing measurement properties, see Chapter 4 on Variables.

5 If the reader is not conversant with this terminology, he should return to this section after reading Chapter 4.

6   There are a number of introductions to graph-theory written for social scientists – Flament (1963), and Busacker and Saaty (1965).

7   The following terminology is by no means universally established amongst graph-theoreticians so some caution should be exercised when comparing this book with others.

8   The type of relationship referred to here should be distinguished from a contingent relationship between structures (see Chapter 6), where, for example, we speak of a causal relationship between structures.

9   There are some rather difficult conceptual problems associated with the idea of graphs (i.e. structures) having relationships, as total entities, with one another. The question naturally arises as to whether they can ultimately be reduced to relationships of one sort or another relating the primary units of the structures. See Abell (1969a). This is, of course, the old problem of emergence.

10   The uninitiated reader may like to return to this section after reading the next four chapters.

11   We do not lose any generality in the argument by thinking in terms of dichotomous variables (i.e. two-valued variables). We here consider proportions of a given variable which is, of course, entirely equivalent to the mean of a cardinal variable if we adopt the values 1 and 0 for the dichotomous variable.

3 Concepts

1   Perhaps Nagel (1961) is the best text on these matters. A shorter and more elementary book is Carl S. Hempel (1966).

2   See, for instance, P. Berger and T. Luckman (1966).

3   Nagel has shown how difficult it is to draw the distinction between O- and T-concepts even in the physical sciences.

4   If the actor is a social collectivity then there will be a problem of relating individual internal concepts to collectivity concepts. This is one aspect of constructivism (see below).

5   It is clearly an impossibility for actors to have an explanation or description of phenomena they do not cognise.

6   Peter Winch (1958) and Alfred Schutz (1967) are perhaps the most significant internalists. Although, as we noted, they both allow the use of concepts constructed out of internal ones. But neither gives sufficient reasons for ruling out of court descriptions or explanations of non-cognised phenomena.

7   It is possible, of course, that the sociologist may use the actor's explanatory concepts in a logically *different way* to explain the phenomena rather than external concepts. That is, use the actor's concepts in a manner unfamiliar to him. I think most internalists would not accept this as a legitimate enterprise.

4 Variables

1   The idea of mathematical structure will become clear as the chapter progresses.
2   The naming of these types of ordering is by no means universally adopted.
3   In an entirely trivial sense if there were an infinity of objects this property would have meaning.
4   I am ignoring the distinction between 'mass' and 'weight'. It should be noted that the objects themselves will have equivalent values with respect to the property in question. But the actual *values* form a linear order (see below).
5   See James S. Coleman (1964) for a further treatment of these points.
6   Boolean addition is defined as: $1 + 1 = 1, 1 + 0 = 1, 0 + 1 = 1$, and $0 + 0 = 0$.

5 The Treatment of Theoretical Variables

1   See, for instance, Lazarsfeld (1961).
2   Note the relationship between this and the definitional approach to T-concepts.
3   A lattice is a special type of partial order such that each pair of points has, in effect, a least common superior point (technically a least upper bound) and a highest common inferior point (technically a highest lower bound).
4   The operationalist approach to T-variables has as we noted often verged upon the causal approach. Techniques like factor analysis can be construed as a search for underlying causal variables (i.e. the factors), so the interrelations amongst the observed variables is as a consequence of their separate 'causal' relations to the underlying factor.

6 Propositions

1 For the sake of simplicity of argument in the next few paragraphs we concentrate on the *conditional* relationship between status disequilibrium (*A*) and political liberality (*B*), i.e. the conditional probability that an *A* is a *B*. So when this is less than unity we are concerned with why some *A*s are not *B*s. The correlation measure is, of course, a symmetric measure and reflects also the possibility that some *B*s are not *A*s. To account for these, as we shall see later, additional variables sufficient for *A* have to be introduced.

2 The product-moment correlation coefficient will only be appropriate if expression (6.1) is in stochastic form, in other words, the relationship between X_1 and X_2 is not exact or deterministic. As we shall see later this means that a variable μ must be added to 6.1 giving $X_1 = a + \beta X_2 + \mu$ (see Chapter 8).

3 A dummy variable is a dichotomous variable scored 1 and 0.

4 For continuous variables a negative catalytic effect can be 'partially' captured by taking the reciprocal of the value of the variable.

5 See Blalock (1969) for a detailed examination of the equilibrium of feedback processes.

8 Some Salient Features of Sociological Covariation and Model Building

1 Not all mathematical functions can be expressed explicitly but this is of little consequence in practice.

2 It is possible also to express a variable as a function of itself, which normally implies that its current value is a function of its past value.

3 In the context of estimation μ will also account for errors of measurement in the explained variable. It is also sometimes suggested that μ can be included in the light of a basic indeterminism of human behaviour. This would, however, seem to involve unwarranted philosophical problems of 'uncaused' events (i.e. events that are not effects).

4 This problem does not, of course, arise if there is only one explanatory variable.

5 α and β values of zero would indicate no relationship.

6   The usual assumptions of ordinary least squares estimation
     are
     (a) The expected value of μ for all values of the explanatory
     variable is zero.
     (b) The covariation of the disturbances for different values of
     the explanatory variables is zero.
     (c) The variance of the disturbance term is constant.
     (d) The stochastic variable and the explanatory variable are
     independent.
     (e) It is also usually assumed that the disturbances are
     normally distributed so standard tests of significance can be
     applied.
     These assumptions will be examined in a little more detail in a
     later section.
7   The reader should note that lower case roman letters stand for
     least squares estimators. It is important to remember that the
     Greek letters refer to parameters at the population level and
     models are specified at this level. Then the problem is to estimate
     these parameters on the basis of observations on a sample.
8   For an elementary introduction to the use of these tests, see
     Blalock (1960) for a more advanced treatment see Johnston
     (1960).
9   This assumes that all the coefficients are significant in any
     particular model (see below, Section 8.12).
10   There are no interaction (initial) conditions accompanying X_2
     and X_3 in this model. It may be assumed that they are specified
     in the definition of the population to which the model pertains.
11   The reader should remember that lower case roman letters stand
     for ordinary least squares estimates. These estimates rest, as with
     the two-variable model, on a series of assumptions (note 6), and
     also that the two explanatory variables do not covary themselves.
     If they do, we have the problem of multicollinearity (see below).
12   It is easy to see how this dependency arises: assume interest is
     centred upon the relationship

$$X_1 = a_1 + \beta_{12} X_2 + u_1$$

     and that X_2 is observed with measurement error so that its
     observed values X'_2 are related to the 'true' values by

$$X'_2 = X_2 + v$$

Then substituting this expression in the original equation we obtain

$$X_1 = a_1 + \beta_{12} X_2 + w$$

where $\qquad w = \beta_{12} v + u.$

So w is not independent of X_2.

13 We are ignoring the possible ambiguity introduced by changing the units of measurement. Perhaps for the purposes of this argument it would be best to think in terms of standardised regression coefficients.

14 The identification problem is, in a rather more sophisticated guise, the old question about having as many equations as unknowns. For an authoritative (but sometimes technically difficult) statement see Fisher (1966); Blalock (1969) gives an elementary introduction. Any text on Econometrics will have a section on this problem.

15 Variable X_1 is exogenous as it is determined outside the model by u_1.

16 See Fisher (1966) Chapter 4, for a full treatment of these restrictions.

17 For an easy introduction to these equivalences, see Alker (1965).

18 Dummy variables are ones scored 0, 1, and dummy regression refers to standard regression practice when the variables are scored in this manner.

19 Expressions like (8.46) can also be used when some of the variables are cardinal. For example X_1 may be cardinal. In fact if the explained variable is dichotomous an estimation difficulty is introduced since the assumption of homoscedasticity breaks down (see Johnston, 1963, p. 227).

20 An alternative restriction is to assume the β values are identical which, as we saw earlier, is similar to forming a composite index out of the explanatory variables.

21 If the explained variable is dummy (dichotomous) and the explanatory variables cardinal then a technique known as probit analysis is applicable.

Analysis of variance is also a possible type of analysis when the explained variable is cardinal.

22 In the unlikely situation where the condensations and expansions

tend to off-set the scatter around the true relationship this will not be true.

9 Causal Models

1 The reader should read expressions like Cor $(AB) > 0$ and $b_{12} > 0$ as indicating values significantly greater than zero and Cor $(AB) = 0$, $b_{12} = 0$ as measuring no significant departure from zero.

2 X_2 and X_3 will be openly necessary (see Chapter 6).

3 The quasi-deductive nature of the enterprise follows from the deductive form of the argument: *if* causal model so and so, *then* certain parameter values. So if on the basis of the data these values can be 'established' this will be corroboration of the model. But the data will, in general, be equally compatible with other models. Furthermore, since we are dealing with a probabilistic phenomenon a failure to establish the predicted values does not refute the model outright but gives it a low probability of being correct.

4 We can, of course, never be certain that other variables are not involved. For example, if we establish a correlation between two variables and preclude many potential third variables as spuriously generating the correlation, it is always possible that a yet untried third variable is responsible for the correlation. This once again emphasises the quasi-deductive aspects of causal modelling.

5 By equilibrium model we mean that the values of X_1 and X_2 are in aggregate equilibrium (see Chapter 1). The regression model implies that if changes in X_2 cause changes in X_1 then there will be an appropriate value of X_1 for each value of X_2. But if X_1 does not change its value instantaneously when X_2 changes, then it is possible to observe values of X_2 and X_1 that are not in equilibrium. In the dichotomous case it would be possible to have cases of X_2 that are not X_1 even if X_2 causes X_1.

When using regression models to reflect causal processes, it is therefore assumed that the variables are in their equilibrium values.

6 Note that we have automatically considered a stochastic representation. u represents all the other variables causing X_1 (not related to X_2). If X_2 is the only cause of X_1 then the

disturbance term disappears and we have a perfect linear relationship but, in practice, situations like this never occur.

7   X_2 and u_1 may intercorrelate if the model has not been specified in the correct value of n (see Chapter 8).

8   It is, as we noted in Chapter 8, possible to obtain an insignificant value for r with α and β significant.

9   Blalock (1969), has developed the theory of models of this sort. The determinant has the value $k_{11} k_{22} - k_{12} k_{21}$.

10   From here on we will assume the causal models are linear. This is for the sake of expositional clarity. But from what has been said earlier, we must often anticipate non-linear models. The logic of causal modelling is, however, not materially altered.

11   The subscripts on the β coefficients correspond to the numbering for a normal recursive system.

12   The zero predictions have not been written into this system of equations.

13   The cyclic (intransitive) structures will be considered below in terms of a time-flow diagram. They will exhibit stability/instability properties similar to the two-variable feedback processes (see Blalock, 1969).

14   This practice is common where path-analysis is used. Path-analysis is identical to the procedures outlined here except that the variables are entered into the models in standardised form (i.e. divided by their standard deviations). Path-analysis has the advantage that the coefficients of the 'paths' into a variable add up to one and so quick calculations can be made of the relative importance of different causal variables in their effect on the caused variable. Boudon (1967) has made extensive use of path-coefficients (under the name dependence coefficients). But it appears to this author advisable to think in terms of the more traditional econometric models and techniques for the statistical details and problems are well detailed. For example, see Goldberger (1969). The traditional path-analysis literature seems not to clearly distinguish between parameters of a model and estimates of the parameters.

Bibliography

ABELL, P. (1968) 'Measurement in Sociology', *Sociology*, 2.
  (1969a) 'Measurement, Structure and Sociological Theory', *Sociology*, 3.
  (1969b) 'Some Problems in Structural Balance Theory' in *Structuralism*, (ed.) Michael Lane, Jonathan Cape, London.
  (1971) 'Social Theory and Ontological Depth: The Need for a Paradigm', *University of Sussex Series on Methodology* (forthcoming).
ALKER, HAYWARD (1965) *Mathematics in Politics*, Macmillan, New York.

BERGER, PETER L., and THOMAS LUCKMAN (1966) *The Social Construction of Reality*, Doubleday, New York.
BLALOCK, H. M., Jnr. (1960) *Social Statistics*, McGraw-Hill, New York.
  (1964) *Causal Inference in Non-Experimental Research*, University of North Carolina Press, Chapel Hill.
BLALOCK, H. M., Jnr. and BLALOCK, A. M. B. (1968) *Methodology in Social Research*, McGraw-Hill, New York.
  (1969) *Theory Construction, From Verbal to Mathematical Formulations*, Prentice-Hall, Englewood Cliffs, New Jersey.
BLAUNER, ROBERT (1964) *Alienation and Freedom*, University of Chicago Press, Chicago.
BOYLE, RICHARD P. (1966) 'Causal Theory and Statistical Measures of Effect: A Convergence', *American Sociological Review*, 56.
BUSACKER, ROBERT G., and SAATY, T. L. (1965) *Finite Graphs and Networks: An Introduction with Applications*, New York.
BOUDON, RAYMOND (1967) *L'analyse mathematique des faits sociaux*, Plon, Paris.

CARNAP, RUDOLF (1936, 1937) 'Testability and Meaning', *Philosophy of Science*, 3 and 4.

COLEMAN, JAMES S. (1964) *Introduction to Mathematical Sociology*, The Free Press, Glencoe, Ill.

COOMBS, C. H. (1964) *A Theory of Data*, John Wiley, New York.

COSTNER, H. L. (1965) 'Criteria for Measures of Association', *American Sociological Review*, 30.

COSTNER, H. L., and LEIK, R. K. (1964) 'Deductions from Axiomatic Theory', *American Sociological Review*, 56.

CURTIS, R. F. and JACKSON E. F. (1962) 'Multiple Indicators', *American Journal of Sociology*, 68.

FISHER, FRANKLIN M. (1966) *The Identification Problem in Econometrics*, McGraw-Hill, New York.

FLAMENT, CLAUDE (1963) *Application of Graph Theory to Group Structure*, Prentice-Hall, Englewood Cliffs, New Jersey.

GALTUNG, JOHAN (1967) *Theory and Methods of Social Research*, George Allen and Unwin, London.

GARFINKEL, H. (1967) *Studies in Ethnomethodology*, Prentice-Hall, Englewood Cliffs, New Jersey.

GOLDBERGER, A. (1969) 'On Boudon's Method of Linear Causal Analysis', Mimeo, University of Wisconsin.

GOODMAN, LEO A. (1959) 'Some Alternatives to Ecological Correlation', *American Journal of Sociology*, 64.

HARARY, F. (1959) 'On Measurement of Structural Balance', *Behavioral Science*, 4.

HARARY, F., with R. Z. NORMAN, and D. CARTWRIGHT (1965) *Structural Models: An Introduction to the Theory of Directed Graphs*, New York, 1965.

HEMPEL, CARL (1966) *Philosophy of Natural Science*, Prentice-Hall, Englewood Cliffs, New Jersey.

JOHNSTON, J. (1963) *Econometric Methods*, McGraw-Hill, New York.

KISH, LESLIE (1959) 'Some Statistical Problems in Research Design', *American Sociological Review*, 60.

LAZARSFELD, P., and MENZEL, H. (1961) 'On the Relation Between Individual and Collective Properties', in *Complex Organisations, A Sociological Reader*, (ed.) A. Etzioni, Holt, New York.

LENSKI, GERHARD E. (1954) 'Status Crystallisation: A Non-Vertical Dimension of Social Status', *American Sociological Review*, 19.

LUCE, DUNCAN R. (1959) *Individual Choice Behaviour*, John Wiley, New York.

MALINVAUD, E. (1966) *Statistical Methods of Econometrics*, North Holland Publishing Co.

MACINTYRE, ALASDAIR (1967) 'The Idea of a Social Science', Proc. Aris. Soc.

MAXWELL, A. E. (1961) *Analysing Qualitative Data*, John Wiley, New York.

NAGEL, E. (1961) *The Structure of Science*, Routledge and Kegan Paul, London.

NORTHROP, F. S. C. (1947) *The Logic of the Sciences and the Humanities*, Macmillan, New York.

ORCUTT, G. H.; GREENBERGER, MARTIN; KORBEL, JOHN; and RIVELEN, ALICE M. (1961) *Microanalysis of Socio-economic Systems: A Simulation Study*, Harper and Row, New York.

RICHARDSON, LEWIS F. (1960) *Arms and Insecurity*, Boxwood Press, Pittsburgh.

ROBINSON, W. S. (1950) 'Ecological Correlation and the Behavior of Individuals', *American Sociological Review*, xviii.

SCHUTZ, ALFRED (1967) *The Phenomenology of the Social World*, Evanston.

SANQUIST and MORGAN (1969) *Detection of Interaction Effects*, Michigan Monograph.

STINCHCOMBE, ARTHUR (1968) *Constructing Social Theory*, Harper and Row, New York.

SUITS, D. B. (1957) 'Use of Dummy Variables in Regression Equations', *Journal of American Statistical Association*, 52, pp. 548–51.

TORGERSON, WARREN S. (1958) *Theory and Methods of Scaling*, John Wiley, New York.

WHITE, HARRISON (1963) *An Anatomy of Kinship*, Prentice-Hall, Englewood Cliffs, New Jersey.

WILLER, D. (1967) *Scientific Sociology*, Prentice-Hall, Englewood Cliffs, New Jersey.

WINCH, PETER (1958) *The Idea of a Social Science*, Routledge and Kegan Paul, London.

ZETTERBERG, H. L. (1965) *On Theory and Verification in Sociology*, Bedminster Press, Totlowa, New Jersey.

Index

Abell, P., 18, 30, 67, 71, 72, 74, 96
accumulation effect in sociological covariation, 174–5, 179
aggregate equilibrium, 214
aggregates, 12, 13, 14, 17, 18–19, 21, 22, 23, 24
algebraic ordinal graph, 74
algebraic structures: group, 71; gruppoid, 70; semi-group, 70–1
analysis, units of, *see* units of analysis
autocorrelation, 187–8
axiomatic structure, 64, 140–1, 152–4, 162–4

behaviour and action, 125–9, 130–3
binary operations: 65–70; associativity, 68–9; closure, 66–8; commutativity, 68; units and zero, 69–70
binary relations, 41–9
Blalock, H. M., Jnr., and Blalock, A. M. B., 94, 187, 209, 212
Boolean addition, 71

Carnap, Rudolf, 76
Cartesian product, 65
causal connectives, 115–21
causal models, 213–36
causality in sociology, place of, 129–33

causation in sociology, logical features of, 121–5
cause and anthropomorphic concepts, 125–9
coefficient of variability, 100
collectivity, 12–13
concepts: 1, 5–6, 7, 27–37, 38–40, 49; constructivist, 31, 133; external, 30–1; external explanations, 33–6; internal, 30–1; explained, 30; radical externalism, 36–7; radical internalism, 32–3; secondary, 31; technical, 31; types of sociological explanation, 31–7
conjoined conditions, 121–3
contextual variables, 101
Coombs, C. H., 58
correlation coefficients, 102, 108, 109, 111, 155–61, 173, 178, 180, 181
Costner, H. L., 114, 155, 158
covariation, 165–212
Curtis and Jackson, 190

di-graphs, 14, 15, 16, 18, 71, 73
disjunctions, 123
distortions, 205–6
dummy regression, 199–204
Durbin-Watson *d* statistic, 188

empirical collectivities, 13, 18–19